Hitler's Exiles

Related titles:

Hitler's Bureaucrats – Yaacov Lozowick
Leni Riefenstahl – Rainer Rother

Hitler's Exiles

The German Cultural Resistance in America and Europe

VOLKMAR ZÜHLSDORFF

Translated by Martin H. Bott

continuum
LONDON • NEW YORK

Continuum

The Tower Building	15 East 26th Street
11 York Road	New York
London SE1 7NX	NY 10010

First published by © Ernst Martin Verlag, 1999
Translation © Continuum 2004

Originally published as *Deutsche Akademie im Exil. Der vergessene Widerstand* (The German Academy in Exile. The Forgotten Resistance) by Ernst Martin Verlag, 1999.

British Library Cataloguing-in-Publication Data
A catalogue record for this book is available from the British Library.

ISBN: 08264 7324 5 (hardback)

Typeset by RefineCatch Limited, Bungay, Suffolk
Printed and bound in Great Britain by MPG Books Ltd, Bodmin, Cornwall.

Contents

Translator's Preface

In the first place I should point out that, being an organization created by and for Germans, the 'German Academy for Arts and Sciences in Exile' was generally known as the *Deutsche Akademie der Künste und Wissenschaften im Exil*.

For the convenience of non-German-speaking readers I have endeavoured to provide equivalent details of any published English translations of German books cited in the text or notes. Even where this has been possible, however, quotations from books written in German are my own translations from the original text unless otherwise indicated. The exceptions are generally from English editions which acquired particular importance by (for example) appearing before the German ones, as was the case with a number of works written in exile.

For the sake of clarity and consistency I have given precedence to the original titles of German books, films and works of art. Where an English translation has been published, the title follows in parenthesis and in italics. In the absence of an English edition, I have supplied a translation – in parenthesis but not in italics – if the meaning of a title is relevant. In both cases, subsequent references are to the German title only.

All quotations from books and other extant documents written in English are, of course, from the original text and cited accordingly. It is worth noting that this applies to several books by German authors who sooner or later 'adopted' the language of their new homes in Britain and North America.

A term which crops up several times and perhaps requires elucidation is that of 'inner exile'. This should not be confused with 'internal exile', i.e. with punitive banishment within a country's borders. Rather, it refers to the situation of the many Germans hostile to the Nazis who remained in the country but withdrew from public life. As US Secretary of the Interior Ickes put it in 1939: 'Under a tyranny the best and noblest of a people submerge or go into exile. Those in retirement bide their time until the bright ray of freedom again breaks through the lowering clouds . . .'

I am very grateful for the assistance of Frau Asmus and Herr Maaske at the Deutsche Bibliothek's *Exilarchiv* and the staff of the Zentralbibliothek Zürich, particularly its 'Fernleihe' department. I am, once again, indebted to Pilar and her eagle eyes. Above all, I must express my gratitude to Volkmar Zühlsdorff, who could not have been kinder or more cooperative. My work on his book has been an honour and a pleasure.

Martin H. Bott
Zürich, April 2003

Author's Dedication

I dedicate this book to that great European, Prince Hubertus zu Löwenstein, founder of the German Academy in Exile. During the dark years of an infamous regime, he and his Academy helped maintain the world's belief in a Germany of justice, liberty and human dignity with a place among the reconciled peoples of Europe.

And to his courageous comrade-in-arms, Princess Helga: as a Dutchwoman, born in Norway and imbued with the spirit of Europe, she adopted Germany's fate as her own.

Volkmar Zühlsdorff

Foreword: Culture as a Weapon

In unserem Lager ist Deutschland – 'Germany is in our camp' – was the title Alfred Kantorowicz chose for a collection of his speeches and essays which was published in Paris in 1936. Kantorowicz was a journalist and writer living in exile in France, where he was general secretary of the *Schutzverband Deutscher Schriftsteller im Exil* (League of German Writers in Exile) and director of the *Deutsche Freiheitsbibliothek* (German Freedom Library) in Paris. The title of his book was inspired by a letter Romain Rolland had written to the *Schutzverband*: 'The whole of the Germany we love and revere is in your camp. Goethe and Beethoven are with you, as are Lessing and Marx. They are with you in your struggle. I do not doubt that you will triumph.' The French Nobel Prize-winner's words ascribed a mission to the German writers in exile: that of representing another, better Germany and preparing the way for a post-Hitler nation of the future. It was a mission most exiled intellectuals were indeed eager to be part of.

Intellectuals were responsible for the earliest, most determined resistance to Hitler during the period of the Weimar Republic. Ernst Toller, Kurt Tucholsky and Lion Feuchtwanger were among the writers involved, along with scientists such as Emil Julius Gumbel and Theodor Lessing, pacifist journalists Kurt Hiller and Berthold Jacob, and the artists George Grosz and John Heartfield. They fought with the weapons of irony and satire, scorn and derision, and finally the pathos of despair. Together with the new regime's political opponents, intellectuals were therefore among the first victims of Nazi persecution and emigrants. Their books were thrown on the bonfire of 10 May 1933 and many of them featured in the initial lists of those deprived of their German nationality. A good deal of such persecution was directed at Jews.

The intellectual exodus began in the weeks after the Reichstag fire. The foremost representatives of German-language literature, arts and sciences left their native land. Between 1933 and 1939 a total of well over 10,000 artists, writers, journalists and scientists emigrated after experiencing persecution for reasons of politics and/or race.

Most writers and artists saw their expulsion from Germany as a turning-point from which their lives and work could never fully recover. There were, however, some – optimistic – attempts to unite the many voices of a cultural emigration which embraced all the social levels and intellectual impulses of the Weimar Republic. Such initiatives sought to create larger or smaller groups capable of showing the world at large and the host countries in particular that the exiles did indeed represent the other Germany. Thus, a 'German P.E.N. Club in Exile' was founded as early as the winter of 1933–4. It was recognized by International P.E.N. and used that body's annual congresses to speak up for the silenced people of Germany and alert the international public to the Nazi regime's atrocities, just as its president, Heinrich Mann, had demanded.

Probably the most significant attempt to organize the cultural exiles was the foundation of a German Academy in Exile, together with its aid organization, the American Guild for German Cultural Freedom. This was Prince Hubertus zu Löwenstein's way of enabling the scattered and often isolated German-speaking intellectuals to work together constructively (and of creating a material basis for that work).

The spirit of the Academy and the American Guild was rooted in their founder's vision of a future Germany. Born in 1906, Löwenstein – who also became the organizations' general secretary – was a Doctor of Law who acquired a reputation as the 'Red Prince' of the Weimar Republic. He was one of the few members of the German high nobility publicly to pledge his allegiance to Weimar democracy. His political and journalistic activities soon earned him the hatred of the Nazis. Goebbels derided the 24-year-old prince in *Der Angriff* as early as 10 January 1931. After the Nazis seized power, Prince Löwenstein's home in Berlin was searched and a few weeks later he left for Austria with his wife, having been warned of his imminent arrest. He continued actively to oppose Hitler from his exile.

Prince Löwenstein drew strength and confidence for his struggle against the 'Third Reich' from his vision of a 'Future Reich'. This clearly revealed the influence of Stefan George's idealistic concept of a 'New Reich', to which Graf Stauffenberg, likewise, was deeply indebted. The basic idea was as follows:

For as long as Germany was occupied by the enemy, it would be impossible to realize the Future Reich. The 'task for the present', therefore, was to construct a 'territory of the German spirit': 'it is vital to create "Germany" even before there is a German Reich again.' How was this to be achieved? At first Prince Löwenstein thought of establishing an alternative, legitimate, German government, perhaps in London or in the Saar territory – which was still, at that time, a non-Nazi fragment of Germany. He aimed to recruit all the Germans outside the 'Third Reich' – exiles and other Germans living outside the German borders alike – as representatives of the 'true Germany'. Löwenstein was doubtless conscious of how utopian his idea was, for there were clear divisions at least among the political exiles, and most Germans living in other countries were under the influence of the 'Third Reich'. Realistically, then, the only potential 'representatives of the new Germany' were the intellectuals.

That he was able at least to begin putting his vision of a 'territory of the German spirit' into practice – by founding the Academy and the American Guild – was largely due to the concrete suggestions made by his friend Richard A. Bermann. In a memorandum for Prince Löwenstein, probably at the end of 1934, the Austrian author and journalist summarized the upshot of their joint deliberations on how to help German writers, artists and scientists in exile. Bermann wanted the prince to set up a 'German Sanctuary' ('Deutsche Freistatt' – the title of his memorandum). On 4 April 1935 the 'American Guild for German Cultural Freedom' was officially registered with the signatures of five American citizens and Prince Löwenstein. Its primary duty was to raise the funds needed to build a 'sanctuary'.

In the early summer of 1936, when the idea of a 'German Sanctuary' had developed into the plans for a German Academy of Arts and Sciences in Exile, Richard A. Bermann and Peter de Mendelssohn (probably at the prince's instigation) drafted a 'memorandum on the formation of a German Academy in New York'. The principle underlying this second document was that the Academy should, as the representative organization for the exiled German intellectual community throughout the world, 'act as the ultimate patron and protector of Germany's whole imperilled cultural tradition'. Mendelssohn also listed the practical tasks which the Academy and the Guild would later undertake. It would:

– award scholarships to needy intellectuals to enable them to continue their work, without regard to their political affiliation, religion or philosophy;
– put up prizes for literature and art; and
– provide subsidies for printing costs.

The memorandum was sent to a number of well-known writers, scientists and artists and it, together with Peter de Mendelssohn's tour of the main centres of exile in Europe, did much to win the support of nearly all the eminent German-speaking intellectuals for an Academy *Senat*, or Council. Those who agreed to join included Lion Feuchtwanger, Bruno Frank, Sigmund Freud, Otto Klemperer, Heinrich Mann, Robert Musil, Rudolf Olden, Max Reinhardt, Erwin Schroedinger, Paul Tillich, Ernst Toch, Ernst Toller, Fritz von Unruh, Veit Valentin and Franz Werfel. Peter de Mendelssohn was certainly instrumental in recruiting Thomas Mann as president of the Council. Mann was, together with Albert Einstein, the most prominent of all Germany's exiled intellectuals, so his demonstration of solidarity with the Academy's aims and endeavours carried particular weight. It also persuaded the Nazis that this dual organization represented a serious threat.

The crucial question was what would happen after the excitement of foundation had died down, in the harsh reality of life in exile.

To obtain the necessary resources, the Guild quickly turned to American-style 'fundraising'. In April 1937 a dinner in honour of Thomas Mann achieved a great deal of valuable publicity for the organization in the United States. It was, however, not until the beginning of 1938 that the first scholarship awards could be made. By then the hardship among the exiled intellectuals had increased to such an extent that it was no longer just the younger, lesser-known authors who required assistance. Among the first recipients, each of whom received a scholarship of 30 dollars a month – barely enough to survive on in most of the countries of asylum – for an initial period of three months, were writers of repute such as Oskar Maria Graf, René Schickele, Annette Kolb, Wilhelm Speyer, Alfred Polgar, Gustav Regler and even Joseph Roth. From 1938 until 1940 the Academy and Guild succeeded in helping more than 160 intellectuals continue for a while with their work.

In the summer of 1938, Prince Löwenstein managed to persuade Sigmund Freud – who was gravely ill in exile in London – to become president of the Academy's Scientific Division. Thomas Mann was already president of the Arts Division. Events later in the year, however, and particularly the escalating persecution of German Jews, meant that the flow of donations was substantially diverted to other causes. The Guild resorted to public appeals and imaginative schemes such as an auction of manuscripts (to which Albert Einstein and Bertolt Brecht contributed items) in the quest for the means to address the growing poverty of the intellectual exiles. It achieved a further public relations coup in April 1939 with its dinner at the Waldorf Astoria, at which US Secretary of the Interior Harold L. Ickes spoke as the guest of honour.

The beginning of the war in Europe and the unfortunate developments in the literary contest (the American publisher refused to publish the work selected by the European jury, which included Thomas Mann and Lion Feuchtwanger) led to a crisis in the Guild. Another followed in the spring of 1940, this time sparked by a newspaper article in which Prince Löwenstein objected to, as he put it, the 'policy of annihilation directed against Germany'. The prince's article, published in the *New Yorker Staatszeitung und Herold* of 17 March 1940, was influenced by his idea of a future Reich. It led to a break with the whole Mann family and ultimately, in the summer, to his resignation as general secretary and director of the American Guild. By this time it was virtually impossible for the Academy to fulfil the role for which it had been created, of patron to the exiled intellectuals. The main priority now was to save the lives of those stuck in France, most of them as internees, and in danger of being handed over to the Gestapo. This was the hour of Volkmar Zühlsdorff, Prince Löwenstein's closest friend and collaborator, who had shared his exile with him from the start and had been the

Guild's acting secretary since autumn 1938. Zühlsdorff worked tirelessly to obtain the affidavits and visas needed for entry to the United States. He collected money to pay for ocean crossings and tried to offer hope and encouragement in letters to desperate individuals even if he also had to break bad news. He, the Academy and the prince worked closely with the Emergency Rescue Committee which had been formed specially to deal with the problem in France. It was led by Frank Kingdon, who was one of the Guild's directors. The ERC took over all the rescue projects which were still underway when the Guild eventually had to cease its operations at the end of 1940 – 'because of our inability to raise further funds', as Treasurer Villard told the directors in his letter.

The 'great and . . . lasting achievement of the German Academy in Exile founded by Prince Löwenstein and his friends', according to Wolfgang Frühwald, is that it 'retarded that often fatal feeling of alienation'. It was 'the last bastion and the last institution of a humane German culture', founded on both 'the spirit of the European Enlightenment and Germany's civic culture'. As such it – along with the resistance within Germany and the activities of political exiles – helped to keep alive the idea of a humane and democratic Germany in the world at large, an idea which would serve as a starting point when Germany was reconstructed after the war.

The issue of 'culture as a weapon' has lost none of its topicality. Forced emigration and exile are still important in our modern world; indeed they seem even to be on the increase. Among those persecuted in their own countries and living in our midst are, of course, many intellectuals. One indication that we are willing to listen to them – as the cultural representatives of their nations, like the German intellectuals in exile – was the election of one of them, the Iranian writer SAID (who has been in exile in Germany since 1979) as president of the German P.E.N. Centre. An awareness of German history and of the lessons to be drawn from it is indispensable to any understanding of the foundations and perspectives of German politics. This applies not just to us Germans, but also to our neighbours, allies and partners who value Germany as a civilized nation at the heart of Europe. For that reason I wish this historical eyewitness account by Volkmar Zühlsdorff every success.

Klaus-Dieter Lehmann

CHAPTER ONE

The Background

Freedom and spirit are one and the same thing. Free spirit is a pleonasm and unfree spirit is a contradiction in terms.
Thomas Mann, *Letter to the editor of the*
New York Times, *12 December 1936*

After the National Socialists seized power in 1933, their bloody reign of terror rapidly smothered all open opposition and forced it abroad or underground. It was the German Academy of Arts and Sciences in Exile that came to embody the other Germany – the Germany of justice, freedom and human dignity for which all friends of liberty had been struggling even in the Weimar Republic. The Academy in Exile acquired its tremendous political significance not least because – irrespective of the political outlook and activities of each individual émigré – the roots and character of German emigration were political. The resistance of a determined minority within Germany, which produced over 40 attempts to assassinate Hitler,[1] represented a continuation of the fight against the enemies of democracy that had begun immediately after 1918. In exile, meanwhile, the Academy's spiritual and intellectual campaign against the regime belonged to the same liberal tradition.

The Weimar Republic founded after World War I was born 'of blood and tears'. When Philipp Scheidemann, the Social Democrat who became Germany's chancellor, proclaimed the Republic on 9 November 1918, he was only a few hours ahead of communist leader Karl Liebknecht. The latter was planning a proclamation from the *Berliner Schloss*: 'All power to the workers' and soldiers' councils!' Scheidemann resolutely opposed any such development:

> So Germany is to be a Russian province, a Soviet offshoot? I
> saw the madness of Russia before me, the exchange of the
> Tsarist rule of terror for that of the Bolsheviks. No, no, at least
> spare us that in Germany after all the other misery![2]

This was soon followed by the communist Spartacist uprising in
Berlin in January 1919, the declaration of the Soviet Republic in
Munich in April, the communist revolt of 1920 outside the Reichstag, which cost 42 lives, and finally by a series of revolts in Saxony
and the Ruhr. The Right instigated the Kapp *putsch* in March 1920;
the murder of government minister Matthias Erzberger in 1921;
that of Foreign Minister Walter Rathenau in 1922; and Hitler's
putsch in Munich of 1923, which collapsed in a hail of machine-gun
bullets fired by the Bavarian police.

Unfortunately these internal strains were accompanied by even
greater pressures arising from Germany's defeat in the war. In this
respect the Treaty of Versailles was of particular significance. The
treaty was such that Reich Chancellor Scheidemann refused to sign
it and his government showed its solidarity by resigning with him.
His successor and fellow Social Democrat Gustav Bauer also lodged
a 'protest against this treaty of violence and destruction – against
making a mockery of the right to self-determination, against the
enslavement of a great and good people, against the new threat
to world peace masked by a ceremonial peace treaty.'[3] It is worth
noting that the United States refused to sign the treaty and came
to a separate peace accord with Germany.

On top of all this, in 1923 the French army seized on a trivial
pretext to march into the Ruhr. Inflation was rampant; at its height
at the end of the year, one dollar was worth 4,200 billion marks. The
horrendous reparations accelerated the world economic crisis of
1929 and led in turn to mass unemployment in Germany, which
ultimately reached a record of nearly seven million.

All this created the background to the subsequent democratic
crisis and Hitler's staggering and grotesque popular appeal. In
their campaign of lies, the right-wing radicals blamed the democrats for the Treaty of Versailles and even for the defeat itself, as well
as for the growing economic hardship. Hitler never achieved a
majority while elections remained free, but the three-quarters
majority initially enjoyed by the democratic parties did shrink very

rapidly. In 1930 they lost even their simple majority. This development was, according to the historian Karl Dietrich Bracher, triggered partly by the Treaty of Versailles. Coercing Germany to sign the treaty 'put an end to the period of initially overwhelming support' for the democratic Republic.[4]

It required moral strength to rise above the bitterness created by injustice and to realize that hate cannot be overcome by hate, that it is wrong to counter violence with yet greater violence. It was not easy to see that sometimes it is necessary to endure injustice – without thereby licensing it but also without taking up arms – for as long as it takes for the other side to recognize that its conduct is indeed unjust. It was this insight that informed the politics of reconciliation in that era of European rapprochement associated with the names of Gustav Stresemann, Aristide Briand and Sir Austen Chamberlain. It also became the ethos of Germany's liberally-minded youth in the years of the Locarno Pact (1925), of Germany's admission into the League of Nations (1926) and of the French withdrawal from the Rhineland (1930): that short, happier post-war period which has been dubbed a 'springtime for the nations of Europe'.[5]

Those years also saw a blossoming of German culture and science. Literature, theatre and film, music, the plastic arts, architecture and many scientific disciplines all flourished. The roots of this wealth of creative modernity extended back into the pre-war era. Frank Wedekind's *Frühlingserwachen*, for example, had appeared as early as 1891 (in English as *Spring Awakening*, 1909). Thomas Mann followed with *Buddenbrooks* in 1901 (translated in 1924), *Tonio Kröger* in 1903 (translated in 1928) and *Der Tod in Venedig* in 1913 (*Death in Venice*, 1928). Heinrich Mann published *Professor Unrat* in 1908 (translated as *The Blue Angel*, 1932, and *Small Town Tyrant*, 1944) and *Der Untertan* in 1918 (*The Patrioteer*, 1921, and *Man of Straw*, 1947). Walter Hasenclever completed his first expressionist drama *Der Sohn* in 1914 (*The Son*, 1986). Sigmund Freud's Psychoanalytic Society arrived in Berlin in 1910. In 1912 Wassily Kandinsky published his programmatic text *Über das Geistige in der Kunst* (*Concerning the Spiritual in Art*, 1947, first translated as *The Art of Spiritual Harmony*, 1914) and painted 'Der Blaue Reiter' (The Blue Rider), which gave its name to the group of artists in Munich around Franz Marc, Paul Klee, August Macke, Alfred Kubin and

Gabriele Münter. In the world of music, composer Arnold Schönberg had already advanced as far as atonality on the way towards
dodecaphonic technique.

The *Novembergruppe* of artists of every ilk – writers such as Bert
Brecht and Ernst Toller, painter Emil Nolde, architects Walter Gropius and Erich Mendelsohn, musicians Kurt Weill, Alban Berg and
Paul Hindemith – had been formed immediately after the revolution of 1918. Its members declared: 'The future of art and the gravity
of the present moment compel us as revolutionaries of the intellect
(expressionists, cubists, futurists) to unite and collaborate closely
together.'[6] Max Beckmann's remark about himself might also apply
to his whole generation: 'What I want to show in my work is the
idea which hides itself behind so-called reality. I am seeking for the
bridge which leads from the visible to the invisible.'[7] Paul Klee
insisted: 'Art does not reproduce the visible, it makes visible.'[8] '*Die
Brücke*' – The Bridge – was in fact the name chosen for the circle of
expressionist artists including Ernst Ludwig Kirchner, Karl
Schmidt-Rottluff, Fritz Bley and Erich Heckel which formed in
Dresden in 1920.

In the same year the first expressionist film, *Das Cabinett des Dr
Caligari* (*The Cabinet of Dr Caligari*) with Werner Krauss and Conrad
Veidt, achieved an international breakthrough for German filmmaking. It was produced by Erich Pommer with his own company,
Deutsche Eclair Decla, which was later absorbed into Ufa (Univer-
sum Film AG), of which he became director. In 1921 Fritz Lang
made his film *Der müde Tod* (released in English as, variously,
Destiny/Between Two Worlds/Beyond the Wall, all 1921), following it
a year later with *Dr Mabuse, der Spieler* (*Dr Mabuse, King of Crime/Dr
Mabuse: The Gambler*, both 1922). These films were only the begin-
ning of a long series of successful productions in the 1920s.
Examples include Wilhelm Dieterle's *Das Wachsfigurenkabinett*
(*Waxworks/Three Wax Men*); Ernst Lubitsch's monumental *Madame
Dubarry* (the first major German success in the United States);
Erich Pommer's *Varieté* with Emil Jannings; Fritz Lang's films *Die
Nibelungen, Metropolis* and *Die Frau im Mond* (*By Rocket to the
Moon/Girl in the Moon/Woman in the Moon*); Friedrich Murnau's
Der letzte Mann (*The Last Laugh*) and *Faust*; and finally Pommer's
Blauer Engel (*The Blue Angel*) with Marlene Dietrich, based on
Heinrich Mann's *Professor Unrat* and scripted by Carl Zuckmayer.

During this period German filmmaking exerted international influence.

Walter Gropius had founded his school for architecture and the applied arts – the *Hochschule für Bau und Gestaltung*, or 'Bauhaus' – in Weimar in 1919. He demanded a new 'altered form of architecture', which 'is not there for its own sake, but rather springs from the *essence* of the building, from the function that it is intended to fulfil.'[9] The architect or 'master builder', he therefore insisted, needed to return to his basic craft. Gropius believed that the same should apply to sculptors, painters and graphic designers. 'The artist', he explained, 'is the highest form of craftsman: the apotheosis of the craftsman.' This tenet was reflected in the fact that, as well as architects such as Marcel Breuer and Ludwig Mies van der Rohe, artists such as Paul Klee, Lyonel Feininger, Wassily Kandinsky and László Moholy-Nagy worked and taught at the Bauhaus. In the same spirit, in 1921 Erich Mendelsohn built the 'Einstein Tower', the observatory at Potsdam which Albert Einstein visited and admiringly described in a single word: 'organic'.[10]

Einstein had been awarded the Nobel Prize for his theory of relativity that same year. Before him, Max Planck had received the Prize in recognition of his quantum theory, whilst in 1925 it was won by physicists Gustav Hertz and James Franck for their work on atomic theory. The Nobel Prize also went to several German chemists: Walter Nernst in 1920; Richard Adolf Zsigmondy, Heinrich Wieland, Hans Fischer and Friedrich Bergius between 1925 and 1931. Biologist Jakob Johannes von Uexküll, who founded the *Institut für Umweltforschung* (Institute for Environmental Research) in Hamburg, was a winner in 1920, as was biochemist Otto Meyerhof in 1922.

1924 saw the founding of the *Institut für Sozialforschung*, affiliated to the University of Frankfurt am Main, which subsequently rose to great eminence in exile as the International Institute of Social Research, first in Geneva and then, from 1934, at Columbia University in New York with Theodor Adorno, Erich Fromm, Otto Kirchheimer, Paul Lazarsfeld, Leo Löwenthal, Herbert Marcuse, Franz Neumann and Karl A. Wittfogel.

Music, literature and theatre also enjoyed something of a boom in Weimar Germany. Those of us who were young at the time knew so many of Rainer Maria Rilke's poems by heart that we were able to engage in long dialogues consisting entirely of quotations. We would not have had the temerity to do the same with the classically strict poetry of serious, élitist Stefan George. In our eyes he stood for the poet as a prophet.

George left Germany even before Hitler came to power, and in his will he stipulated how many decades had to pass after his death before his remains could be returned there. Of those in the Stefan George circle, poet Karl Wolfskehl emigrated to New Zealand as early as 1933 and historian Ernst Kantorowicz, author of the work on the Hohenstaufen Kaiser Frederick II, went to America. Theodor Heuss, the first German federal president after the Second World War, records in his memoirs how significant the 'great works of historical prose produced by the Stefan George circle' were to him.[11]

The cultural focal point of Germany at this time was Berlin; the great, lively, stimulating Berlin of the Weimar period, a cultural centre not just for Germany but also for Europe and far beyond. During my exile and subsequently as a diplomat I have seen many important cities, but none to overshadow the creative modernity and cosmopolitan wealth which characterized that Berlin of the 1920s.

This was not the first time Berlin had taken on such a leading role: it had occupied a similar position at the end of the nineteenth century, in the age of Naturalism. After the turn of the century it was briefly eclipsed by the Vienna of the neo-romantics, represented by Hugo von Hofmannsthal, Arthur Schnitzler and Richard Beer-Hofmann, and by the Munich of the Stefan George circle and the young Bert Brecht. Very soon after the war ended in 1918, however, it was once again Berlin that became the undisputed centre of art and culture in the German-speaking region, first with the 'boldness of expressionism',[12] then with the overlapping Dadaist, cubist and futurist movements, and then with the *Neue Sachlichkeit* (New Objectivity) movement. 'Many talents were born in Vienna,' wrote Richard Bermann, co-founder of the Academy in Exile, in retrospect, 'but later they moved to Berlin. Only when they had achieved success in Berlin did they win recognition at home as well.'[13]

In Berlin there were approximately 40 theatres, including the *Deutsches Theater* and *Kammerspiele*, where Max Reinhardt was director, and the *Staatliches Schauspielhaus*. It was the *Schauspielhaus* that staged Leopold Jessner's experimental expressionist production of *Wilhelm Tell*, starring Albert Bassermann and Fritz Kortner. This was a deliberately provocative rejection of tyranny and war, which led to heated protests from both the Right and the Left. The productions at the *Staatsoper*, such as Alban Berg's *Wozzeck* and Leo Janáček's *Jenůfa*, were similarly controversial, as were the *Kroll Opera* with its musical director Otto Klemperer, the Philharmonic concerts given by Wilhelm Furtwängler and Bruno Walter, and the *Dreigroschenoper* (*Threepenny Opera*) by Bertolt Brecht and Kurt Weill, which had its premiere at the *Theater am Schiffbauerdamm* and became an international success. The Berlin cabarets which shot up like mushrooms after World War I (there were 38 of them by 1922) also achieved international renown. Notable examples include Max Reinhardt's *Schall und Rauch*, Rosa Valetti's *Grössenwahn* and Trude Hesterberg's *Wilde Bühne*, where the young Brecht made his debut and provoked uproarious protests.

In view of this cultural diversity, it is hardly surprising that Berlin became the focus for arts journalism and above all for theatre criticism, which was still widely read at that time. Alfred Kerr, Herbert Ihering, Siegfried Jacobsohn, Julius Bab, Alfred Polgar, Bernhard Diebold and Emil Faktor were among the leading figures to emerge. Moreover, Berlin became the centre of political journalism, represented by men such as Kurt Tucholsky or Carl von Ossietzky and his *Weltbühne*. About 120 newspapers and magazines appeared in Berlin; pre-eminent among them were the *Berliner Tageblatt*, the *Vossische Zeitung*, the monthly magazines *Querschnitt* and *Uhu* and the innovative *Berliner Illustrirte*, which featured Erich Salomon's photographs. Berlin was also home to major publishing houses such as Ullstein and Fischer. The latter published the work of Thomas Mann, Hermann Hesse, Gerhart Hauptmann, Stefan Zweig, Carl Zuckmayer and Alfred Döblin among others.

The vast majority of the leading figures in culture and science, many of whom were Jewish Germans, regrouped after 1933 in exile, and a considerable number of them joined the German Academy of Arts and Sciences in Exile. Peter Gay, a historian at Yale University who was born in Berlin and emigrated in 1939, has referred to the 'greatest collection of transplanted intellect, talent, and scholarship the world has ever seen'.[14] It was as if the main representatives of a whole cultural region had gone into exile, where they now stood up for an alternative Germany, repeatedly reminding the world that Hitler and his murderous mobs ought not to be equated with Germany itself.

CHAPTER TWO

Prince Hubertus zu Löwenstein: Founder of the German Academy in Exile

No sooner had I entered the German embassy in Mexico in 1964 than a man approached me with outstretched arms: 'Amigo, you must still remember me: Barcelona, Valencia, Madrid – I organized your radio addresses to the Germans everywhere!' He enabled me to speak on over two dozen radio stations. He introduced me as 'an old anti-Fascist friend of mine, from the time of the war in Spain'.

Prince Hubertus zu Löwenstein, Botschafter ohne Auftrag[1]

When he went into exile in 1933, Löwenstein, a dedicated democrat whom Joseph Goebbels dubbed the 'Red Prince', was only 26 years old. Yet he was already one of National Socialism's most prominent opponents. His extraordinary commitment to social issues, his political far-sightedness and the heated reactions to his publications had contributed to that prominence. His first editorial, entitled 'The Third Reich', appeared in the respected *Vossische Zeitung* of Berlin on 12 July 1930. In it, even at this early date, he compared and contrasted the Weimar constitution and its merits with Italian Fascism, and the latter with the aims and intentions of the German National Socialists. He came to the conclusion that 'while Fascism had not upset the peace of Europe, Nazism in power would mean another war'.[2]

Löwenstein was ahead of his time in coming to that conclusion. It was informed by his detailed study of Italian Fascism – the subject of the thesis for which he was awarded his doctorate in Hamburg in 1931. His supervisor was Professor Albrecht Mendelssohn Bartholdy, the founder of the *Institut für Auswärtige Politik* (Institute for International Politics). In his dissertation, entitled *Umrisse der Idee des faschistischen Staates und ihrer Verwirklichung (unter Vergleichung mit den wichtigsten Gebieten des deutschen Staatsrechts)* (Sketches of the Idea of the Fascist State and its Realization (in Comparison with the Main Areas of German Constitutional Law)), Löwenstein asserted that every totalitarian regime, be it of the Left or the Right, was inherently contrary to the basic laws of society among the Christian peoples of the Occident. Wherever there was a fundamental violation of human rights, and if all legal means were of no avail, there was a right to resist which went beyond the law: indeed, every individual would then have 'not just a right, but the duty to revolt'.[3]

He meant this literally, for Löwenstein consistently followed through from his theoretical insights to their practical political consequences. When the growing power of the Nazis became a threat, he responded by joining the republican *Reichsbanner Schwarz-Rot-Gold* (the cross-party, SPD-dominated paramilitary formation named after the black, red and gold standard of the Republic) in October 1930. And in 1937, when Hitler sent his troops to Spain to support the caudillo, Generalissimo Franco, in his struggle against the Republicans, socialists and Communists, Löwenstein decided to travel to Spain and – despite being a devout Catholic – take up the Republican cause. His prescience enabled him to recognize even then – earlier than most of his contemporaries – that Hitler's military intervention was more than just an attempt to create a shield against atheist Communism. Rather, the war against the democrats of Spain amounted to a dress rehearsal, staged by Hitler and Mussolini, for World War II. Furthermore: 'if these powers are successful, their next victims will be Czechoslovakia and other Central European states, until the Fascist bloc [is] strong enough to turn against the East and against the Western democracies.'[4]

Löwenstein's committed statements regarding the civil war, his espousal of a Christian socialism beholden to neither Communism nor National Socialism and his desire for the peoples of a united Europe to live in peaceful coexistence were widely welcomed abroad. His reports on the Spanish Civil War in the *New York Post*,

the *Atlantic Monthly*, the *Baseler Nationalzeitung*, Prague's *Neue Weltbühne* and other media were also greeted warmly, along with his
book *A Catholic in Republican Spain*, which appeared in English in
1937 and in my German translation in 1938.[5] The Nazi authorities
were among those who followed the Prince's public activities very
closely. On 8 September 1937, for example, the German embassy in
Madrid made the following report to the Foreign Ministry in Berlin:

> Prince Löwenstein, the former leader of the democratic youth
> associations and head of the Christian movement, recently
> received a series of journalists in Barcelona. He described to
> them at length the conditions allegedly prevailing in Germany
> at present and the interest being taken there in the events in
> Spain. Among other matters, he mentioned that the Spanish
> people was not involved in a class battle or a battle of the
> religions, but was in fact defending itself against the barbarism
> which was attacking it, and that the magnitude of this battle
> was not yet fully understood in Europe. In particular, it was
> not yet common knowledge that a Fascist Spain would be a
> direct threat to France and that the consequence of this would
> be that all the democratic powers of the West would be at the
> mercy of the aggressive barbarism of Hitler and Mussolini. He
> said he must also add that the victory of democracy in Spain
> would mean liberation for oppressed peoples, including those
> of Germany and Italy. The same criminals who had destroyed
> Guernica were also terrorising the German people.[6]

That a member of the aristocracy should plead with uncomprom-
ising passion for the preservation of democracy and not only draw
on his whole fortune but also, on several occasions, risk his life to
pursue that end, was quite extraordinary in Germany at that time.
His wide open mind (which made him detest any whiff of provin-
cialism), his inner independence and assuredness were largely the
result of his background and his consciousness of a long historical
inheritance.

Prince Hubertus zu Löwenstein belonged to the Wittelsbach
dynasty, which had produced several German emperors. As the son
of Maximilian Prince of Löwenstein-Wertheim-Freudenberg, he
was the descendant of Frederick 'the Victorious', Elector Palatine.
He was born and grew up in Austria and was of English descent on

his mother's side. His mother, Constance, was the youngest daughter of Baron Henry de Worms, whom Queen Victoria had raised to the peerage as Baron Henry Pirbright of Pirbright and who was appointed to the Privy Council as Parliamentary Secretary to the Board of Trade.[7]

Prince Löwenstein was given a classical education and grew up in a stimulating, often paradoxical, environment. World War I and the overthrow of the monarchy also made an impression on him, and he soon developed a keen interest in politics and a profound aversion to all obsessively violent, totalitarian movements, whether they stemmed from the Left or the Right.[8]

I had met Löwenstein in Berlin in 1929 and collaborated with him politically for the first time in the *Reichsbanner Schwarz-Rot-Gold*. He was much in demand as a passionate speaker who galvanized the masses on behalf of the Republic. Even at that time, it was clear from the galloping unemployment in the wake of the world economic crisis and the growing strength of those hostile to the parliamentary system that the Republic was entering a critical period. Neither the coalition of the centre, nor the forces of the Left or Right, could now command a majority in the Reichstag, so Germany was governed by a presidential cabinet founded not on parliamentary support but rather on the emergency powers of Reich President Paul von Hindenburg under Article 48 of the constitution. On 28 March 1930, Hindenburg appointed the parliamentary leader of the Centre Party, Heinrich Brüning, as Reich chancellor. Brüning formed a minority government of the centre and moderate Right and issued a series of emergency decrees needed to deal with the economic crisis. When the Reichstag, at the request of the Social Democrats (*Sozialdemokratische Partei Deutschlands* or SPD), demanded their repeal, Hindenburg dissolved the Reichstag without further ado.

Brüning at least attempted to win the tolerance, if not actually the backing, of a majority in the Reichstag. The man who succeeded him on 1 June 1932, the reactionary, unscrupulous Franz von Papen, had no time for such niceties. His 'cabinet of national concentration', as he called it, survived only by one dissolution of the Reichstag after another.

With the disempowerment of parliament, the radicals became more confident and more vociferous. They were spurred on by considerable gains in the Reichstag elections: the National Socialists, who had managed to increase their number of seats from twelve to 107 on 14 September 1930, achieved a total of 230 on 31 July 1932, thereby becoming the strongest parliamentary party. Drunk on success, the National Socialists and their paramilitary forces, the SA and SS, began treating the Party's opponents outside parliament with increasing brutality. We of the *Reichsbanner*, responsible for security at democratic rallies and demonstrations, were forced into the front line to grapple with the Nazis' aggressive shock troops. It is worth pointing out that we also had to deal with the forces of the Communist paramilitary organization, the *Rote Frontkämpferbund* (Red Front Fighters' League). The Communists, after all, were also bent on destroying the Republic. To that end they were prepared, if necessary, to form alliances even with the National Socialists, as they did in the referendum of 9 August 1931 concerning the dissolution of the Prussian Landtag (state parliament) and in the Berlin transport strike of November 1932. These were not merely instances of chumminess between the thugs of the Left and Right; they were concerted policies.

Because we of the *Reichsbanner* came to the conclusion that National Socialism and Communism could not be combated by purely parliamentary means, the *Reichsbanner*'s federal council decided after the success of the National Socialists in the Reichstag election of 14 September 1930 to create potent defence formations (*Schutzformationen*, commonly abbreviated to *Schufos*). After only a few months they were 160,000 strong; 250,000 men had joined by the start of 1932 and ultimately 400,000 by 1933 – a membership which put them on an equal footing with the SA.

On 11 October 1932 the reactionary *Deutschnationale Volkspartei* (German National People's Party), which still imagined it could hitch Hitler to its own wagon, made an alliance with Hitler in Bad Harzburg, known as the 'Harzburg Front'. The horror this provoked among the democratic public deepened when, soon afterward, the 'Boxheim document' came to light. This consisted of plans for a seizure of power which had been drafted by Nazi officials and foresaw, among other things, the arming of the SA and a *Landwehr* (territorial army) troop, the implementation of courts martial with unrestricted powers, the death sentence with immediate execution for any offence and the abolition of private property.

Thoroughly alarmed, the republican forces – the *Reichsbanner*, the *Allgemeiner Deutscher Gewerkschaftsbund* (the association of German trade unions), the Social Democratic Party, the workers' sports movement (known as the *Arbeitersportler*) and the *Allgemeiner freier Angestelltenbund* (Afa – an umbrella organization for white collar unions) – responded by forming the *Eiserne Front* (Iron Front) alliance. They chose as their symbol three downward slanting arrows. Soon every swastika, whether 'official' or daubed, was pierced by such arrows.

In June 1932 Papen succeeded by means of an intrigue in toppling the most powerful democratic bastion, the Prussian coalition government, which had been duly elected and was led by two Social Democrats: *Ministerpräsident* (State Prime Minister) Otto Braun and Interior Minister Carl Severing. In order to end the disturbances, Chancellor Brüning had allowed his interior minister, Wilhelm Groener, to ban the SA and SS, but Papen rescinded the ban on 14 June 1932. This prompted a fresh outbreak of terror on the streets, bloodier and more brutal than ever before.

This, however, was simply the excuse Papen had been waiting for: he now blamed the Prussian government for the bloodshed he himself had made possible. On 20 July 1932, he informed the Prussian state administration that the president of the Republic had appointed him, Papen, as Reich commissar for Prussia under Article 48 of the constitution, 'because public security and order in Prussia [was] no longer guaranteed'. At the same time he relieved Braun and Severing of their offices.

In this new situation, we of the *Reichsbanner* waited expectantly for a signal from the leadership of the Iron Front, but first and foremost from the Prussian government, giving us the go ahead to avert a coup at the last moment by coordinated mass protests, demonstrations and marches throughout Germany. 'We were raring to go,' states one of many contemporary reports, 'we were waiting for the call to arms! To the streets! General strike!'[9] Another commentator affirms: 'In all German cities formations of the Reichsbanner and Iron Front were standing by . . . and waiting for a call to action.'[10] Yet we waited in vain. The Prussian ministers merely lodged a protest; Severing famously declared: 'I only yield to force!' Their motivation was entirely honourable: as democrats, they wanted 'no bloodshed'. They were unable, in a constitutional state such as the

Weimar Republic, to conceive of the crimes to which capitulation to Papen (and thus to the Nazis) would ultimately lead.

We, the younger generation, allowed our imaginations to run wild: we saw the disaster coming and were ready to lay down our lives to preserve a free Republic. Our mistake was to accept abstention from all forms of violence as the decision of a democratically legitimate government, instead of weighing in against that government's will if necessary.

Severing soon regretted his politically fatal mistake. At an SPD party conference on 19 June 1933 he admitted: 'It is awful when I look back today on my determination to prevent bloodshed in July 1932 . . . Now I have to tell you that my efforts were in vain. Now a sea of blood and tears awaits us.'[11]

As the events were unfolding, Prince Löwenstein, already one of the leading figures in the *Reichsbanner* at the age of 25, attempted to take decisive steps to embolden the ministers and force them to act. When we learned of Papen's manoeuvre on 20 July 1932, Löwenstein was leading a training camp at Erkner, near Berlin. We pleaded with him to do something.

Löwenstein knew that the *Länder* of Southern Germany had lodged a protest with Hindenburg five weeks earlier, after the ministerial conference of 11 June, against any possible interference by Papen in Prussian rights of state. He therefore decided to try to win their support for the Prussian ministers. Late in the evening of the same day, 20 July 1932, he received a sealed authorization from the secretary of state in the Prussian interior ministry, Wilhelm Abegg. Early the following morning he and Dr Sigmund Nathan, a *Reichsbanner* confidante, flew to Munich. Since the Bavarian prime minister, Heinrich Held, was in Stuttgart for a *Länder* conference, Löwenstein spoke to his deputy, Interior Minister Karl Stützel, who, after briefly consulting the cabinet, promised the support of the Bavarian state government.[12] Löwenstein was then able to inform Held personally in Stuttgart. The state president of Baden, Joseph Schmitt, declared his *Land*'s readiness to endorse a formal complaint about Papen's infringement of the constitution.

The Hessian government received Löwenstein and Nathan with open arms. Wilhelm Leuschner, the Social Democrat interior minister who was later executed in connection with the Hitler assassination attempt of 20 July 1944, not only promised Löwenstein every assistance against Papen, but also declared that he was ready to convene a conference of the Southern German state governments without delay. The Hanseatic cities, he said, would be sure to join the campaign. Moreover, he assured Löwenstein that his government was prepared to offer the Prussian ministers a 'seat of government in exile' in Darmstadt for the duration of the conflict. Darmstadt was at that time in the demilitarized zone under the Treaty of Versailles and thus not liable to attack from the *Reichswehr*.

A Prussian government in exile would have shown up the illegality of the 'Prussian coup' for all the world to see. Recognition of such a government would have represented the signal for which so many people were waiting and which could have set the democratic masses in all of Germany into motion. The prime ministers of the *Länder*, however, insisted on a firm resolution from the Prussian ministers, together with a public declaration that they – as the rightful government of Prussia – had sought support from the Southern German *Länder* to defend the Reich's constitution and to restore constitutional order. Leuschner, Stützel and Schmitt expected such a declaration that same day (23 July) or by the following day at the latest.

They waited in vain.

Neither Severing nor Braun could bring himself to issue such a declaration. They wanted to leave the decision solely to the *Staatsgerichthof* (the German Supreme Court for Constitutional Conflicts) and the electors in the imminent Reichstag election of 31 July. The National Socialists emerged from that election as the strongest party in parliament, with 37.8 per cent of the votes and 230 seats. And by the time the *Staatsgerichthof*, which had already rejected the Prussian government's application for a temporary injunction against Papen on 25 July, concluded on 25 October 1932 that the ministers could only be relieved of their authority temporarily, Papen's control of Prussia was so secure that the judgement did nothing to change the situation.

The disaster took its course; Germany's fate was sealed. On 30 January 1933, Hindenburg appointed Hitler as chancellor.

After Hitler's seizure of power, Löwenstein attempted to continue the struggle illegally, by forming the *Deutsche Legion* resistance group. The Nazis responded with blood and terror. Armed SA men broke into the homes of members of my local

Reichsbanner unit in central Berlin and beat them up so badly that they required hospital treatment. The *Reichsbanner*'s lawyer Günter Joachim was arrested by SA men wearing *Hilfspolizei* (police reserve) armbands; in the notorious SA torture centre at the former 'Ulap' exhibition grounds, he was blinded, castrated and tortured to death.

Löwenstein himself was tipped off by a loyal police captain that he was about to be arrested and sent to a concentration camp. On 30 April 1933 he and his wife, Princess Helga née Schuylenburg, emigrated to Matzen, near Brixlegg in the Tyrol. I followed them two weeks later, on 15 May, after witnessing the barbaric book burning on Berlin's Opernplatz. As Löwenstein's closest collaborator, I wanted to be by his side in exile too.

For us, emigration stood not for resignation but rather for political struggle as the only alternative to a concentration camp or elimination. We were, however, far from secure in Austria, for Hitler's secret police – the *Geheime Staatspolizei* or Gestapo – soon attempted to kidnap the 'Red Prince', his wife and me. Accomplices were then supposed to smuggle us over the nearby border into Germany. We were indebted to Social Democrat friends in Matzen for foiling that plan by guarding our house day and night. In Innsbruck, however, we were repeatedly forced to take up arms in self-defence. When Princess Löwenstein was set upon in front of the University of Innsbruck and fired a shot at one of her assailants, the incident was reported by the domestic and foreign press; the *New York Times* of 2 June 1933, for example, included the story on page two under the headline: 'Princess Fires Shot at Austrian Nazis'. This prompted the Tyrolean state government to station a detachment of Austrian *Bundeswehr* soldiers in a building adjacent to the house in Brixlegg for our protection.

Prince Löwenstein had left Germany with virtually no money. Fortunately, the British government chose that moment to release his share to the inheritance of his maternal grandfather, Lord Pirbright of Pirbright, who had died in World War I. Before long, however, these funds too were exhausted, for Löwenstein provided frequent and generous assistance to other exiles. Later he had to depend on his income from journalism, lecture tours through England and America and what he made from sales of his books until, in 1937, the Carnegie Endowment for International Peace in

New York offered him a post as Visiting Carnegie Professor for International Relations, which was renewed annually.

We saw exile as a continuation of the political struggle by different means but with the same goal: that of deposing Hitler. From the very start, therefore, Löwenstein made plans for the post-Hitler future. Among his efforts to this end were two books about the situation in Germany: *The Tragedy of a Nation. Germany, 1918–1934*,[13] a critical treatment of the reasons for the downfall of the Weimar Republic (published in 1934 and translated into various languages) and *After Hitler's Fall*,[14] the vision of a liberated, democratic Germany in a united Europe (completed in the same year). Both works enjoyed a wide international readership.

Internationally, Hitler was initially able to profit from the general spirit of reconciliation persisting in Europe due to Gustav Stresemann's peace policies. Löwenstein's activities in exile were therefore designed to show Hitler up for what he really was: a disaster for Germany and Europe. This, Löwenstein hoped, would strengthen the domestic opposition to Hitler and encourage a coup, as well as convincing the people of free Europe and the USA that Hitler and Germany were not synonymous, that, contrary to all the Nazi propaganda, there was still another, liberal Germany which would resume its role as a civilized nation in the heart of Europe after the dictator's inevitable downfall. It was, of course, also essential to undermine the notion that Hitler represented a trustworthy potential ally against the Soviet Union, which was rearming to an ever greater extent, but Hitler himself soon shattered any such ideas through his campaigns of conquest – the invasion of Austria, the extorted cession of the Sudeten German areas, the occupation of the 'rest of Czechoslovakia' – culminating in his pact with Stalin, in which the two of them carved up Poland and coordinated their invasions: Hitler's on 1 September, Stalin's on 17 September 1939.

Initially the Western powers hoped to satisfy the dictator's appetite by granting him territorial concessions. Löwenstein, however, had never been under any illusions about Hitler's intentions. He warned against the appeasement policy adopted by Britain's prime minister, Neville Chamberlain, which was intended to serve the cause of peace but which in fact merely intensified Hitler's aggressiveness and greed.

In order to bolster the liberal forces against the Nazi regime, Löwenstein planned to activate the hundreds of thousands of German-speaking émigrés spread among 75 countries on five continents. He wanted to bring together their spokesmen in a prestigious institution. It was an ambitious undertaking, in which he was helped by influential figures and close friends.

Among them was the journalist Rudolf Olden, a friend of the family, who had been deputy editor of the *Berliner Tageblatt* newspaper before emigrating. In London, Olden founded and led the German P.E.N. Club in Exile, and he was also the author of a series of standard works on Stresemann, Hitler and Hindenburg. One of Löwenstein's principal collaborators was the respected Austrian writer and journalist Richard A. Bermann, better known by his pen-name of Arnold Höllriegel. In the course of his considerable travels Bermann had accumulated close contacts with numerous influential, well-placed figures in all parts of the world. His friendship with Löwenstein was built on a profound spiritual and political basis. When the prince returned from the Spanish Civil War in 1937, Bermann wrote to him:

> I congratulate you for everything you have done and especially for your baptism of fire. I too have repeatedly risked my life, but I have never had the chance to do so for what I believed to be a just cause. . . . I have never doubted you and therefore see no reason to be especially proud of you. And please do not doubt that I too would be prepared to sacrifice my blood if it were necessary.[15]

Their friendship began in February 1934 after the semi-Fascist Dollfuss regime's bloody suppression of the Viennese workers' revolt. In response to Bermann's appeal for help, Löwenstein had successfully campaigned for an end to the fighting in Vienna. At the time he was writing his book, *After Hitler's Fall*, in which he contrasted the barbarism of National Socialism with a free, just Germany, part of a European community of free peoples, which he predicted would be resurrected in a fresh form after the overthrow of Hitler. Löwenstein and Bermann both believed that this future Germany depended not just on those who went into 'inner exile' or who emigrated abroad, but also on all the friends of German culture among the 35 million Germans abroad.

Such considerations ultimately led to the plan for a German academy of arts and sciences in exile. This organization was intended to put on show the wealth of creativity which had been banished abroad when German-speaking intellectuals – writers, artists, musicians, architects, scholars and scientists – were driven from their homeland.

In his *After Hitler's Fall* Löwenstein wrote:

> A Reich is coming into being, supported by men all over Europe; it still possesses no territory, but is united and throbs with a guiding will, a creed and a ready spirit. That is the new Germany . . . Its political realization is yet to come, but spiritually it may be achieved at once.[16]

In order to make his concept clear, he offered the example of the Catholic church, which might be restricted in terms of statehood to the tiny territory of the Vatican City, but which had an importance extending far beyond that territory and which was recognized under international law.

The aim of founding an academy was a forward-looking one, and Richard Bermann shared Löwenstein's view that it represented no more than a first step:

> It is, however, important never to forget that there can only ever be *one* real sanctuary for the German spirit: a liberated, reconstructed German Reich. Our little Sanctuary must aim, so far as possible, to bring the greater one closer. To that end we will build a site hut, a model, a nursery. And that is why we must never allow temporary details to distract us from our future purpose, from our great cause: the fight for the political, social, spiritual and intellectual freedom of all Germans.[17]

One of the most urgent questions to be settled before realizing such plans was that of where to locate the future Academy in Exile. One of the German-speaking regions beyond the Reich's borders at the time was the Saar territory, which had been taken from Germany under the Treaty of Versailles to be administered for a period of fifteen years by France under League of Nations supervision. Here, in Saarbrücken, adjacent to Germany but out of the Gestapo's reach, the Academy in Exile might have found a home.

There was to be a plebiscite on 13 January 1935 on the Saar's future. The options were a reunion with Germany, incorporation into France or the prolongation of the League of Nations mandate. Rudolf Olden was the first to urge Löwenstein to 'go to Saarbrücken and help to convince the people that national as well as religious reasons should prevent them from submitting to Hitlerism'.[18]

With an eye to the future Academy in Exile, Löwenstein concluded in 1934 that

> . . . a victory of the *status quo* policy would mean a clear defeat for Hitlerism only, not for Germany. A twofold aim could be achieved: first, a possibly mortal blow to the prestige of Nazism; and second, the winning of a German territory to form the center of national opposition against the shameful misuse of the German name by the Nazis. If on free German soil all liberty-loving forces could be gathered, a German exiles' government might be established on its own territory, one day to be transplanted to a liberated Berlin.[19]

It was, however, most unlikely that the Saar's population would vote against returning to Germany: even Hitler's opponents were too afraid of ultimately being annexed by France, as Alsace-Lorraine had been before. Aware of this, Löwenstein saw clearly that the Saar could only remain separate from Germany until Hitler's fall, and the possibility of returning to Germany at a later date must therefore be left open. To this end he lobbied the League of Nations to take the precaution of preparing the way for a further plebiscite even as the present one took place. The League of Nations indeed passed a resolution to that effect on 6 December 1934.

In the plebiscite of 13 January 1935, the people of the Saar nevertheless voted against preserving the *status quo* – that is, against prolonging the League of Nations' mandate – and for reunion with Germany. When the government in Paris again insisted on the Saar's cession to France after the war, Löwenstein and the civil-rights movement he had founded, *Deutsche Aktion* (German Action Movement), campaigned vehemently and successfully for the League of Nations resolution to be honoured. In 1954 the French premier, Pierre Mendès-France, gave in and on 23 October 1955 there was another plebiscite, in which the great majority of the people of the Saar again voted for Germany. On 1 January 1957 the Saar was finally reunited with Germany.

After the Saar's reincorporation into Germany in 1935, the search for a headquarters and organizational centre for the Academy in Exile focused above all on the traditional host country for political refugees: the United States of America. Löwenstein, by now a figure of international repute, was engaged at the time in giving various lectures in England, including appearances at the Royal Institute for International Affairs and the League of Nations Union. He was then invited to undertake a lecture tour of the USA. His theme was to be the situation in Germany. After the failure of the Saar campaign, he immediately travelled to America.

In order to realize his plan to found a German academy for the arts and sciences in exile, it was essential to create an American aid organization. This was the only way to raise the necessary funds for the academy. It says a great deal for Löwenstein's energy and powers of persuasion that even on his first visit to the United States he was able to set up such an organization in the course of his three-month lecture tour, which took him right across the continent and to Canada. His success is also a measure of the sympathy and understanding of the Americans – including many German-Americans – for those whom the Nazis had driven from Germany and who were now taking up intellectual arms against the Hitler regime from exile.

Löwenstein had announced his ideas for an academy in exile as soon as he arrived in New York on 2 February 1935:

> Modern Germany is no longer a home to German culture, to German intellectual life. The real Germany survives only outside the Reich's borders, wherever Germans are able to live in freedom. My idea is to unite all these Germans, not into a political Reich, but rather into a spiritual and intellectual one. . . . We German patriots, currently living in exile – we, whom usurpers have banished from the land of our birth – shall soon be forced to assume responsibility for Germany's destiny. . . . Over the course of history, Germans who cherished their liberty have often come to the United States. It is therefore my desire to win friends among the people of America, people who are ready to understand our situation.[20]

Löwenstein's pronouncements received considerable attention not just in New York, but also in the rest of America. The *Los Angeles Times* went furthest; under the headline 'Hitler's Public Enemy No. 1', it speculated on Löwenstein's political future: 'Many persons in Europe think he will succeed Hitler when and if the Nazis lose power.'[21]

When the ship docked, Löwenstein was greeted on the quay by members of the New York *Reichsbanner* section, the 'Friends of German Democracy', waving black, red and gold flags. In the press and through a poster campaign, the *Reichsbanner* called for a mass demonstration of Germans: 'Prince Hubertus von Löwenstein-Wertheim-Freudenberg, Count zu Löwenstein-Scharffeneck will speak on: "The Tragedy of my Fatherland – Nazi Germany is not the Real Germany".'[22] Over 1,000 German-Americans took part in the demonstration. Attempts by a mob from the Nazi 'German-American Bund' to cause a riot against the demonstration were so violent that ultimately police intervention became necessary. As early as February 1934, a parliamentary investigative committee in Washington had ascertained that the Hitler regime's representatives in America assisted the Bund in such exploits.[23]

The German embassy and the German consulates general and consulates in the United States and Canada informed Berlin regularly and with mounting concern – but sometimes with ill-concealed satisfaction – about the effect of Löwenstein's activities and his subsequent lecture tour to Montreal, Washington, Chicago, St Louis, Cincinnati, San Francisco, Los Angeles and Philadelphia. The consulate general in San Francisco, for example, reported that two of Löwenstein's lectures (given on 17 and 19 February) 'seemed to make a strong impression on those present, as the lengthy debates which followed also indicate'. It summarized Löwenstein's lecture as follows:

> In the course of time the sections of the population with anti-National Socialist sympathies will unite with the army to topple the current German regime. The forces outside Germany are of the utmost importance in these struggles against barbarism and suppression. The whole world should join in these struggles, as it is a campaign for the reinstatement of the ideals of freedom, justice and peace.[24]

In his speeches and publications, Löwenstein repeatedly insisted that Hitler was not entitled to speak for Germany. After a lecture at the Californian University of Berkeley, for example, he explained in the *Wiener Tag* newspaper of 24 March 1935:

At present Professors M. [Moritz Julius] Bonn and C. [Carl] Landauer of the *Handelshochschule* are lecturing in lecture halls which are full to overflowing in Berkeley. There has been no place for them in Berlin since Germany stopped concerning itself with people's intellect and their present abilities, and focused instead on their grandmother's pedigree. Painful though it is that our own youth should have to do without such leading lights, the role that these exiles and expellees play abroad is also important. They are living, creative examples of what 'Germany' is – the land of knowledge and research, the land of philosophy and humanity; not the land of barbarism, pernicious ideology, bondage and the jackboot, which is the distorted image some superficial observers may have obtained.[25]

The wide coverage he received in the press showed just how strong an impression Löwenstein made in his public appearances and utterances, not just on German-Americans with democratic sympathies but also on the population at large, irrespective of class or origin. Klaus and Erika Mann made this point at the time in their book *Escape to Life*, which appeared more than half a century later in Germany with the subtitle *Deutsche Kultur im Exil* (German Culture in Exile). In it they also describe the German Day celebrated each year in New York, on the occasion of which Löwenstein gave one of his many speeches:

A big hall had been hired out in the Bronx, but it turned out that it could not hold half of the crowd which had gathered. A second great hall was opened: more than ten thousand men and women must have come together to demonstrate for Germany and against Hitler. For that is the neatest form of the German anti-Fascist motto: For Germany, against Hitler.[26]

Klaus and Erika Mann added that Prince Löwenstein had made many friends through his personality and his spirited and eloquent manner; he had already succeeded in filling eminent and influential Americans with enthusiasm for his plan to found a German academy in exile.

Encouraging experiences such as these redoubled Löwenstein's confidence that a 'sanctuary for German culture' would be received in America with a great deal of sympathy and support. This confidence, nay certitude, lent him the energy and persuasiveness he needed to found an aid organization for the exile academy in the short time available to him in New York between completing his lecture tour of the USA in March 1935 and returning to Europe: the American Guild for German Cultural Freedom.

Löwenstein had already won considerable respect and was generally acknowledged as one of the leading figures in the German exile community. The nine books he published in exile, his teaching work at American universities under the auspices of the Carnegie Foundation and his numerous essays and radio talks about Germany and the future of Europe would enhance his reputation still further in the years ahead. In November 1941, for example, when the New York monthly *Scoop* demanded that the Allies recognize a 'German Victory Government-in-Exile', it added:

> Germany's greatest day in these eight bloody years of Hitler rule will come when President Heinrich Mann, Foreign Minister Prince zu Löwenstein and the cabinet of Germany watch in a room in London while [the Allied leaders] sign a treaty with the new government. It must be a treaty of peace, a treaty offering the German people, not the vengeance of armies of occupation, but the weapons of peace: food and ballots, for a nation hungry for peace.

CHAPTER THREE

Richard Arnold Bermann: Co-founder of the Academy

So what is my purpose in the unexplored regions of the Libyan Desert? I have an answer to that question: to stick my head in the sand. I set out on this wildest, most adventurous and most dangerous of my many journeys and know that it is simply an escape, an escape from political circumstances in central Europe which have become intolerable, from the news, from events, from the professional situation of a German writer behind whom the German intellectual world is collapsing like a rotten building.

Richard A. Bermann: Sahara expedition diary, 1933

Richard Arnold Bermann, the eminent Austrian writer and journalist, is today better known by his pseudonym, Arnold Höllriegel. He was born in 1883 in Vienna and grew up in Prague until the age of fourteen. Later, from 1908 to 1933, he was almost more at home in Berlin than in Vienna. It was the Berlin of the inter-war years – that liveliest, most culturally bountiful of cities – to which he, like many of his Austrian contemporaries, was indebted for his rise to literary prominence. Hitler's seizure of power brought his world crashing down around him. Soon, however, he became an active spokesman for the exiles and, together with Prince Löwenstein, emerged as one of the spiritual and intellectual father figures of the German Academy of Arts and Sciences in Exile.

Our first encounter was in 1934, after the Löwensteins and I had left Germany. Until then we had known Bermann/Höllriegel above all as the author of astute arts-section articles and fascinating travel stories which appeared, along with Löwenstein's leading articles and other contributions, in the *Vossische Zeitung* and *Berliner Tageblatt* of the early 1930s. The latter included the following tribute to him in 1929:

> Arnold Höllriegel . . . has been to America for us, to the islands of the South Seas; he has struck up friendships in Hollywood with Chaplin and all the great film stars; he has participated in the New York and London seasons; lastly, he has also enjoyed and described life in the English countryside.[1]

We were also familiar with some of Bermann's books, such as *Das Urwaldschiff* (1927; published in English as *The Forest Ship, a Book of the Amazon*, 1931), 'the epos of a world traveller unable to find the dreamland for which he longs', *Die Erben Timurs* (1928), about the end of the last great Mogul, and *Die Derwischtrommel* (1931; published in the same year in English as *The Mahdi of Allah. The Story of the Dervish, Mohammed Ahmed*), a book about the revolt led by the Mahdi, with whose son Bermann was able to obtain a personal interview. Winston Churchill, who wrote the Introduction to the book, called it the 'final word said about that chapter of history'.[2] We had also read the magical *Das Mädchen von St Helena*, which was dedicated to Elisabeth Bergner. This was a novelistic tale about Betsy Balcombe, the 'spoilt darling' of Napoleon's second and final exile. We did not read Bermann's charming little travel book about Polynesia and New Zealand, *Tausend und eine Insel* (1927), until the author gave a copy to the prince during a visit to Matzen, near Brixlegg in the Tyrol, our first stopover in exile. Bermann's last great novel, *Home from the Sea*, about Robert Louis Stevenson on Samoa, which he considered his own finest work, was not published until 1939, in America, shortly after the author's death.

Bermann drew a wealth of literary material from an exhausting enterprise upon which he embarked in 1933. He joined a desert expedition led by Ladislaus von Almásy, a Hungarian who was searching in the Sahara for a site steeped in legend: the oasis of Zarzura. In the course of the expedition the two men came across hundreds of prehistoric cave-paintings on the Gilf Kebir plateau. Similar to those of Altamira and Lascaux, the paintings featured cattle, gazelles, giraffes, lions and people – sometimes swimming – and thus dated back to a time when the Sahara was still fertile and blessed with water. Bermann's reports of this discovery in the Austrian press later formed the basis of his book, *Zarzura, die Oase der kleinen Vögel*.

The discoveries made during the expedition caused a sensation and have excited the imaginations of novelists, screenwriters and directors ever since. In his award-winning film *The English Patient*, for example, Anthony Minghella – like Michael Ondaatje, author of the bestseller on which the film is based[3] – drew partly on one of Bermann's lectures[4] (Bermann appears in both the film and the novel) and on Almásy's book 'Unknown Sahara', which was published in the original Hungarian in 1934 and in German in 1939. In 1997 a new German edition was published under the title *Schwimmer in der Wüste*.[5]

After the war, Arnold Höllriegel and his work largely fell into oblivion for many decades. Several other major exiled writers shared that fate. It is, however, quite incomprehensible that his name should appear in so few of the major literary histories. It was only in the 1990s that the books referred to above, the film and, in particular, the exhibition of 1995 at Germany's national library, the Deutsche Bibliothek (with an accompanying publication[6]), and the posthumous publication in 1998 of Bermann's autobiography (entitled *Die Fahrt auf dem Katarakt*, edited by Hans-Harald Müller[7]), generated new interest in and recognition of Bermann/ Höllriegel.

By the time Bermann boarded the *Ausonia* in Venice in 1933, bound for Cairo, Hitler was already Reich chancellor. Bermann's reaction was one of despair. In his diary of the 1933 Sahara expedition he noted: 'Here ends – through its own fault – the German republic that once inspired me: here ends the world in which I have lived, the only one I can conceive of.'[8]

By the time he returned to Vienna in the summer, a resurgence of his old fighting spirit had displaced his depression. This was when he made contact with Löwenstein. In November 1933, he spontaneously congratulated the prince on a plan that the latter had presented to the Dutch minister of education, Hendrik Pieter Marchand: the plan to found a 'European Youth League of Nations'. This was meant to combat the influence the Nazis were exercising over young people not just in Germany but also in neighbouring countries such as the Netherlands and Austria.

Löwenstein's memorandum on the subject was forwarded to Queen Wilhelmine by Johan Huizinga, who was then president of the Humanities and Social Sciences Division of the Royal Netherlands Academy of Arts and Sciences and had formerly been tutor to Crown Princess Juliane. Löwenstein also contacted other influential politicians such as the Austrian minister of justice and education, Kurt von Schuschnigg. When Bermann read press reports about the scheme – among others, an article by Löwenstein in the *Prager Tagblatt* – he wrote to the prince again: 'I have read your proposal for a Youth League of Nations. I heartily agree, but don't forget that also a Youth migration must be organized between the young of all countries, to promote real international friendship and combat hatred and war.'[9]

Löwenstein and Bermann belonged to different generations – Bermann was 23 years older – and their backgrounds and upbringings were quite dissimilar. Nevertheless, they got on well together from the start and were united in their dedication to the fight against any form of totalitarianism. Bermann's constitution had been delicate since his youth, but, as Löwenstein noted: 'His physical frailty never prevented him from risking dangers and fighting courageously for his democratic convictions.'[10] Bermann proved his courage whilst still a young man, during World War I. Convinced pacifist though he was, he went to the front as a war reporter – 'doubly courageous,' as Hermann Broch later testified, because

> on the one hand [he], as a pacifist, laid himself open to prosecution for high treason; on the other, he demonstrated so much genuine bravery that the army commanders – who were far from kindly disposed towards him – felt constrained to decorate him for bravery in the face of the enemy, an honour conferred on very few other non-combatants and no other war reporters.[11]

Bermann, for his part, admired Löwenstein – initially in Germany and subsequently in exile – for his passionate defence of democracy and his consistent opposition to Hitler and National Socialism. He wrote that Löwenstein was 'almost the only one of the hundred or more German princes to declare his support for the German Republic in the pre-Hitler years and to fight in the ranks of the *"Reichsbanner Schwarz-Rot-Gold"* against the rising reactionary tide.'[12]

Bermann was also a committed enemy of the semi-Fascist Austrian corporative state led first by Federal Chancellor Engelbert Dollfuss and then by Kurt von Schuschnigg. Neither Bermann nor Löwenstein were members of any socialist political party, but in the struggle against totalitarianism they stood firmly on the side of the workers. In February 1934, during the Viennese workers' revolt, which Dollfuss bloodily suppressed and in the course of which even severely injured men were seized from their stretchers on the way to hospital and hanged, Bermann begged Löwenstein for assistance in stopping the bloodbath: 'Come to Vienna, Prince, you are needed here. It is a matter of life and death!'[13]

Löwenstein, who was in London at the time, immediately sprang into action. With the help of Labour Member of Parliament Clement Attlee he collected 60 signatures from members of both Houses of Parliament for a telegram of protest to Dollfuss, demanding an end to the massacre. He then boarded the first available flight to Vienna.

Only a few hours after my messenger had telephoned him [writes Bermann] the prince was with me in Vienna. He had boarded a scheduled flight, without regard for the dangerous fact that it passed over German territory in a stretch between Innsbruck and Vienna. An emergency landing would have spelled death for the prince.[14]

Löwenstein succeeded in persuading Cardinal Archbishop Theodor Innitzer to make energetic and effective representations to Dollfuss. 'After the initial murderous frenzy, after a number of terrible executions, after prisoners had been tortured, the little chancellor – with blood on his hands – returned to a conciliatory approach with conspicuous alacrity,' noted Bermann, deeply moved by the success of the intervention. He added: 'Thus began my friendship with Prince Hubertus zu Löwenstein.'[15]

After sharing that dramatic experience, the two men began to collaborate closely. Long and intensive discussions took place during Bermann's many visits to Matzen at Brixlegg in the Tyrol, our first refuge in exile. They led, in June 1934, to the idea of creating a representative institution for the exiled writers, artists and scientists. At Bermann's suggestion, this was to be called the 'German Sanctuary in Exile' (*Deutsche Freistatt im Exil*). It was also Bermann who produced a detailed blueprint,[16] which Prince Löwenstein took with him on his American journey of 1935 and used as a basis in founding the American aid organization for the Academy in Exile, the 'American Guild for German Cultural Freedom', in New York.

Bermann had many friends and prominent acquaintances in America and did all he could to assist Löwenstein's efforts. He too travelled to the United States, in order to visit Albert Einstein at the scientist's summer house at Old Lyme in Connecticut and enlist him for the Academy, thereby contributing to the organization's speedy development. Bermann also helped to recruit sponsors for the American Guild and to organize benefit events. Moreover, he became the official representative of the Guild and the Academy in Vienna – on an honorary basis, needless to add. The Austrian press was not alone in noting with interest the news of his appointment as leader of the Academy in Exile's first European office.

After the American Guild had helped create a secure footing for the Vienna office, Bermann prepared the initial recommendations for a series of financial grants to support the work of individuals such as Walter Mehring and Hans Flesch von Brunningen. These were writers whose output Bermann greatly admired and who were experiencing severe material hardship.[17] He also attempted to realize his plan for a book club, which he had sketched out in his blueprint for a 'sanctuary'. He hoped that this would create additional opportunities for exiles seeking to publish their work. In this case, however, the obstacles both in America and Europe were too great to overcome. In 1937, for example, the attempt to collaborate with the 'Erasmus Foundation for the Dissemination of Good Writing' in The Hague, Wassenaar, fell through. On 9 November 1937, the Foundation's director wrote to Prince Löwenstein in New York:

> I must tell you that the difficulties facing the appeals for the 'Erasmus Foundation' and its book club, in central Europe and elsewhere, are very considerable. There is a panic fear of incurring the displeasure of present masters and those masters whose dreaded arrival people await with fixed stares, as if possessed by a spectre. With only a few exceptions, that fear has bled former democrats and socialists dry. In Prague the 'International Culture League' and other friends were a great disappointment; Scandinavia along with Denmark (I used the addresses you kindly provided . . .), Hungary and

Poland were enthusiastically in favour, but failed in practical terms.[18]

The success Bermann was finally able to report to Löwenstein on 24 February 1938 was short-lived. He had managed to win over Frederick Ungar from the Saturn publishing house in Vienna for the foundation of 'an initially small "book association" '. It was intended that it should, at first, be restricted to Austria and Czechoslovakia and have its headquarters in Bratislava. There, unlike in Schuschnigg's Austria,

> the books can be produced under more liberal censorship regulations and can, at least for the time being, be brought to Vienna without any difficulty . . . It is a small beginning, but at least it is a beginning at last. Please make it clear to our friends in the 'Guild' that I want their moral help above all. Something *must* happen immediately, and so I am doing it.[19]

This appeal for help came just before Hitler's invasion of Austria. We were well aware that Austria was in danger. As early as December 1937, Bermann had informed Löwenstein of the secret negotiations between the Austrian federal chancellor, Kurt von Schuschnigg, and Hitler:

> I would prefer to tell you what I know of the matter face to face; it is, at any rate, enough to make me request this favour: help me to prepare my exile! Speak to all your American friends about it! I know what I am talking about . . .[20]

On 31 December he appealed to Oswald Garrison Villard, the American Guild's treasurer:

> I have already told you that my personal situation in Austria is becoming intolerable. But what can I do? Can your tremendous influence and Einstein's recommendation not secure me a chair at one of those innumerable American colleges? I know I would make a very decent professor.[21]

Nevertheless, his sense of duty and responsibility for the exiles in his care detained him in Vienna, where he remained as head of the European office of the Academy in Exile and the American Guild until the bitter end. The work became ever more difficult. It was not just the applications for scholarship awards: there were also

desperate cries for help from exiles who feared expulsion from their
host countries, requests for representations to be made to the
authorities to help secure asylum or for assistance in moving on
overseas, as well as distress calls from people facing starvation –
among them Robert Musil, Alfred Polgar and Joseph Roth.

When Bermann found himself in immediate danger after Hitler's
invasion on 12 March 1938, Löwenstein and I were in New York. It
was two weeks before we were able to embrace him in Paris after a
dramatic rescue operation; only then did we hear the details of
what had taken place.

On the eve of that 12 March, in the Café Herrenhof in Vienna, he
had learned from his lawyer friend Otto Müller of Federal Chancellor Kurt von Schuschnigg's resignation. He had immediately
boarded a train, which was full to bursting with refugees, and
attempted to escape via Lundenburg on the border with Czechoslovakia. Unfortunately, the Czech police – themselves in a state of
panic – sent all the refugees back to Austria on the next train. During the return trip, Bermann destroyed those documents he had
with him relating to his work for the Academy. On arriving in
Vienna he was arrested by the SA with all the other refugees and
imprisoned in a waiting room. His luggage was ransacked. He was
lucky: a list bearing the names of people awarded and applying for
scholarships from the Academy in Exile, which he had forgotten to
destroy, was not discovered. On the evening of 12 March 1938 he
was finally released. He then went to his home and burned all his
correspondence, the European office archive and numerous books.

That was when Löwenstein tried to reach Bermann by telephone
from New York. On 13 March he managed to get through, although
the danger of being overheard by the Gestapo forced them to communicate obliquely. The conversation made it clear that only an
intervention from abroad could now save Bermann. That same day,
Löwenstein sent a telegram to President Eduard Beneš in Prague,
asking him to issue a Czech passport for Bermann and forward it to
him via the legation in Vienna. In the USA Oswald Garrison Villard,
with the backing of the president of the American Guild, Governor
Dr Wilbur L. Cross, asked US Secretary of State Cordell Hull to
approve and issue an American visa. Both statesmen immediately
instructed their representatives in Vienna to take the necessary
action.

In the meantime, however, Bermann had made a second escape attempt after his telephone conversation with Löwenstein. This time he headed for Italy, only to be ejected from the train by the SA shortly before reaching the border and detained in a prison at Bruck an der Mur. After his release he hid in a small pension at Küb am Semmering. This was where emissaries from the two legations finally tracked him down.

On May 3, Bermann – now bearing a Czech passport and the American visa – succeeded in escaping to Prague, where he was confined to bed for three weeks due to high blood pressure. Ignoring the urgent advice of his doctors, he next flew from Prague to Strasbourg and then on to Paris. There we were finally able to welcome him on 24 May 1938, as if he had risen from the dead.

Bermann immediately got down to work. In June and July 1938 he travelled to London. There he spoke to Sigmund Freud, who shortly afterwards agreed to be nominated as president of the Academy in Exile's Scientific Division. He encouraged the actress Elisabeth Bergner to join the Academy in Exile and persuaded the Archbishop of Canterbury to back the foundation of a British branch of the American Guild – a 'British Guild for German Cultural Freedom'. Before long, such an institution was indeed established: the 'Arden Society', led by the young English poet Stanley Richardson.

After joining the Löwensteins and I for a short holiday on the Isle aux Moines in Brittany, Bermann travelled to America. There he dedicated much of his time and energy to the Academy and the Guild – in an honorary capacity, as ever, despite the fact that he no longer had any means of his own. He had great difficulty in supporting himself and sometimes had to go hungry – an experience that was only too familiar among the exiles. Nevertheless, he did everything he could to help others. When his old friend Andrew Green, who was on the island of Dominica but had learned of Bermann's situation and knew how selfless he was, sent Villard a cheque for 300 dollars to forward to Bermann, he added cautiously:

> My guess is, that it would be safer to tell him that it comes from me, rather than from some relief fund. He is so magnanimous, that he might feel that he was getting what might be used more advantageously elsewhere.[22]

Soon after his arrival in New York, Bermann was elected to the American Guild's Board of Directors. He worked closely with us for some months. The correspondence with members, scholarship recipients and the Academy in Exile's protégés throughout the world was continually expanding; one matter of particular urgency was the rescue of those who had not yet managed to flee from Austria. Bermann also received many private pleas for help from friends and acquaintances, some of whom were already in Czechoslovakia.

The literary competition which the American Guild organized for the work of German-speaking émigrés was an additional burden. The Guild collaborated on this competition with the American publisher Little, Brown and Company, and with eight major European publishing houses including William Collins in London, Albin Michel in Paris, Sijthoff in Leiden and Querido in Amsterdam. Having been appointed to head the competition committee, Bermann undertook to give a preliminary reading to all the manuscripts submitted and to divide them into five categories for the Academy's five judges: Thomas Mann, Lion Feuchtwanger, Bruno Frank, Alfred Neumann and Rudolf Olden. On 2 December 1938, he told Stefan Zweig:

> I never have time to write at all; in my 'free time' I have to read about 100 [in fact 177] German novel manuscripts which have been submitted for the competition ... I have taken on the initial sorting for the judges. Amazing how many *good* manuscripts are among them.[23]

Despite the massive workload generated by the honorary posts he occupied during this period, Bermann also tried to continue his work as a committed political journalist. In this respect too, however, his situation was more difficult. He was, as he once complained, a 'journalist without a newspaper' for the first time.

When I left for France again with Löwenstein and the princess in the spring of 1939 to coordinate the work of the European office in Paris, Bermann accompanied us to the ship in New York. He seemed almost to sense that this was a final goodbye. His last words were addressed to Löwenstein: 'Your old critic has to admit that you have become more realistic since we first met in 1933. You know: not too many ideas all at once, please. And, please understand Prince Hubertus – a bit more realism wouldn't go amiss.' And then, deeply moved, he added: 'Oh, for heaven's sake, don't get too realistic; it would be horrible, and – most unrealistic!'

On our return to New York on 29 September 1939 we waited on the quay for Richard Bermann – in vain. After learning that war had broken out he immediately wanted to play a part in Europe. On 3 September 1939 he wrote to Theodor Meisels in Jerusalem that this event would

> change various things in all our lives. I assume that you will not just sit there, and I cannot imagine that I will either, regardless of my blood pressure. I have already written to all the influential people I know in London, asking them to use me as an interpreter or as an anti-Nazi propagandist.

On the morning of 5 September he was found dead of heart failure in his bathroom in the artists' colony of Yaddo, Saratoga Springs, where he had been offered hospitality during the summer after Albert Einstein and Thomas Mann had each put in a good word for him.

Richard Bermann received many obituaries, not just in America but also – despite the war – in Europe. Alfred Polgar, an old friend who had been at Bermann's side through thick and thin, wrote a tribute to him for the Parisian journal *Die Zukunft*:

> His friends – and everyone who knew this honourable, ungrudging, appreciative individual was his friend – have lost a comrade whose desire and constant endeavour it was to be a guardian angel to those of whom he was fond. His honest heart knew nothing of malice. He was a . . . comprehensively educated man, a talented writer and a brilliant journalist . . . who told the truth even when doing so was dangerous . . . An unquenchable thirst for travel took him to the most remote corners of the world, until frontiers began turning into prison walls . . . If anything could still trouble such a passionate globe-trotter and journalist after leaving the sullied earth behind him, it would doubtless be that he is unable to send us a report about the shores on which he has now landed.[24]

CHAPTER FOUR

The American Guild for German Cultural Freedom: The American Aid Organization and its Sponsors

About a year ago, a society called the 'American Guild for German Cultural Freedom' was founded in the United States. Its purpose is to secure the freedom and continued existence, for the present and the future, of an artistic and scientific German culture which is not tied to any political party. . . . It aspires to help German artists and writers without regard to their religion, race or their particular nationality, and irrespective of their political allegiances within the front which opposes the political system currently prevailing in Germany.

Die Stunde, *Vienna, 30 October 1936*

Before founding a German academy in America, it was vital to secure authorization from the host country and the active – and financial – support of the American public. The academy was intended to be an entirely German institution. It would have German roots, membership and aims; it was to be set up in exile only because its members had been driven from their homeland by the Nazi tyranny. It was to be a cultural equivalent to what, in politics, would be termed a government in exile. It would thus, as Löwenstein once observed, also be 'a sharp political weapon, without there ever being any need to mention the word "political" '. Its long-term goals, moreover, were to be identical to those of a government in exile: the overthrow of the iniquitous regime and the return of the expellees to their homeland. Unlike a political institution, however, the academy would have only intellectual and spiritual ammunition at its disposal.

In order to gain the necessary political backing and financial resources for the planned German academy – the impoverished exiles were not in a position to fund its activities without outside help – an American aid organization had to be set up. This would function as a midwife for the birth of the academy itself. State patronage for such institutions was a concept alien to the whole social structure of the United States at the time. American citizens therefore had to be enlisted as members and sponsors – a task which Löwenstein, as described above, set about successfully as early as 1935, during his first lecture tour of the United States.

One of the most important patrons was the distinguished German-American Oswald Garrison Villard. Born in Wiesbaden in 1872, he had never lost touch with the land of his fathers. He visited Germany frequently and devoted three of his eighteen books to it. He followed the new political developments there with profound concern. As a democrat and a loyal friend to the Germans, he ideally embodied the spirit of the 'Guild', as Prince Löwenstein confirmed when he described their first encounter (which took place before Löwenstein went into exile) in his autobiography *Towards the Further Shore*:

> It was in late autumn 1930 that I received a telephone call from Oswald Garrison Villard, publisher and editor-in-chief of the New York weekly *The Nation*. He had come to Berlin to collect material for his book *The German Phoenix*. As it happened, I was wearing the uniform of a republican youth leader when I met him, as there had not been time to change. Villard pointed at my black-red-gold badge and said: 'These are the colours which we in America love and respect!' We were friends ever after.[1]

Villard had inherited his love for the colours of freedom from his father, Henry Villard,[2] who was born in Zweibrücken in 1835 as Ferdinand Gustav Hilgard and took an enthusiastic interest in the ideas of the German liberal reformist movement of 1848 even as a schoolboy. After the failure of the revolution, he left home. He arrived, penniless, in New York in 1853, where he initially earned a living working for German-American newspapers. During the Civil

War he quickly made a name for himself reporting for major English-language newspapers in the liberal states of the North. In 1864 he married the daughter of William Lloyd Garrison, the famous and pioneering anti-slavery campaigner. He accumulated a considerable fortune as a financial advisor to German investors, then as a shareholder and finally as president of the Northern Pacific Railroad Company during the expansion of this and other railways. In 1900 he bequeathed that fortune, together with the *New York Evening Post* and the magazine *The Nation*, to his son, who was thus able to pursue a career as an author and journalist of independent means.

Oswald Garrison Villard was strongly critical of the Treaty of Versailles. Right from the start he expressed his fear that it would lead to another European and world war, into which America would ultimately be dragged. Despite subsequent developments, he maintained a deep-seated faith in the development of a free, democratic Germany, as he made clear in the Foreword to his book *The German Phoenix*, which was published in December 1932 – shortly before Hitler's seizure of power:

> That the Republic, for the moment, is but a shadow of what it was intended to be is undeniable. Yet it is difficult to believe that Germany with its traditions and its heritage will long remain at the mercy either of dictators or demagogues. The circumstance, however, that the Republic is, temporarily, in its twilight has made it seem the more desirable to record the efforts of its founders to establish a true democracy upon the ruins of the Empire and the extraordinary progress since 1918 toward a socialized State. Many of the changes, much of the new orientation, cannot be lost no matter what the form of the new governmental control.[3]

It was this indestructible belief in a democratic future for Germany that moved Villard to invest all his energy in realizing the idea of a 'sanctuary' for German culture. He was particularly instrumental in helping the American Guild to overcome all the difficulties involved in planning and founding the Academy in Exile. It was also he who provided the Guild and subsequently the Academy with a headquarters, by making rooms available in his handsome ten-storey office building on Vesey Street, New York: the

'Garrison Building'. Whenever problems arose, he stepped in with generous assistance.

The other German-American whose support Prince Löwenstein secured, having contacted him on the very day of his arrival, was George Nauman Shuster. Born in 1894, Shuster was a university lecturer, literary scholar, author and editor of a liberal Catholic weekly, the *Commonweal*. He later became president of Hunter College, which is now affiliated to New York University. Like Villard, he was the son of a political refugee from the period following the failure of the 1848 revolution, when over a million Germans emigrated to America, the land of freedom. He too sympathized with the liberal ideals of this second generation of Germans forced to leave their native land and seek refuge and assistance in America.

George Nauman Shuster spent three years in Germany studying literature, returning in 1930. The impressions and experiences he gained in the land of his fathers led to the publication of *The Germans* in 1932. After the war, Shuster was appointed as deputy US high commissioner from 1950 to 1951. As the *Land* commissioner for Bavaria, he proved himself a loyal friend to, and advocate for, the Germans. In grateful acknowledgement of his efforts he was subsequently awarded the Order of Merit of the Federal Republic (*Grosses Bundesverdienstkreuz*) and an honorary doctorate from the University of Freiburg.

With Shuster's enthusiastic assistance, Löwenstein was rapidly able to win the support of prominent personalities for the foundation of the American aid organization. As treasurer, Shuster also laid the Guild's financial foundations.

A New York attorney named Samuel R. Wachtell, of Austrian descent and a friend of Richard A. Bermann, undertook the legal work necessary for the Guild to be recognized as a body corporate in the form of a registered society. In the years ahead he would act as the Guild's legal counsel. He was responsible for the 'Certificate of Incorporation', which set out the Guild's legal framework and status and defined its background and objectives.

The certificate was based on a draft which Wachtell, Villard and Shuster had worked on together, and which was in turn indebted to Bermann's aforementioned blueprint.[4] It specified that the Guild's purpose was to facilitate the free development of German culture in exile, safe from censorship and oppression by the Nazi regime. It was to make creative activity possible by fostering exiled writers, artists and scientists. The Certificate of Incorporation also author-ized an independent, organized union of German intellectuals, in order further to protect and foster 'the cultural tradition of the German-speaking people as one of the great treasures of civiliza-tion' and the 'true spirit of Germany as expressed by such writers as Lessing, Kant, Schiller and Goethe'.[5]

On 4 April 1935 the Certificate of Incorporation was ready for signing by Löwenstein and five American citizens. It was approved and registered on 27 April 1935 by the New York State Supreme Court.[6] The other American signatories with Shuster and Wachtell were Horace Meyer Kallen, Emil Lengyel and Freda Kirchwey. Horace Meyer Kallen was a Silesian by birth, who had come to the USA in 1887 at the age of five. He was the author of numerous books and had now become a professor at the New School for Social Research, which was unofficially dubbed the 'University in Exile' on account of its high proportion of émigré academics. The histor-ian and political economist Emil Lengyel was born in 1895 in Buda-pest. After a rough time as a very young volunteer in World War I, he was forced to spend two years in Siberian prison camps, before arriving in America in 1921 as a convinced pacifist. His book about his experiences in Siberia, *Cattle Car Express* (published in 1931, also in German as *Im Viehwagen-Express: Als Kriegsgefangener in Sibirien*), was reprinted many times both in Europe and America. Freda Kirch-wey was a colleague of Villard's at *The Nation* magazine, and was preferred to him in order to have a woman signatory. She was a liberal journalist of considerable repute; already editor-in-chief, two years later she would become *The Nation*'s publisher when Villard made the magazine over to Maurice Wertheim (one of the Guild's sponsors).

The legal formalities having been completed, the organization was now officially the American Guild for German Cultural Free-dom 'Inc.'. The next step was to recruit further well-known, respected figures for the Board of Directors and, from among their number, a president, vice-president and treasurer, along with the other staff needed for the Guild's practical, day-to-day work. This was the most pressing duty of the founding consortium that was in charge until the first general meeting of members.

The Guild's foundation caused considerable interest in Europe as well as America. The *Wiener Tag* newspaper, for example, published a detailed report by Löwenstein, in which he described the organization's political background and the support it enjoyed from the American public:

> The Nazis in America fight all the more doggedly because of the vehemence with which the enlightened sections of the German population and the freedom-loving American people of all religions reject their cause. Germans and Americans have therefore created an organization called the 'American Guild for German Cultural Freedom', which has already received approval from the New York Supreme Court. Its purpose is to promote German culture, free of Nazism, in the United States. ... The greater the oppression of intellect and civilisation in Germany in the months ahead, the stronger the counter-pressure in America will become.[7]

At the general meeting on 11 June 1936, another sixteen public figures were elected to the Board of Directors along with the six founding members. The treasurer, charged with raising much-needed funds, was George N. Shuster. The members approved Samuel R. Wachtell's articles of association or 'By-Laws' for the Guild[8] and not only welcomed the idea of a German academy of writers, artists and scientists in exile but expressly called for one. Such an institution, as the upholder and representative of free German culture and thus of the 'other' Germany, was guaranteed every assistance and all the financial resources the Guild could muster.

Some future members of the Academy who were already established in the United States were present at this meeting. They included economist and social scientist Eduard Heimann of the New School for Social Research, Austrian composer Ernst Toch, radiologist Gustav Bucky, internist Leopold Lichtwitz of Columbia University and Hans Staudinger, a former secretary of state for trade in Prussia and lecturer at Berlin's *Hochschule für Politik* who was now professor of economics at the New School. These men were the key members of an advisory committee within the Guild, the European Council. Led initially by acting chairman Robert McIver of Columbia University, they were actively involved in laying the groundwork for the Academy and its formation. Under the chairmanship of Thomas Mann and later Sigmund Freud, the

European Council (the members of which were known as 'senators') grew over the years to include more than twenty members. They were listed in the Guild's letter-heading and in all its official representations.

At Löwenstein's instigation, the general meeting appointed several committees: one for scholarship awards, chaired by Oswald Garrison Villard; another for literary prizes, with Samuel Barlow and his wife Ernesta as members and Henry Seidel Canby as chairman. Barlow, Canby and Villard also formed the American Guild's finance committee, which assisted the treasurer. When Shuster's professional commitments as a newly elected member of the social sciences research group at Columbia University forced him to step down a year later, first Barlow and later Villard took over as treasurer.

Dr Henry Seidel Canby, whose Quaker upbringing had instilled in him a strong sense of social duty, was a liberal, a literary scholar and a professor at Yale University. He had already made his name as the author of numerous books in the fields of literary studies, linguistics and historical biography when he took on the editorship of the *New York Evening Post's Literary Review* in 1920. In 1924 he founded the *Saturday Review of Literature*, which he developed into the foremost literary journal in the United States. In 1926 he became the first editor-in-chief of the large and influential Book of the Month Club, an office he held for almost 30 years. His standing in American cultural life enabled him to make a considerable contribution to the activities and reputations of the Guild and the Academy.

The same is true of the composer and writer Samuel Latham Mitchell Barlow, the first (and at that time only) American to have an opera premièred at a French national opera house: *Mon ami Pierrot*, at the Opéra Comique in Paris in 1934. He worked with numerous cultural organizations and committees: he was, for example, president of a citizens' committee for government cultural projects, as well as being involved in groups concerned with civil rights, democracy and intellectual freedom. He lived in Gramercy Park, New York, with his sophisticated wife Ernesta (formerly married to Ambassador William Bullitt); their residence was a focal point of cultural activity and was sometimes made available for Academy events. The Guild was also indebted to Barlow for his short, succinct appeals for donations, which we sent out in thousands of letters and which proved particularly persuasive and successful.

The Guild's other directors included Dorothy Thompson, a noted journalist and wife of the writer and Nobel Prize-winner Sinclair Lewis. *Time* magazine once called her the most influential woman in America after First Lady Eleanor Roosevelt. Dorothy Thompson had spent several years in Germany as a reporter and despised Hitler. When her book *I Saw Hitler* was published, she became the first foreign correspondent to be expelled from Germany. Hitler personally ordered that she be given 24 hours to leave Berlin.

Her political acumen enabled her to recognize at an early stage that the policy of appeasement pursued by the Western powers, particularly by Great Britain under Neville Chamberlain, was bound to end in war. She attacked the appeasers incessantly in her 'On the Record' column in the *New York Herald Tribune* and in countless speeches, radio talks and other articles. Later she campaigned just as passionately against Roosevelt and Churchill when they insisted on unconditional surrender at the Casablanca conference in 1943: she called the demand an 'absurdity', an 'insanity', and warned that it would undermine 'the forces in Germany that were anxious for peace',[9] for it would convince all Germans that 'a lost war means a lost nation'.[10] She also objected to the plans for dividing Germany and dismantling its industry in the spirit of the Yalta and Potsdam conferences, which she summed up in her diary as a fatal, 'hundred per cent Russian victory'.[11] She claimed that some of the very groups and persons who had once led the way in appeasing Hitler were among those who now favoured erasing not just him and National Socialism but the whole of Germany from the map – thereby again inviting disastrous and predictable political consequences.

In 1937 the internationally renowned president of New York's Columbia University, Professor Nicholas Murray Butler, arranged for Wilbur Lucius Cross, governor of the state of Connecticut and a literary scholar and professor at Yale, to take on the presidency of the Guild. The honorary chairman was a member of the American upper house, Senator Robert Ferdinand Wagner, architect of the National Labor Relations Act, which became known as the 'Wagner Act'. There was nationwide interest – reflected in the *New York*

Times, *Washington Post*, *Los Angeles Times* and local newspapers alike – in the readiness of such eminent figures in America's public and political life to lead an organization for the benefit of Germany's hard-pressed culture in exile, and their support meant that Americans took the Guild seriously from the start.

It became clear that the Guild represented the formation of a cultural, 'alternative Germany', in contradistinction to the barbarism of National Socialism. On 12 April 1937, *Record* magazine commented:

An admirable idea is involved in the new technique to be adopted in this country by men who want to demonstrate their confidence, and admiration of, the life and spirit of German culture outside of the Reich [*sic*].

For years it has been a source of much regret to many that the beloved memories of old Germany were being overcast by the sinister shadows of New Germany as illustrated in the Hitler policies.

They saw with menacing swiftness, the time honored culture of Germany as represented in the arts, professions and sciences, being rudely eliminated to make room for a nondescript so-called totalitarian scheme which subjugates everything to the State as represented by Herr Hitler and his cohorts . . .

So accustomed has the world become to consider all things pertaining to Germany as being confined within the area which has been Hitlerized, that it is difficult to realize that 'outside the borders of the Reich there are living thirty-five million people whose intellectual and spiritual life takes place more or less decisively within the German language.'

Among this sizeable number are Germans who represent the creative part of the traditional German culture which, before the World War, was the wonder and delight of all Christendom. It is the appreciation of this type and the resentment felt for the obvious intention of the German State as represented by Hitler *et al.*, to curb it to submission or to eliminate it completely, that the creation of the Guild is hailed with satisfaction by all who believe in justice and tolerance [*sic*].

The *Jewish Exponent* newspaper in Philadelphia went so far as to describe the alliance, born of the necessity of exile, as the chance for a rebirth of German culture:

> The hopelessness of seeing German culture grow in the Reich, under the present regime, made these exiles unite in a compact body, and with the help of the thousands of other intellectuals who esteem the contributions of German culture and are anxious to maintain it, the organization was effected and began its operations . . .
>
> German culture, torn out of its moorings, may also grow and prosper in exile as long as its standard-bearers are still impregnated with a great love for the land and entertain the hope of a restoration. It is not unlikely that in this way it will expand into a more healthy growth because of the closer contact with other cultures, while its influence on the outside world will be much more direct and much more salutary. The experience of the Jewish people in this direction should serve as a comfort to the intrepid spirits who would not be cowed by the tyrants who now sway Germany, but are ready to make heavy sacrifices in order to maintain the glorious traditions of German culture and its contributions to the sum total of human civilization.[12]

The Guild's president, Governor Cross, was not often able to leave his office at Hartford, the state capital of Connecticut, and could make only brief visits to New York, chiefly to attend the annual general meetings of the Guild and Academy. In the intervening periods the vice-president was therefore largely responsible for running the Guild. At the meeting of the Board of Directors on 14 December 1936, the director of the New School for Social Research and dean of the Graduate Faculty of Political and Social Science, Alvin Saunders Johnson, was elected vice-president of the Guild. He had taught at several leading American universities – Columbia, Chicago, Cornell, Stanford, Yale – and had then spent six years defining the profile of the respected journal *New Republic* as its editor. When he took charge of the New School in New York in 1923, he quickly enhanced its reputation through his personal influence and above all by taking on top scientists from Europe – thereby creating the 'University in Exile'. Today the institution still has a unique status among the universities of America.

Johnson's duties included convening and chairing the Board's meetings. The 'By-Laws' prescribed four meetings a year, although in practice the rapidly expanding workload caused them to be convened far more frequently. The workload also meant that further vice-presidents were soon required, and on 25 March 1937 Frank Kingdon and Robert Hutchins were appointed. Kingdon was born in England and arrived in America in 1912 at the age of eighteen. Initially he worked as a Methodist minister; in 1934, after studying theology and law, he became president of the University of Newark. As an emigrant himself, he took an active interest in the political developments in Europe. This led him, for example, to co-found the Emergency Rescue Committee, which came to the aid of many victims of persecution who had sought refuge in Vichy France only to find themselves at the mercy of the Gestapo.

Robert Maynard Hutchins had studied law at Yale and then taught there as a professor. In 1929 he was appointed president of the University of Chicago. He won international respect for the almost revolutionary zeal with which he reformed that institution. He turned it into a university for the classical sciences and liberal arts based on the European model, in which teaching and research were kept strictly separate from vocational training. His achievements were such that eighteen universities, including those of Frankfurt, Copenhagen and Stockholm, awarded him honorary doctorates; in 1949 he was elected to the Board of Directors of the Goethe Bicentennial Foundation and awarded the city of Frankfurt's Goethe Medal. He exerted a major influence on the liberal trend in American society and politics.

The Guild's president, honorary directors, the Board of Directors and the European Council were supported by a wide circle of friends and sponsors, whose efforts contributed to the American public's general acceptance of the Guild. Among the most eager of these helpers were several Jewish immigrants or their descendants, who still felt close ties with Germany, their former homeland. The members of the Board of Sponsors, who soon numbered more than a hundred, were listed on the reverse side of the Guild's official writing paper.

One of the most active sponsors was the young New York lawyer Clifford Forster, who was special counsel to the American Civil Liberties Union for many years and subsequently to the International League for the Rights of Man, as well as director of the

International Rescue Committee. He too was the son of an immigrant, Karl von Foerster, originally from Austria, who was a great friend and patron of the arts as well as a gifted pianist. In 1961 the German federal president awarded Clifford Forster the Order of Merit of the Federal Republic, First Class (*Bundesverdienstkreuz Erster Klasse*), for his lifelong efforts on behalf of a democratic tradition of German culture.

Everyday business was handled by the office in the Garrison Building, New York, where the American Guild and later also the Academy had their headquarters. The office was led by Prince Löwenstein in his capacity as general secretary. After my arrival in New York in January 1938 to work for the Academy, the Board of Directors also elected me assistant secretary – that is, Löwenstein's deputy – to the Guild. None of the office-bearers in the Guild or Academy was paid, and neither was any member of the office staff except for a full-time American secretary. All those involved, many of whom were themselves émigrés and dedicated to the cause, lent their support out of their love for German culture and in the hope of building towards a free Germany.

In Cross, Wagner and Hutchins the Guild had three leading figures based outside New York. This reflected the founders' determination that the Guild should be represented across the country. The sponsors also came from all parts of America.

Right from the start, Prince Löwenstein regarded New York as the administrative centre for both organizations, but he also wanted the Academy in Exile to be known and active throughout the world and the American Guild throughout the United States. To that end he began setting up local groups during his lecture tour of the USA in February and March of 1936, even before the general meeting in June of the same year. He managed to create such groups in the Midwest, Chicago, Milwaukee and elsewhere, all the way to the Pacific.

The American Guild's first public events, which also helped raise the necessary funds, took place in Los Angeles. This was the second most important literary and artistic centre for German exiles after New York. Representatives of the film industry and associated activities in Los Angeles took a warm interest in the needy intellectuals and were keen to help them, particularly in the early years of their exile.

The first event in Los Angeles was a benefit dinner in honour of Prince Löwenstein at the fashionable Victor Hugo restaurant, on 26 April 1936. The man behind the event was an emigrant named Otto Katz, who worked under the pseudonyms of Rudolf Breda and André Simone and had directed for Erwin Piscator at the latter's *Theater am Nollendorfplatz* in Berlin until 1933. Breda had excellent contacts in Hollywood and he wasted no time in introducing Löwenstein to celebrities such as Charlie Chaplin, Clark Gable, Irving Thalberg, William Dieterle, David Selznick, Greta Garbo, Norma Shearer, Ernst Lubitsch and Joseph Scott. The patron of the dinner was the Archbishop of Los Angeles and San Diego, John Joseph Cantwell, who also delivered the opening address. The organizing committee, chaired by Donald Ogden Stewart, included Fritz Lang, Frederic March, Irving Berlin and Dorothy Parker. It was, as the newspaper reports confirmed, a 'glittering social occasion', which attracted 300 guests including most of Hollywood's leading figures.

Amid all this, Breda did not forget how important the financial aspect was to the American Guild. He 'wooed and begged', as an amused but admiring Prince Löwenstein observed, concentrating on the 'Hollywood magnates [and] hammering away at their guilty social conscience until they reached remorsefully for their chequebooks'.[13] The proceeds were among the earliest funds the Guild had at its disposal when it met in New York on 11 June.

The American Guild organized another event in Los Angeles in the autumn of 1936. Through the composer Ernst Toch, who had moved to California, Löwenstein had made the acquaintance of Arnold Schönberg and the conductor Otto Klemperer. All three spontaneously agreed to collaborate in a benefit concert for the Guild. Princess Löwenstein and Richard Bermann took an active part in the preparations; Schönberg and Toch supplied compositions specially for the occasion and Klemperer conducted.

The concert was a considerable social and artistic success. The media reported it in detail, characterizing it as a kind of musical foundation ceremony. It helped get the Guild and the Academy off to an auspicious start on the West Coast.

CHAPTER FIVE

The German Academy of Arts and Sciences in Exile: Formation, Development and Structure

It is the intention of the emigrants to convince the American public that they are the true heirs and representatives of the German cultural tradition. Through contracts with publishing houses, musical institutions and art galleries and by founding book clubs they aim to secure future sales for the dross turned out by emigrants and to exclude young, National Socialist Germany . . . There is no doubt that the plan represents the most far-reaching and dangerous attempt . . . to exclude National Socialist Germany from exerting influence on the cultural life of the United States.

Report from the German embassy in Washington to the
Reichsminister *for Enlightenment of the People*
and Propaganda, Joseph Goebbels, 14 December 1936

With the founding of the American Guild, an effective basis had been laid for the formation of the German Academy of Arts and Sciences in Exile. There were many German writers, artists and scholars in exile and they were distributed among various countries on four continents; the aim now was to bring together those of them who were to be appointed to the Academy. Financial constraints made this an even more difficult undertaking. It was a lack of funds that made it impossible for the first general assembly of members in Geneva, announced by Thomas Mann in 1936, to take place as planned. As a result, New York – where the Academy had its headquarters – became the regular location for annual general meetings.

Regional conferences were only possible in the émigré centres such as London, Austria (until Hitler's invasion in 1938) and above all, until the outbreak of war, Paris.

The fact that the Academy's members were strewn across the face of the globe was, however, a positive, indeed almost indispensable, asset in raising its public profile. It meant that it was represented and recognized throughout the world from the very start. It was, after all, the Academy's efficacy in the international public arena that constituted its bottom line, for although it was indeed an intellectual and cultural institution, the Academy very soon developed into an important political weapon against National Socialism, just as its founders had intended.

One of the first figures Prince Löwenstein managed to enlist as a future member, during his second lecture tour through the United States in 1936, was Albert Einstein in New York. Privy Councillor Fritz Demuth pursued further contacts in the sciences to great effect. In Switzerland in 1933 he had co-founded the '*Notgemein-schaft deutscher Wissenschaftler im Ausland*' (Emergency Society for German Scholars in Exile), which he subsequently represented in the advisory committee to the League of Nations' high commissioner for refugees from Germany. The *Notgemeinschaft* was based in London from 1936 and dealt with teaching and research appointments to foreign universities and institutes, which meant that it was generally well informed about where eminent émigrés were living and what they were doing. Demuth was also co-founder of a '*Vereinigung deutscher Ausgewanderter*' (VdA – a union of German émigrés) and he later – together with Sudeten German and Austrian émigrés – attempted to create a common representative body for German-speaking émigrés.

In a letter to Demuth, Löwenstein mentioned that scholars such as the economist and social scientist Eduard Heimann, internist Leopold Lichtwitz, radiologist Gustav Bucky and former Prussian secretary of state Hans Staudinger had already undertaken to support the Academy. He also told Demuth to expect the writer Peter von Mendelssohn, who had taken on the task of informing the exiles in Europe of the German Academy's aims and of convincing them of the need for an international union.[1]

Löwenstein had met Peter von Mendelssohn through Richard Bermann in 1934 in Vienna. In the Saarland campaign of 1934–5,

Mendelssohn had followed Löwenstein to Saarbrücken and had collaborated on the prince's anti-Nazi weekly paper *Das Reich* – anonymously, to avoid endangering his relatives who had remained behind in Germany.

My friendship with Mendelssohn began in 1935 after the Saarland plebiscite, when he came to Matzen as the Löwensteins' guest for six months. During this period he wrote his novel about the Tyrolean Minnesinger Oswald von Wolkenstein, which was published in Germany the same year under the pseudonym Carl Johann Leuchtenberg.[2]

The Wolkenstein novel was Mendelssohn's fifth book. Reclam had published his first, *Fertig mit Berlin?*, in 1930 when he was aged just 22. On completing his school-leaving examinations in 1926 he had joined the *Berliner Tageblatt* as a trainee, and the newspaper had then sent him to London as an assistant correspondent until 1928. After returning to Berlin he had spent a year as an editor at the *United Press of America* before becoming his own master on his 21st birthday, 1 June 1929. He went to the South of France, acquired his first house at Cagnes-sur-mer and settled in Paris as a freelance writer until 1932.

The fruit of that sojourn was another autobiographically-inspired book, *Paris über mir*. This was followed by the publication in Berlin of *Schmerzliches Arkadien* (actually his first work although it did not appear until 1932), a story in which he bid goodbye to his youth, very much in the spirit of the times. It was, as Pamela Wedekind put it, an expression of the 'emotional situation of the cream of our generation'.[3] A further pre-*Wolkenstein* novel, *Das Haus Cosinsky*, was published as early as 1934, in exile in Paris, by the German-language publishing house of Europäischer Merkur, which he had helped found when he left Germany again in April 1933 (Hutchinson brought out the English translation, *The House of Cosinsky*, in London in 1936).

And now, in the summer of 1935, Mendelssohn worked on his new novel at the Löwensteins' home in Matzen, inspired by our excursions to the castle of Wolkenstein in the South Tyrol, where the Minnesinger had once resided. Occasionally he read us chapters aloud, and we and Richard Bermann also organized musical evenings and historical amateur theatrical performances, scripted by Mendelssohn and Bermann.

When Prince Löwenstein returned from America in May, our discussions focused on what he had to tell us about the newly founded
American Guild and above all on the idea of, and planning for, the
German Academy of Arts and Sciences in Exile. Mendelssohn took
an increasing interest in these discussions. He was therefore
well prepared when Löwenstein asked him to make contact with
potential members of the Academy in Europe in the spring of
1936.

By then we had already moved on from Matzen, our first base in
exile. In October 1935, the Löwensteins travelled to England to give
lectures and undertake other work on behalf of the Guild and the
Academy in Exile, and early in 1936 Hubertus went on to New
York. When the princess was about to return to Matzen, the
Austrian ambassador in London, Baron Georg von Franckenstein,
warned her confidentially that political developments and the
consequent danger of being abducted over the nearby border to
Germany meant that if she or her husband did go back they would
be taking their lives in their hands. He also hinted that there was a
real possibility of Austria being coerced into an *anschluss* – as
indeed it was just two years later. Franckenstein himself never
returned to Austria and later became a British citizen.

We therefore had to abandon Matzen. After completing my
studies at Innsbruck by passing the state examination and, in February 1936, obtaining my doctorate, I cleared the household with
the help of Peter von Mendelssohn, who then went to Vienna. I soon
followed him in order to do some work on behalf of the Guild,
Bermann having left in June of that year to help the Löwensteins in
America.

I was then stuck in Austria, as my German passport had expired.
There would have been no point in attempting to renew it in Innsbruck after my armed encounters with the Nazis and the coverage
in the international press which had followed the princess's shot at
one of her assailants. I could only hope that my luck might improve
at some future date in Vienna – and three years after the riots I did
indeed get my opportunity. To this day I do not know whether my
good fortune was due to an oversight or to a secretly sympathetic
consular official at the German embassy. At any rate, a passport
bearing a swastika was handed over to me – with a wink, or so I
fancied, and with an emphatic instruction: 'Only for your return to

Germany.' The next day I was in Paris, and a week later I reached England.

In 1936 Peter von Mendelssohn, in Vienna, had wasted no time in getting preparations for an exiles' academy in Europe underway. First he and Bermann drafted a document in which they presented the academy and its aims.[4] This was forwarded without delay to a select circle of eminent émigrés involved in cultural activities. In a letter from New York of 12 June, Löwenstein had this to say about the criteria for admission: 'The academy should be receptive to everyone and help everyone. But not everyone should be admitted as a member. Admission is an honour, not a formality.'[5]

Mendelssohn then embarked on a tour of several countries, meeting potential members individually in order to gather the information which would be needed later for the admissions procedure. Löwenstein provided 200 pounds for this work, partly from his own pocket and partly from a donation made by his English friend Sir Victor Schuster, who had previously helped finance the weekly paper *Das Reich* during the Saar campaign. This was a considerable sum at the time: most émigrés lived on 10 to 15 pounds a month in England, and on 30 dollars (about 8 pounds) in France. Peter von Mendelssohn's journey took him from Vienna via Salzburg to Zürich and Basle and then to Paris and London. On his way back to Vienna via Amsterdam he paid a second visit to Paris before travelling through the South of France and revisiting Zürich. At the same time he was corresponding diligently with other figures whom he was unable to visit, setting out for them the kind of activities in which the exiles' academy was to engage.[6]

Not all the plans came to fruition, but without the confidence, vigour and dedicated determination of all those involved, the extremely adverse circumstances in exile would surely have made it impossible to form the Academy at all. It was, moreover, the impression of self-sacrifice and idealism that leant the Academy its peculiar spiritual resonance. No comparable state institution could have had such an inspiring effect.

The long list of those Mendelssohn recruited for the Academy was encouraging in itself. Headed by Thomas Mann, Martin Buber, Alfred Döblin, Lion Feuchtwanger, Bruno Frank, Emil Ludwig, Heinrich Mann, Otto Klemperer and Alfred Neumann, it also included Rudolf Olden, Max Reinhardt, Joseph Roth, Ernst Toller,

Bruno Walter, Franz Werfel, Arnold Zweig, Stefan Zweig and Professors Karl Barth, Albert Einstein, Hermann Kantorowicz, Alfred Mendelssohn-Bartholdy, Erwin Schrödinger and Veit Valentin. It was not long before the Academy could boast illustrious representatives from a broad spectrum of German culture and science.

Mendelssohn made sure that the public got to hear of this progress through the German-language newspapers in Austria, Czechoslovakia and Switzerland and through exile publications, which published detailed reports. Later he also gained coverage in the international press. He ensured, in particular, that the media publicized the London address of the Academy's European office; this immediately led to inquiries, suggestions, calls for help and applications for scholarships from all parts of the world.

Unfortunately, Peter von Mendelssohn soon gave up his efforts on behalf of the Academy. On his tour of Europe he had succeeded in gaining enthusiastic acceptance of the Academy; encouraged by that achievement and the general interest in its formation, he now harboured hopes of turning the special mission Löwenstein had given him into a permanent position funded by the American Guild. Unlike Richard Bermann, who ran the Academy in Exile's European office in Vienna on a purely honorary basis, Mendelssohn hoped for a fixed salary in charge of a second such office in London.

When I arrived in London in December 1936, I undertook the management of the European office, at first working with Mendelssohn. That same month he notified me of an application he was making to Löwenstein for a permanent appointment.[7] It included a description of his successful European tour and of the media coverage, resulting from his work with the press, that had raised the Academy's profile in Europe. Because of this considerable publicity, he said, the European office in London was receiving many letters from exiled German poets, writers, journalists, painters, sculptors, musicians, actors and scientists – not just from Europe, but also from as far afield as South Africa and the Far East. Many of them were in desperate straits, but all of them took fresh heart from the news about the Guild's formation and the development of the Academy.

Mendelssohn went on to state that the file arising from this correspondence already ran to over 300 names and would probably expand to about 2,000. It should, he suggested, serve as a basis for an archive relating to intellectual emigration in general with the aim of providing information not just about names, addresses and so forth, but also about the exiles' characters, careers, works, circumstances and artistic plans: an archive which, being 'an outstanding, exceedingly valuable, in fact a unique documentary resource, could serve in future as a reliable basis for the whole work of the Guild and the Academy'. He had, he said, already embarked on this project. Everything – correspondence, information from the Academy members, supervision of scholarship recipients, public relations work, the preparation and organization of a pan-European congress of exiles, the construction and maintenance of an archive and any further activities which might come to seem necessary or desirable in the future – should come under the auspices of the European office in London.

It was an impressive concept and one which certainly made good sense, particularly at a time when the overwhelming majority of intellectual émigrés were unable to leave Europe. Moreover, when Hitler overran Austria in 1938 and most of the continent in 1939, England turned out to be the only European country other than Switzerland in which it was possible for the Guild and Academy to continue their activities.

Regrettably, however, the Guild's directors were not in a financial position to pay Peter von Mendelssohn a fixed salary. So impoverished were the émigrés pleading for scholarships and subsidies from every part of the world that the organization's entire income was needed just to deal with the most urgent cases. This was why all the representatives of the Guild and the Academy were basically unpaid, except for a secretary at the head office in New York. This even applied to Löwenstein, whose work as general secretary was nothing if not gruelling, and to me as assistant secretary. Mendelssohn therefore received a mere 120 dollars from the Guild towards his expenses and no salary as such, although Löwenstein arranged to send him 20 pounds a month out of his own pocket for the time being. This was despite the fact that Löwenstein himself no longer had any means of his own and had, like Mendelssohn, to live on the income arising from his lectures, books and newspaper articles. When, after returning from America in April 1937, he was no longer able to pay Mendelssohn, the latter decided that he could not or would not continue his work in an honorary capacity and ended his involvement altogether.

Mendelssohn joined the British civil service as early as 1939 and initially served as an official in the Ministry of Information, where he took charge of the intelligence services dealing with Portugal and Switzerland. In 1941 he anglicized his name to de Mendelssohn and became a British citizen. In 1944 he was transferred to the press and information department of the Supreme Headquarters Allied Expeditionary Forces (SHAEF), and worked on psychological warfare, first at the headquarters in London and then in Paris. In April 1945 he arrived in Germany as a press officer with the British troops, where he was involved in, among other projects, founding the *Süddeutsche Zeitung*, *Tagesspiegel* and *Telegraf* newspapers. He then took charge of the Berlin edition of *Die Welt* as editor-in-chief. In 1949 he returned to London, where he worked as a correspondent for Bavarian Radio from 1954. In 1970 he elected to become a German citizen again and returned to his native city of Munich.

His life's work as a writer eventually ran to 30 works: novels, stories, essays, biographies and non-fiction, along with about 80 translations from several languages, predominantly English. His unfinished biography of Thomas Mann, intended as a two-volume work and entitled *Der Zauberer*, attracted particular acclaim. In 1975, when Mendelssohn was awarded the City of Lübeck's Thomas Mann Prize, Golo Mann said of the biography:

> Peter de Mendelssohn's achievement outshines those of all other Thomas Mann scholars. . . . I happen, purely by force of circumstance, to know a great deal about the life of Thomas Mann, but even I found myself repeatedly coming across facts that were new to me as I read this first and probably last truly valid, literally exhaustive biography.[8]

After 1937 I did not see Peter de Mendelssohn again until many years later in Germany, long after the war, and then only briefly. We occasionally met at the Julius Glückert House in Darmstadt, the headquarters of the German Academy for Language and Literature (*Deutsche Akademie für Sprache und Dichtung*), over which he presided from 1975.

Following Mendelssohn's withdrawal from the Academy in Exile, Prince Löwenstein and I continued the work in London in 1937, then in Switzerland and from 1938 in New York, although during the summer months, which we always spent in Europe until the outbreak of war, we were based in Paris. After returning from America in 1936, Richard Bermann continued to lead the Academy in Exile's office in Vienna in an honorary capacity and largely without reimbursement of his expenses, whilst Rudolf Olden – a member of the Academy from the very start and also the secretary of the German P.E.N. Club in Exile – took over as its representative in London. When Löwenstein persuaded Stanley Richardson to found an English sister association to the American Guild under the patronage of the Archbishops of Canterbury and York – in a letter to Olden, Löwenstein described it as 'a parallel, but autonomous organization, a "British Guild for German Cultural Freedom", as I term it'[9] – it was Olden who, as the Academy's representative, strove both determinedly and diplomatically to achieve close ties and collaboration between the American Guild and its new British counterpart. Richardson came up with a more poetic name for the organization: the Arden Society, an allusion to the banished duke's haven in *As You Like It*.

As its name suggests, the German Academy of Arts and Sciences in Exile consisted of two divisions of equal status, each led by a president (sometimes also referred to as a chairman) selected by the members of the division. For the Arts, also known as the Literary Division or Division of Arts and Letters, this was Thomas Mann and for the Scientific Division it was Sigmund Freud. One of the two was also to act as the overall president of the Academy; the statutes stipulated that this office would change hands each year. After his election on 14 December 1936, Thomas Mann became the first president of the Academy.

All 'scholars, writers and artists of unblemished repute' who were 'held in general respect on account of their outstanding achievements' were eligible for appointment as full members, irrespective of their nationality. Persons whose cultural background was not German could also become corresponding or honorary members. The precondition for any form of membership was a public commitment to 'intellectual and spiritual freedom'.

The Academy was based in New York, where it had an office led by a full member, Prince Löwenstein, as general secretary: 'The office prepares conferences and meetings, undertakes the tasks delegated to it, drafts proposals, is responsible for correspondence and manages the archive. It maintains relations between members and with other, allied organizations.' Since the aims and activities of the Academy and its fundraising organization, the American Guild, were closely entwined, it was natural that the services of the office which had been opened for the Guild should now also be made available to the Academy, and that Löwenstein, elected as general secretary by the Academy as well as the Guild, should run the office for them both. Similarly, the Guild's treasurer also served the Academy, for the latter's only funds were those raised by the Guild.

The fact that its members were scattered across the globe meant that the Academy could not convene general meetings except for its annual congresses, and that some members would not even be able to attend once a year. The statutes therefore accorded procedures in writing – which by force of circumstance became almost the norm – the same validity as oral resolutions. In the course of its day-to-day work on behalf of the Academy the American Guild needed to be able to contact an advisory body, so it formed a European Council composed of full members termed 'senators'.

The Academy in Exile and its aid organizations – the American Guild and its British 'offshoot', the Arden Society for Artists and Writers Exiled in England – together created a network spanning every continent. The strings of that network came together at the headquarters shared by the Academy and the Guild at 20 Vesey Street in New York. It was there that the extensive programme of assistance and aid, involving scholarships and prize competitions, advice and mediation, approaches to authorities and all sorts of other support, was coordinated, with the aim of relieving the creative and material troubles of numerous exiled intellectuals. It was there too that funds were made available for further rescue operations and for recent arrivals embarking on a new life in America.

Yet the Academy in Exile was more than an aid organization; its members saw it above all as a mouthpiece for a national culture which had been gagged by the terror of the Nazi dictatorship, indeed as an action group for the overthrow of the dictator and the reconstruction of a democratic Germany in a united Europe. That the Academy made such a considerable and widespread impact was due in no small part to its decentralized presence. In addition to more than 80 senators and members – male and female – there were 163 scholarship recipients and many individuals who were linked to the Academy as helpers or dependants: the thousand or so personal files in the *Exilarchiv* (Exile Collections) of Germany's national library, the Deutsche Bibliothek in Frankfurt, bear impressive witness to the breadth of the organization. Each such person acted as a disseminator in their host country, as well as enhancing the Academy's profile and prestige through his or her activities and reputation.

Before long, ordinary people throughout the world came to regard the Academy as something like an 'intellectual army' against the barbarism of National Socialism and as powerful evidence of the fact that, contrary to Nazi propaganda, Hitler and Germany were not identical and that there was always, even in the horrific years of the Third Reich, another Germany. In fact, intellectual exile was to some extent just the 'tip of the iceberg', just the most visible and conspicuous section of the 600,000 people throughout the world who, driven from their home by an infamous and mindless regime, kept alive the idea of a free and just Germany, a Germany with respect for human dignity. And even these refugees were in their turn just the most obvious representatives of those Germans who were not Nazis – the hundreds of thousands of Germans in the concentration and extermination camps, the millions in 'inner exile', the men and women engaged in active and even armed resistance, as well as all those countless Germans who, though not supporting National Socialism, went along with it at a superficial level in order to survive.

The overwhelming majority of émigrés wanted to return to Germany as soon as possible. Alfons Söllner affirms, for example, 'that the émigrés' emotional and cognitive ties with their native land survived for a long time and remained a decisive factor in their life-stories'. And although, as time passed and the regime endured, the exiles 'turned from refugees and émigrés into "immigrants" ', many of them continued, undeterred, to keep their gaze 'fixed on Germany'.[10] At the same time, regardless of how they might prefer to see themselves, in their new home they were generally regarded as Germans, or at least as immigrants of German origin.

CHAPTER SIX

Thomas Mann: President of the Academy's Literary Division

It was soon perceived that [the Academy's programme] could not be carried out without the active cooperation of the emigrated bearers of German culture themselves. They are the ones who must actually build up the movement by means of which the values that the German spirit has made precious to the world may be preserved, further developed and transmitted to future generations. Out of this realization was born the idea of the German Academy . . .

I have written in such detail about this matter because my heart says yea to it and my good wishes are with it – the wishes of a German to whom it would be a heavy blow if the word German should become, without any mitigating connotation, merely another name for threats of war, coercion of the spirit and of other peoples.

Thomas Mann, Letter to the editor of the
New York Times, *12 December 1936*

Towards the end of his European tour, Peter von Mendelssohn had called on Thomas Mann at Küsnacht, near Zurich. Mendelssohn had been friends with Klaus and Erika Mann ever since their youth in Munich, when the three, along with Pamela Wedekind and several others, were known as the 'poets' children', although Mendelssohn's own father, Georg von Mendelssohn, was a gold-smith and craftsman rather than a writer. Peter von Mendelssohn himself, however, had begun writing very early, as a schoolboy, as did his father's brother Erich, who published the novel *Nacht und Tag* in 1913, with a foreword by Thomas Mann, shortly before his premature death.

In his diary, Thomas Mann recorded Mendelssohn's visit to Küsnacht on 14 July 1936: 'The young v. Mendelssohn here for dinner. Later discussed the New York German Academy, its composition and plans, with him, Klaus and Erika.' He added: 'Whether the Viennese Beer-Hofmann and Musil are allowed to join, a good measure of the way things are going in Austria'.[1] Richard Bermann had already spoken with both these Austrians about their possible collaboration, but they were still hesitant. After his conversation with Mendelssohn, Thomas Mann put their misgivings down to the fear that they might encounter difficulties in the semi-Fascist corporative state, which was already coming to terms with the Nazi regime in Germany.

Thomas Mann himself had hesitated for a long time before stepping into the political arena. He was keen that his works should remain freely available to his German readership and was influenced by his publisher, Gottfried Bermann-Fischer. In 1933, for example, he had yielded to pressure from the official office responsible for 'furthering German literature' (*Reichsstelle zur Förderung des Deutschen Schrifttums*) to join Alfred Döblin, René Schickele and Stefan Zweig in a public statement to the effect that he refused to work on the exile journal edited by Klaus Mann in Amsterdam, *Die Sammlung*.[2] This made it possible for another of his books, *Leiden und Grösse der Meister*, to appear as late as 1935 in Germany.[3]

Only after a long inner struggle could he finally bring himself to make a clean break with National Socialism. In a poem written in his youth (which he quoted in 1938 in a lecture at Yale University) he had admitted: 'A vision of a slender crown of laurels, / Oft drives the troubled sleep from me at night.' And when he was just 29 years old he had revealed to his brother Heinrich that he sensed 'a princely talent for representation'. Mann felt a powerful need for recognition, indeed for acclamation, and secretly aspired to model his own life on that of Goethe. To such a writer, exile, as he confided to his diary in 1933, seemed 'a grave error of style and destiny in my life, and it appears to me that my attempts to reconcile myself to it are in vain'.[4]

In fact he was quite unlike Goethe in his stature and physiognomy, in contrast to Gerhart Hauptmann, another writer who harboured similar ambitions. This probably explains a certain stiffness in the dignified persona Thomas Mann tended to cultivate in public. The *New Yorker* once compared him ironically to an old-fashioned, ramrod-straight walking stick topped, in the accompanying caricature, by a finely engraved head.

That was also the impression I received the first time I encountered this hero of my youth in person, the author of internationally successful works such as *Buddenbrooks, Tonio Kröger, Tod in Venedig (Death in Venice)* and *Der Zauberberg (The Magic Mountain)*. I met him early in 1938, immediately after his arrival in New York, at the Hotel Bedford, which was then a meeting-place for émigrés and where Klaus and Erika Mann and the Löwensteins regularly stayed. It was 21 February, the same day on which he famously and proudly declared in a radio interview: 'Wherever I am, Germany is' – a pronouncement reported in the *New York Times* the following day which went on to resonate throughout the world. I immediately seized on it to formulate a motto for the Academy in Exile: 'Wherever the Academy is with its president Thomas Mann and Germany's cultural elite, Germany is.'

I approached Thomas Mann as soon as he entered the hotel lobby. After Erika had introduced me I was able to give him the good news that we had just forwarded initial instalments to the first twelve recipients of Academy scholarships, who included those authors whom Thomas Mann had particularly recommended: René Schickele, Gustav Regler, Oskar Maria Graf and A. M. Frey.

As he chatted with his daughter and with me – a young man of 25 – his manner lost all its stiffness. He seemed relaxed, even affable, and went on to mention the names of other authors such as Joseph Roth, Annette Kolb, Alfred Polgar, Wilhelm Speyer and Franz Blei, along with Ernst Weiss, Ludwig Marcuse, Heinz Politzer and Soma Morgenstern, whom he intended to recommend in writing for scholarships.

Not long afterwards, at a press reception early in March 1938 for the fourth book Prince Löwenstein had written in exile, his autobiography *Conquest of the Past*, I again spoke with Thomas Mann. He had in the meantime delivered lectures at Yale and the Wesleyan University, as well as in Chicago and Detroit. This was immediately before Hitler's predictable invasion of Austria on 12 March 1938, and it was obvious that those members of the Academy in Exile still living in Austria were, as prominent opponents of the regime, in considerable peril, as were the lesser-known recipients of Academy scholarships. We – Thomas Mann, Löwenstein, his wife (who had also been invited to give lectures in America about the situation in Germany) and I – discussed what the Academy could do to rescue them. The Nazis loathed Richard Bermann in particular, and he was therefore in more danger than most before finally effecting his dramatic escape.

By this time Thomas Mann, whose contacts with the other Academy members were mainly by letter after his move to Princeton, had long since broken off his relations with Nazi Germany, notwithstanding his initial efforts to avoid a direct confrontation with the Hitler administration. His eventual decision in 1936 to opt publicly for exile was due in no small part to his eldest daughter, Erika, who was the closest to him of his children and exerted the greatest influence on him. She was a fierce critic of the Nazi regime and had repeatedly urged him to distance himself once and for all from its system. In desperation she even went so far as to threaten to break with him, her own father, if he did not do so.

It was when the literary editor of the *Neue Zürcher Zeitung*, Eduard Korrodi, described literature in exile as the product of 'Jewish authors' and even referred to 'ghetto madness'[5] that Thomas Mann was finally spurred into action. He spoke up fervently in defence of political emigration and protested against demagoguery:

> My brother Heinrich and I are not Jews. Nor are Leonhard Frank, René Schickele, the soldier Fritz von Unruh, that son of Bavaria Oskar Maria Graf, Anette Kolb, A. M. Frey or younger talents such as Gustav Regler, Bernard von Brentano and Ernst Glaeser.

He also cited the names of Bert Brecht, Else Lasker-Schüler and Johannes R. Becher and continued:

> Being nationalistic does not make one German. Germany's hatred of Jews, or rather that of those in power in Germany, is – in spiritual and intellectual terms – actually directed not, or at least not only, at the Jews, but rather at Europe and the higher form of German culture [*Deutschtum*] itself; it is directed, as is becoming ever clearer, at the Christian and classical foundations of Occidental culture. . . . And I am certain to the

depths of my conscience that I am doing the right thing for now and for posterity in joining those to whom the words of a truly noble poet apply: 'Yet he who evil in his heart despises, / Prefers to wander from his native nation, / If slavishly it evil idolizes. / Much wiser to elect expatriation, / Than linger where mob hatred brutalizes, / As part of such a puerile generation.'[6]

This was the breakthrough. After talking to Peter von Mendelssohn, Thomas Mann indicated that he was prepared in principle to work in and with the German Academy of Arts and Sciences. On 14 December 1934 he was elected president of the Literary Division by the *Europäischer Senat*, or European Council, which was composed of the members enlisted so far and represented the Academy in the early stages of its genesis. For the time being Mann was in fact the sole president.

Thomas Mann's appointment was headline news in America and Europe even before the official election. Both the press and the radio broadcasters took a close interest in the development. On 26 August 1936, for example, *New Republic* in New York reported: 'A noteworthy new member of the Academy is Thomas Mann, winner of the Nobel Prize in literature, who now joins his brother Heinrich and his son Klaus in the organization.' After paying tribute to the Academy and the American Guild for German Cultural Freedom, the article goes on to predict that Hitler was unlikely to appreciate the irony in the foundation of the Guild, as it debunked his vociferous *Deutschtum* propaganda for all the world to see. After the election, on 22 December 1936, the *Prager Presse* carried a report entitled 'On the German Academy in New York':

> The European office of the German Academy in New York announces that the Senate of the German Academy has been formed at the general meeting of the American Guild for German Cultural Freedom in New York. It consists of the following figures: president of the Senate: Dr Thomas Mann, members: Heinrich Mann, Professor Veit Valentin, Professor Max Reinhardt, Professor Bronislav Huberman, Professor Otto Klemperer, Ernst Toch, Dr Arnold Höllriegel, Professor Emil Lederer, Dr Lion Feuchtwanger, Franz Werfel, Arnold Zweig, Ernst Toller, Bruno Frank, Professor Sigmund Freud, Professor

Melchior Palyi, Dr Georg Moenius, Dr Rudolf Olden. The general secretary of the German Academy . . .: Prince Hubertus zu Löwenstein.

In order to make the significance of these developments clearer and thus to heighten their impact, Löwenstein had written to Thomas Mann as early as 10 August, asking him to make a public affirmation of support for the Academy in Exile. He argued his case as follows:

> It has long seemed to me that the greatest challenge is that of preserving – and re-creating where necessary – a spiritual and intellectual Reich, as the doors to the political one remain closed to us. Although I quite see the necessity of realizing the Reich politically as well, I also believe that such a Reich can only come about if the strengths inherent in tradition, proportion and form are preserved. After all, one can almost say already that if we stand idly by in the face of current developments, soon there will no longer be any German language. I for one admit that I no longer understand a great deal of what I read from the books and newspapers produced in today's Germany. The barbarism of twisted, corrupted words has assumed dimensions ruinous to the people's linguistic sense. One of the Academy's tasks may therefore consist of ensuring that future generations still have available to them the means by which artists and scientists can express themselves. . . . It is thus our job to preserve a German culture [*Deutschtum*] that does not stop at any borders, a German culture that thinks universally in its art, its science and its political and social lore and bows only to universal criteria. It seems to us that we will then also find the strength required to liberate, purge and renew our nation.
>
> I know that a considerable material basis is vital in order to bring these things within reach. I am doing all I can . . . But unfortunately I am not really suited to the task – I think it would help immensely, Herr Mann, if you could write, in a place where it will generate the maximum amount of publicity, about the plan, the foundation and the help we require. A word along these lines from you would very likely open up considerable resources to us in America at once.[7]

Prince Löwenstein's appeal to Thomas Mann eventually succeeded. In October, as the president elect of the Academy in Exile's Literary Division, he composed an exhortation, affirming fundamental spiritual and intellectual values, which amounted to a kind of manifesto for the Academy. On 12 December 1936 it appeared in the *New York Times*:

> We are living in an age which, among some potent disadvantages, possesses the virtue that it leads our experience back to the roots of things – to fundamental truths, fundamental facts, and again renders noteworthy the eternal realities of which we have more or less lost sight because of their very obviousness. One such simple truth – a truth to be experienced as new and deserving of new expression – is that the spirit must be free if it is to possess any interest or evoke any curiosity.
>
> A regimented, commanded, terrorized spirit is not worth a shot of powder ... A 'Life of the Spirit' in the compulsory service of a political power concentration, under the dictatorial thumb and in dictatorial leading-strings, is devoid of all moral credit; it exists only in quotation marks.
>
> I do not believe that the statement of this plain fact places me in contradiction with the better part of my colleagues who live in Germany. I have sufficiently retained contact with my country not merely to surmise but to know that the paralyzing effect of the totalitarian demands of the ruling party upon the cultural life is felt there as deeply as abroad. ... The protest which arises within me against such coordination, against such harnessing of culture to the political chariot, seems to me, at least, genuinely German and entirely normal. German culture has never been geographically confined to the Reich. To the extent to which German culture transcends beyond the borders of the Reich ethnologically and linguistically, its conception is higher than that of the State ... No president of an official chamber of culture can subdue it ...
>
> [The German Academy] is conceived as a representative, practical and effective coalition of all the spiritual, artistic and scientific forces of the German nation which are compelled nowadays to serve Germany, and thereby humanity, abroad, because of the intolerance of a totalitarian State which denies

freedom of conscience and of the spirit at home. The significance of such an organization is obvious. It achieves unity, concreteness and force for what would otherwise diffuse, scattered among individuals without either a joint will or a joint vision. It offers the German artists and scientists who have been exiled and scattered among many nations that united support which spiritual workers in other countries possess at home . . . It will be able to erect a bridge not only between the German culture of yesterday and the German culture of tomorrow but also between the spiritual life of Germany and that of other peoples . . .

One should not forget that Germany is greater than the Reich, and that outside of the borders of the Reich there live 35,000,000 people whose intellectual and spiritual life takes place more or less decisively within the German language. It would be improvident to leave this whole part of the German-thinking and German-understanding world exclusively to the destructive influences of Berlin's Propaganda Ministry. It is possible to create counter-influences. To maintain another tradition of German culture may perhaps be designated as the principal aim of the academy, profoundly important because in this way, through the medium of the German people living abroad, succor can be brought to the finer forces which have undoubtedly still survived in Germany and a salutary influence exerted upon the people of the Reich itself.[8]

The effect of this text was powerful and enduring. In America, Thomas Mann's name already stood for the other Germany, a fact reflected in the extraordinary tributes paid to him in the course of his first two visits. When he came to New York in 1934 at the invitation of his publisher, Alfred Knopf, to publicize the first volume of the American edition of *Joseph und seine Brüder* (*Joseph and his Brothers*), the poet and fellow Nobel Prize-winner, Sinclair Lewis, told him in a telegram: 'As long as T. M. writes in the German language the world will not forget its debt to the people and the culture that produced him.'[9] And in 1935, when Mann, along with Albert Einstein and Henry A. Wallace (who later became the American vice-president), accepted an honorary doctorate from Harvard University to tumultuous applause from the 6,000 people who attended the ceremony, the citation credited him with upholding the dignity of German culture in that period.[10] President Roosevelt also honoured Mann with an invitation to join him and a few selected guests for a meal at the White House.

The manifesto for the Academy attracted considerable attention when Thomas Mann, Rudolf Olden, Konrad Heiden, Dietrich von Hildebrand and others were deprived of their German citizenship and Mann, shortly afterwards, was also stripped of his honorary doctorate from the University of Bonn. For the general public outside Germany this represented a confirmation of the considerable significance of the Academy and its president. Heinrich Mann commented at the time: 'Rather than Hitler depriving Thomas Mann of citizenship, Europe is depriving Herr Hitler of his.'[11]

The German embassy in Washington, alarmed by the manifesto, informed the *'Reichsminister* for people's enlightenment and propaganda', Joseph Goebbels, of the

> impressive appeal by Thomas Mann for support for the so-called 'German Academy' and 'American League [sic] for German Cultural Freedom' . . . The aims of both organizations, as described in the appeal, represent a large-scale plan by which the émigrés will attempt to monopolize Germany's cultural influence in the United States.[12]

As a next step, Löwenstein planned to introduce the international public to the concept behind the Academy by means of a representative event involving Thomas Mann in New York. The Guild's directors had approved the idea on 3 December 1936. Since the Guild itself could not yet afford to cover the costs of inviting Thomas Mann, one of its vice-presidents, Dr Alvin Johnson, extended a parallel invitation in his capacity as president of the New School for Social Research. This involved Mann's giving paid readings as part of the celebrations marking the fourth anniversary of the foundation of the 'University in Exile', as the Graduate Faculty of the New School was often dubbed on account of the many émigrés who taught there. 'Five readings at 500 dollars each', noted Thomas Mann in his diary on New Year's Day 1937, 'Löwenstein vehemently in favour because of the Academy.'[13]

On 12 April 1937, Mann and his wife Katia arrived in New York aboard the *Normandie*. Nicholas Murray Butler, president of

Columbia University in New York and the Carnegie Endowment for International Peace, summed up Mann's reputation in the United States at this time by describing him as 'a truly great author and an outstanding representative of the best that historic Germany has to offer'.[14] The *New York Times* of 13 April carried the following report:

> Denouncing the Nazi regime in stronger terms than ever before and prophesying its end sooner or later, Thomas Mann, the German writer whom the Third Reich recently deprived of his citizenship, said yesterday that dictatorships in Europe in general and Nazism in particular were doomed.[15]

The dinner in honour of Thomas Mann on 20 April at the Ritz Carlton in New York was designed to help publicize the American Guild and the Academy and attract new members. It was organized by a public relations company. Four hundred people attended, including Congressmen and numerous public figures. The governors of 27 of the 48 United States sent telegrams of greeting. Wilbur L. Cross, president of the American Guild and governor of Connecticut, introduced Thomas Mann as 'one of the three foremost men of letters in the world'.[16] In his own speech, the guest of honour spoke up for the Academy in Exile's lofty objectives:

> A comprehensive organization is, then, to be created, within whose boundaries the entire spiritual activity today existing outside the Reich can be included. Not only literary and scientific but also creative artistic production – that is: poetry, research, music, and the plastic arts, shall each take its place therein. . . . But over and beyond this matter of representation, the Academy is to have immediate practical effects on German intellectual life outside of Germany. These can take place in manifold ways; through management of lectures, performances, concerts, exhibitions, through scholarships and contributions to publishers. . . . Above all, behind the idea of the Academy, lies the hope nay the very conviction, that those conditions which have expelled so many intellectual Germans from their country, may not be definitive, but represent no more than an unfortunate interlude. It is our task to help the living spirit of German culture through a period of night and

winter; to keep the flame burning until a better day shall dawn; and, if you will permit the metaphor, the German Academy in New York should be the temple under whose protection this spiritual flame may burn until such time as it may once more flare up on its native hearth.[17]

That same evening, Thomas Mann announced the Academy's first literary prize, of 2,500 dollars, donated by the American publishing house of Little, Brown & Co. on the condition that the winning work must be suitable for the American market.

The Guild's treasurer, the composer Sam Barlow, spoke on behalf of Prince Löwenstein, who had already returned to Europe. He urged those present to support the Guild financially by becoming members. The well-known journalist, Dorothy Thompson, who was married to Sinclair Lewis, concluded with an appreciation:

> We are glad that you are here, Thomas Mann. No nation can exile you. Yours is a large citizenship, in no mean country. Wherever men love reason, hate obscurantism, shun darkness, turn toward light, know gratitude, praise virtue, despise meanness, kindle to sheer beauty; wherever minds are sensitive, hearts generous and spirits free – there is your home. In welcoming you, a country but honours itself.[18]

The press coverage reflected the fact that the German Academy of Arts and Sciences in Exile and its aid organization, the American Guild for German Cultural Freedom, endorsed as they were by so many prominent members, were more than just representatives of Germany's intellectual life. They were also institutions of considerable political significance. The *New York World Telegram*, for example, considered the mere fact that the Nazi regime had forced so eminent a literary figure as Thomas Mann into exile as proof enough that 'cultural freedom cannot exist when economic and political freedom are gone'.[19]

As the editor of a new magazine, *Mass und Wert*, Thomas Mann wrote an introductory essay in which he expressed the hope that exile might create the basis for a new political beginning in a liberated Germany: 'We must not stop hoping – and doing everything in our power to prepare – for a German power, a German state in which the German intellectual spirit can joyfully participate, and which creates a true totality by embracing that spirit as one of its elements.'[20]

Angry about the commotion in the international press and scornful of Mann after the author had been deprived of German citizenship, Joseph Goebbels, the Reich's minister of propaganda, went so far as to address the matter in person in the Nazis' campaigning newspaper, *Der Angriff*, on 27 April 1937:

> The 'great' Thomas Mann spent almost fourteen days in New York on a visit. He arrived on a Czech passport, for six weeks ago he became a citizen of the little village of Brosec in Czechoslovakia. The 'greats' of the 'German Academy in New York', Heinrich Mann, Veit Valentin, Max Reinhardt, Lion Feuchtwanger, Rudolf Olden, Arnold Höllriegel, Ernst Toller, Siegmund [sic] Freud, Prince Hubertus zu Löwenstein and all the other Jews and their comrades wanted to greet their president at least once at the 'Academy's' headquarters. They invited him as the guest of honour to the fourth anniversary celebration of the founding of the 'University in Exile'. And Thomas Mann came – on account of the honour, it goes without saying.
>
> He delivered three lectures about Goethe, Wagner and – Siegmund [sic] Freud and spoke about political freedom and freedom for science, pseudoscience and tales of atrocities dressed up in classic style! The president passed the test and resoundingly justified the trust invested in him by his like-minded comrades from the Academy. There was enthusiastic applause for Mann, the Czech.

At the XVth International P.E.N. Congress from 21 to 24 June 1937 in Paris, Löwenstein formally announced: 'I have the honour to inform the P.E.N. Congress in Paris of the foundation of the German Academy of Arts and Sciences.' In his short address he emphasized that the Academy was an instrument 'through which, above all, the younger generation of German writers, artists and scientists will be able to communicate without being hampered by "racist", political or religious persecution or prejudices.'[21]

Klaus and Erika Mann also hastened to join their father in publicizing the aims, structure, activities, effect and achievements of the Academy and the American Guild. In the book they wrote together,

Escape to Life, they had much to say about the Academy in Exile and its founder, Prince Löwenstein:

> A lecture tour had taken the prince and his wife to America. Both of them are excellent speakers. He lectures in good and fluent English with the slight Austrian accent people accept all over the world with kindness and tolerance; he speaks freely, without notes, and his tone is sincere, cordial and illuminating. He succeeded in awakening the enthusiasm of important and influential Americans for his scheme. As he himself is not only a man of imagination, but a hard worker too, a man of cultured and well-trained mind (he has a degree in law), he had prepared, in addition to the general outline of the Academy, a detailed draft of its purposes and aims, of its constitution and its by-laws.[22]

The book also describes the wide-ranging activities of the Academy and the Guild – their projects, plans and aims, the scholarships they awarded, the subsidies, contributions towards printing costs and many other ways in which the Academy helped enable exiles to continue their work. In a number of cases we were also able to arrange for recipients of scholarships to receive additional grants from American and other aid organizations. Bert Brecht and Robert Musil, for example, were supported by Dorothy Thompson's 'Journalists' Defense Fund'; Ernst Weiss, Hermann Broch and Joseph Roth by Stefan Zweig's 'Jeremias *Fond*'. Our amicable collaboration with William Dieterle and his wife in Hollywood allowed us to help other artists through their generous relief programmes. Thomas Mann personally distributed Dorothy Thompson's one-off contribution of 2,500 dollars, which she had passed on to the Academy through Erika Mann.

Löwenstein had highlighted the Academy's true political aim in a statement published by *Neue Weltbühne* in 1937. He appealed to all émigrés, irrespective of their political leanings or party allegiances, to join forces against National Socialism. This, he insisted, was vital in order to bring about a better future:

> Now it is time to fight, and we must dedicate ourselves solely to the struggle. But is the day really so far off when a coalition of exiles forms a government-in-exile and then – a government

for the Reich? It may be too early to turn our attention to that project, but it is never too early to consider the ultimate goal. And that, surely, must be: the rebuilding of the Reich, with Hitler's downfall as a mere preliminary. This 'afterwards' will be decided *now*.[23]

CHAPTER SEVEN

Sigmund Freud: President of the Academy's Scientific Division

Dear Prince,
When you recently entered my room – unannounced – I hardly looked up
from my writing and merely asked: So where does the island you've come
from actually lie? Such was the air of familiarity surrounding you in my
eyes since my discovery that you are a grandnephew of my old patient
and mentor, Anna Lieben.

Sigmund Freud to Prince Hubertus zu Löwenstein,
London, 23 July 1938

Sigmund Freud and Prince Löwenstein did not meet in person until they were in London in exile. They had, however, been engaged in correspondence regarding the Academy for some time before then.[1] While Freud had hesitated about whether he was still equal to the numerous commitments which bearing office in the Academy would entail, Löwenstein had worked untiringly to persuade him. 'I am all with you,' Freud had written to Löwenstein, 'the cause of intellectual liberty is my own cause. But don't forget, I am a very old man.'[2]

Hitler's invasion of Austria on 12 March 1938 was for Freud, too, a turning-point in his life. He came through the SA's search of his home, and the looting this inevitably involved, unbowed. His long-time scientific assistant, Princess Marie Bonaparte, was a childhood friend of Löwenstein's mother and told her in London about the incident. On hearing of the invasion she had immediately hurried to Freud in Vienna in order to be at his side. In fact the SA men did not dare lay hands on the professor, who watched the plunder with a scornful smile. When they finally discovered a cash box from the Psychoanalytic Society containing 6,000 schillings and stuffed the money into their pockets, he laughed aloud. After their departure, Freud's daughter, Anna, observed that the intruders' behaviour had not struck her as particularly funny. Freud replied: 'Oh yes, it was. I have been a physician for over fifty years, but I never received six thousand shillings for one single "visit"!'[3]

Following representations from Roosevelt and Mussolini, Freud was able to leave Austria in June and move to England. There he found an idyllic new home, at 39 Elsworthy Road in north-west London, which enchanted him from the moment he arrived. Yet his mood remained understandably gloomy, as he confided to his friend and colleague of many years' standing, Max Eitington, in one of his first letters from exile:

> The emotional situation these days is hard to comprehend, difficult to describe. The triumphant feeling of liberation is too thoroughly mingled with grief, for one did, after all, still deeply love the prison from which one was freed. The delight one takes in these new surroundings, which almost makes one yell 'Heil Hitler!', is troubled by uneasiness about little peculiarities in this strange environment. The happy expectations of a new life are damped by the uncertainty about how long a tired heart will wish to continue working.[4]

Although Freud was fond of the house on Elsworthy Road, he soon moved to 20 Maresfield Gardens in Hampstead, which he arranged exactly like his Viennese home on Berggasse, with the same furnishings – including the famous patient's couch and his collection of over 2,000 antique and archeological *objets d'art* from Egypt, Assyria, Greece, Rome, Asia Minor, China and Japan and a Toltec sculpture from Mexico. It was the determined Princess Bonaparte who had rescued all these items, after the Nazis had extorted a quarter of their value from her. When Freud died, not long after the outbreak of war, his daughter Anna ensured that everything was left in its original state. Today the attractive house is home to the Freud Museum.

Löwenstein sought out Freud in London very soon after the psychoanalyst's emigration. The German invasion of Austria and

Richard Bermann's flight to freedom put an abrupt end to the activities of the European office representing the Academy and the American Guild in Vienna. The Löwensteins and I therefore returned across the Atlantic from New York at the end of March 1938 to continue the work of the European office from Paris.

In the course of a long conversation with the prince, Freud mentioned, among other things, a 'remote analysis' of Hitler. When Löwenstein asked him how he intended to use the results, Freud looked at him in astonishment: 'But don't you know that one is not permitted to publish the analysis of a living man without his consent?' Even in this case he was not prepared to diverge from his strict professional code of ethics.[5]

In the course of the same visit, Löwenstein also told Freud about the Academy's other activities and aims. Conscious that Freud had only just completed the arduous process of emigration and was, moreover, undergoing a painful course of treatment for cancer, the prince forbore from pressing Freud to accept the presidency of the Academy in Exile's Scientific Division definitely. Instead, on the advice of Richard Bermann (whose exciting escape from Austria had taken him via Prague to Paris on 24 May and who had arrived in London on 13 June), he promised first to send Freud the statutes.

Bermann had known Sigmund Freud for decades. In 1903, aged just twenty, he had once consulted him as a patient. Freud took such a liking to the interesting and interested young man that he repeatedly invited him back for informal conversations. Many years had passed since their last meeting, but Freud had not forgotten Bermann.

Three decades later, Bermann wrote a tribute in a Viennese daily newspaper, *Die Stunde*, to mark Freud's 80th birthday on 6 May 1936. He observed that even before the advent of the Nazis he had been irked by the fact that Freud was inadequately honoured in his own country, and made a prediction:

> Only in America and Australia have people noticed that the discoverer of undreamed-of regions, the Columbus of the human soul, is the greatest living Austrian. But one day Austria, cured of its complexes, will also acknowledge this old man and be proud of him.[6]

Bermann's interest in psychoanalysis never waned. After his description of a troubling dream appeared in the literary section of the *Wiener Tag* newspaper on 6 February 1938, Freud wrote to him again in friendly and familiar terms as though an interval of 35 years had made no difference to their relationship.

In Bermann's dream, war had broken out and he had fled to America. In a restaurant there, he grabbed the arm of an Italian head waiter, whose features resembled those of Mephistopheles and who attempted to spray him with a bowl of 'red soup' – a mixture of blood and vitriol. Several psychoanalysts contacted Bermann to offer him their interpretations, involving diverse relationships between his dream and his sex life.

Freud's letter was different. Bermann described it in an unpublished manuscript:

> The professor provided me with an interesting and illuminating interpretation of my dream in a few brief words. He had of course immediately recognized the Italian head waiter as Mussolini and realized that my dream was in fact a nightmare about European politics. Behind this, however, Freud also saw the more profound fear of an individual frightened about his own fate.[7]

Freud invited Bermann to visit him again, and after the 'Anschluss', when they were both in exile, he repeated the invitation:

> You cannot evade me so easily. You owe me a visit, and now that we are both lucky enough to find ourselves in London I do not see why I should do without it. None of my many infirmities will spoil my enjoyment of it.[8]

Bermann seized the opportunity to talk again about the Academy in Exile, and on 29 June 1938 he informed Löwenstein:

> Freud spoke of you very affectionately and with a kind of cheerful tenderness. He would like me to tell you that you can use his name whenever you want; in particular, he gladly accepts the (nominal) presidency. He is distressed that he cannot play an active part. He shares our views completely and is a good German European.[9]

Following a second visit, Bermann described on 6 July 1938 the great honour that Freud had been accorded:

He has been made a member of the Royal Society. That in itself is not the whole honour: new members must register in a book which bears the signatures of Newton, Darwin, etc. I saw the book when I visited Freud; it has not left the R.S.'s premises since 1663, but an exception was made for Freud, as he does not go out, and it was brought to his house. The Nazis must have been delighted![10]

In the meantime, Löwenstein had drawn up the draft statutes for the Academy and announced them to Sigmund Freud. In his letter he congratulated him on his appointment to the Royal Society and noted that this was also good news for the Academy:

I was truly glad that the true Germany has been honoured in your person, and no tiding could have been more welcome than the one from Dr Bermann: that in the future you will also take such an active interest in everything we plan.[11]

He added that in sending Freud the papers he would also ask him to accept the presidency of the Scientific Division of the Academy in Exile and select his deputy himself. Thomas Mann, he noted, had already approved the statutes some time ago. According to those statutes, the presidents of the two sections, Freud and Mann, would take turns as overall president of the Academy.

In fact, in addition to expressing his strong support for the concept of the Academy, Thomas Mann had urged the project forward. His brother Heinrich had been president of the literary section of the Prussian Academy of Arts before 1933, and we knew from Klaus and Erika Mann that this was one of the reasons for Thomas Mann's particular eagerness to accept a similar role in the Academy in Exile. He regretted only that the very different circumstances in exile meant the Academy would never be surrounded by the pomp and circumstance of the Prussian, state-financed institution.

He was, however, convinced that appointing Freud would greatly enhance the Academy's reputation. He therefore told Löwenstein in a letter of 13 July 1938 that he thought it would advance their cause considerably to integrate the scientific world under Freud's presidency.

I support this idea very warmly and am delighted about Freud's willingness. I would therefore find it most expedient if

Freud were to head the scientific section and I the artists'. I, doubtless along with all the other members, look forward with interest to the revised statutes you announced. They may help give the Academy a clearer form, not to say more reality and a visible presence.[12]

The relationship between Thomas Mann and Sigmund Freud was founded on mutual respect, although it never evolved into a genuine friendship. In a lecture about Freud he gave in Munich in 1929, Thomas Mann had described Freud's libido theory as 'romanticism divested of mysticism, in scientific form'.[13] Freud wrote to Thomas Mann to thank him for his speech: 'I have always admired and envied poets, particularly if they – like Lessing, the ideal of my youth – subjugated and dedicated their art to thought.'[14]

Freud considered, however, that Thomas Mann hesitated too long before speaking out clearly against National Socialism. His critical attitude is evident in the carefully worded letter of congratulation he wrote for Mann's 60th birthday on 6 June 1935. It concluded pointedly:

> In the name of countless of our contemporaries, may I express our confidence that you would never do or say anything – the words of a poet are, after all, actions – that is cowardly or unworthy. Even in times and situations which confuse people's judgement, you will pursue the right course and direct others along it.[15]

On 2 May 1935, five weeks before Mann's birthday, Freud had remarked in a letter to Arnold Zweig:

> At the instigation of the Fischer publishing company, I have written a short message of congratulation for Thomas Mann's sixtieth birthday (6 June). I interwove it with an exhortation which I hope is unmistakeable. These are murky times; fortunately it is not my job to throw light on them.[16]

Thomas Mann, however, was preoccupied above all with himself and his work. When, a year later, a scientific society in Vienna (the *Akademischer Verein für medizinische Psychologie*) invited him to return the compliment with a speech to mark Freud's 80th birthday on 6 May 1936, he spoke at such length about himself and his

'Joseph' novel, that Klaus Mann commented: 'It is most remarkable how everything he touches ends up as an autobiographical – only too autobiographical – study.'[17]

On 20 July 1938, Prince Löwenstein sent Mann and Freud the Academy's statutes,[18] which had been discussed and approved by the members. In his covering letter he explained that it would doubtless make sense

> to make the circle of full members as exclusive as possible . . .
> in order to set the Academy as high a standard as possible and
> gain it international recognition as a representative entity for
> German intellectual life; we can describe a somewhat wider
> circle when we select corresponding members.[19]

This suggestion was accepted. Yet, despite the strict limitation of membership to the most intellectually distinguished exiles, it soon became apparent that it was not feasible for the Academy to forbear from awarding any prizes or scholarships for work by its own members, as stipulated in the statutes. Even among its most prominent members there were many who could not have survived, and still less worked creatively, without such assistance.

In the same letter, Löwenstein tendered his resignation as acting general secretary of the German Academy to Freud and Mann in their capacities as its presidents, thereby fulfilling the formal requirements for his official appointment as general secretary.

When Freud saw the statutes and realized the true significance of the Academy in Exile and the breadth of its activities, he appealed movingly again to Löwenstein to spare him the considerable burden associated with the honour of the presidency, and place it on stronger shoulders:

> Yesterday's letter from you gave me a veritable shock. Am I
> really to take a place alongside Th. Mann at the head of our
> Academy and fulfil all the functions with which you charge
> me in the statutes? If I previously accepted, as I vaguely
> remember doing, then I ask you now to forget about it. I was
> doubtless just momentarily dazzled by the honour. In justifica
> tion, moreover, I also seem to remember that you assured me
> that it would only cost me my name and would not involve
> any duties. Do not consider me lazy or indifferent for going

back on my acceptance. I still do all that I can; I do not even shirk the details of my work – I continue to write all my letters myself. But I really cannot do much more. I cannot go elsewhere, I cannot leave my room, I cannot attend any meetings.[20]

Freud nominated Albert Einstein as president of the Scientific Division in his place. Einstein, he wrote, was 'without doubt the worthiest counterpart to our Th. Mann. This solution is so obvious that I fear it may already have been attempted, only to fail initially. If this is the case, I beg you to try again.'[21]

Aware of Freud's precarious state of health, Prince Löwenstein had indeed previously approached Einstein about the presidency. He, however, was prepared to join the Academy only as a member, and Löwenstein therefore persisted in his attempt to persuade Freud. He based his appeal on numerous conversations:

Professor Einstein . . . has told me several times that he . . . is only interested in Jewish and Jewish-national issues, whereas the Academy, precisely because it is to administer a universal German inheritance, is super-national. Moreover, Professor Einstein has been a broken man since the death of his wife, and something inside me tells me that I ought not to return to him now with the same request he has previously refused.[22]

The problem was, continued Löwenstein, that Freud was the only other representative of German science in exile whose name carried such weight internationally. And he concluded: 'The fact is . . . that the existence of the whole construction depends on your not withdrawing your acceptance.'[23]

Sigmund Freud could not ignore such an urgent plea. In August 1938 he again brought up the matter of his handicaps, which he insisted would prevent him from contributing much more than his name, but he finally agreed – adding ironically 'that you will have to dictate to me everything to which I must lend my name'.[24]

Thereafter, despite all his reservations and the particular difficulties he faced, Freud went on to play an active part in the Academy by evaluating possible scholarships. Among those he recommended for awards were Kurt Hiller, Ernst Waldinger and Max Fleischer. All of them received funds from the American Guild after the Academy had approved Freud's suggestions.

In February 1939, Löwenstein was able to report to Freud that the process of constructing the Academy was advancing and also that Stefan Zweig had helped it along by donating the royalties from his drama, *Jeremias*, a gesture which carried, 'quite apart from its material significance, a considerable moral value as far as the public is concerned'.[25] After the successful foundation of the Arden Society, with its headquarters in London, Löwenstein was able to make the services of its office available to Freud to help him in his work for the Academy.

Freud, however, was seriously ill, and did not have long to live. He died in the same month as Richard Bermann, shortly after the outbreak of World War II, on 23 September 1939 at his house in Hampstead.

CHAPTER EIGHT

Rudolf Olden: Senator of the Academy and Leader of the German P.E.N. Club in Exile

'The immense German propaganda machine fought against the émigré literature,' Olden wrote. 'It would be a mistake to assume that this literature did not influence German public opinion. Books and newspapers were smuggled into Germany, to be read under faked covers or in the safe rooms of foreign embassies. German travellers pounced upon them when they went abroad. This production had also influence in shaping the opinion of foreign countries. Many of the books were translated, the periodicals were utilized by the foreign press, with or without quotation. But the main achievement was this – the life of the German spirit did not wither; "the debate continued".'

How true this was became apparent after the fall of Hitlerism. Because the debate, i.e. intellectual and political progress, had continued in exile, it could at once be taken up by liberated Germany. The renewal of the cultural and, last but not least, democratic life in a country as devastated as Germany in 1945, would not have been possible so speedily without the intellectual and political achievements of the German emigration.

Prince Hubertus zu Löwenstein (1968), Towards the Further Shore

As observed in previous chapters, the German Academy was built on the model of a democratic government in exile; along with the two presidents, the executive general secretary and the – full, corresponding and honorary – members there were senators, who were also members of the American Guild's European Council. Rudolf Olden was one of the first senators. He and Richard

Bermann were Löwenstein's most important advisers on matters relating to the Academy in Exile.

Unlike Bermann/Höllriegel, who has only recently been 'rediscovered', Rudolf Olden has remained a figure of some significance to many of those with an interest in historical and literary matters. He is known as an anti-Nazi defence lawyer (Carl von Ossietzky was one of his clients), as a journalist (prominent above all for his articles in the *Berliner Tageblatt*), as the author of numerous works of non-fiction (including a biography of Gustav Stresemann) and as the co-founder and secretary of the German P.E.N. Club in Exile, of which Heinrich Mann was president. In founding the P.E.N. Club in Exile he was pursuing the same aims which inspired Prince Löwenstein when he founded the German Academy in Exile.

They had stood shoulder to shoulder against Hitler as early as 1934–5, in the Saar campaign[1] – Olden as the editor-in-chief and Löwenstein as publisher of the weekly newspaper *Das Reich* – but they shared family as well as political ties. Olden's elder sister Ilse, later Countess Seilern, was close to Löwenstein's father, Prince Maximilian, when the latter was still resident at Schönwörth Castle at Kufstein in the Tyrol. This was where Hubertus was born, a generation younger than Rudolf Olden, whom he used to call 'Uncle Rudi'. Olden's father, Hans Oppenheim, was known as an actor and a journalist under the pseudonym of Olden, which Rudolf later adopted for himself.

Rudolf Olden was extremely conservative in his youth. His father having deserted the family at an early stage, he grew up mainly at the home of his aunt Hedwig, who was married to Prince Rudolf von and zu Liechenstein, after whom he had been named. His elder brother, Balder, wrote of young Rudolf:

Rudi, who was destined to become a Michael Kohlhaas in the legal system of the German Republic, a paladin of German liberty – and a martyr to that cause – and who later counted any day without a battle as a day wasted, was at the age of fifteen the complete gentleman. No speck of dust was to be found on his always perfectly pressed suit, his immaculate manners could become decidedly frosty; he was slim, tall, aristocratic in every gesture.[2]

As a student, Olden belonged to a duelling society, a fact betrayed by his scars, and in Vienna he and Arthur Schnitzler – 23 years his senior – were rivals for the affections of the same sweetheart. He went on to serve in the war as a cavalry officer in the Darmstadt Dragoons. After being wounded twice he was transferred to serve in courts martial, having passed the necessary law exams in Bonn shortly before the outbreak of war.

He was a strong personality with a mind of his own, and after Germany's defeat and the revolution he became an ardent liberal and a spirited defender of the democratic Republic. In Vienna he first wrote for *Der Friede*, a journal founded by the socialist pacifist Benno Karpeles, and then for *Der Neue Tag*, other contributors to which included Richard Bermann, Alfred Polgar, Egon Erwin Kisch and Joseph Roth. He later claimed that he learned everything he knew about journalism 'there, from Karpeles and Bermann'.[3] In 1924 Theodor Wolff appointed him political editor at the *Berliner Tageblatt*, which was the leading newspaper in the capital city during the Weimar Republic and enjoyed an international reputation. Within a few years, Olden rose to become deputy to editor-in-chief Wolff, thereby emerging as one of the most influential journalists of the time. It was he who took on the young Hubertus Löwenstein as a freelancer in 1930.

Olden had been registered as a lawyer in 1924 at the Supreme Court (*Kammergericht*) in Berlin. Before long he built up a reputation throughout Germany and even abroad as defence counsel. He favoured cases which offended his pronounced sense of justice and humanity, irrespective of the standing of those involved, the party they belonged to or the political repercussions. The 'Jakubowsky case' is a good example. It concerned the fate of a former Russian prisoner of war, who had been unjustly accused of murdering a child, condemned to death and executed in 1926. Olden managed to get the case reopened and won a posthumous pardon for Jakubowsky. He also conducted the defence in sensational trials such as the one of Carl von Ossietzky, who was accused of betraying military secrets as editor of *Weltbühne*. After the seizure of power von Ossietzky was taken to the remote prison camp of Papenburg-Osterwegen, before winning the Nobel Peace Prize in 1936 and being moved to a Berlin military hospital and subsequently to a private 'ward', where he died in 1938. Olden was also a member – and from 1931 on the board – of the League for Human Rights. In the league representing the interests of German writers, the *Schutzverband deutscher Schriftsteller*, his sympathies were with the left wing.

Rudolf Olden was an impressive personality – one of the 200 figures who really counted for something in Berlin, as Kurt Tucholsky once observed. For all his sympathetic, selfless readiness to stick up for other people, he was also capable of ruthless attacks and cutting judgements when he considered them appropriate. Whenever somebody said something he considered foolish or even reprehensible, he had a habit of inserting his monocle and fixing his gaze on his interlocutor, whom he would finish off without any counter-argument in two words: 'You reckon?'

The first of the books he wrote in those years, and the one for which he remains best known, was his biography of Gustav Stresemann, in which he acclaimed that most pivotal of statesmen as the architect of reconciliation in Europe's post-war *Völkerfrühling* or 'spring of the peoples'. When the book was published in 1929, first in Germany, then in England, France and America, Stresemann had just succumbed to the rigours of his office. His death was a tragic, disastrous stroke of fate for the Weimar Republic. Had he survived and been elected president of the Republic instead of Hindenburg in 1932, Germany's course through the rest of the century would undoubtedly have been very different.

Olden was a man of extraordinary courage. On 19 February 1933 – after Hitler's seizure of power – he organized a congress in Berlin with the theme: 'The Free Word'. Only a week later, on the day of the Reichstag fire, he received a warning that SA troops were waiting for him in front of his house and at the Supreme Court. He spent the night at a friend's home and escaped by pretending to be a holidaymaker and skiing through the woods and over the mountains to reach Czechoslovakia.

Olden remained only briefly in Prague – just long enough to publish his analysis of the Hitler phenomenon: *Hitler, der Eroberer. Die Entlarvung einer Legende* (Hitler the Conqueror. The Exposure of a Legend).[4] This rejects the idea that Hitler had won power through his own efforts; rather, he had been presented with it by Hindenburg, Papen *et al.* in the hope that they could use him to drum up support for their own causes. The pamphlet appeared in May 1933, the first title to be published in Prague by Wieland Herzfelde's Malik publishing company since its emigration. Later Olden donated the manuscript for a book auction in aid of the exiles, organized in New York by the Guild, the League of American Writers and the Booksellers' Guild of America on 19 February 1939.

Olden reached Paris, via Austria and Switzerland, in the summer of the year he escaped from Germany, 1933. There he wrote his *Schwarzbuch* (Black Book),[5] about the position of Jews in Germany, for the *Comité des Délégations Juives*. In November he moved to London with his third wife, Ika (née Halpern). In August 1935, Gilbert Murray, the famous classical scholar and chairman of the League of Nations Union human rights organization, invited him to Oxford and gave him the use of a cottage on his property at Boars Hill.

During the next few years, Olden gave a series of lectures at Oxford University about the history first of the German Reich and then of German liberalism (repeated at the London School of Economics) and, after the war had begun, about the political character of the Germans. He also wrote the rest of his books in Yatscombe Cottage at Boars Hill: *Hindenburg oder der Geist der preussischen Armee* (Hindenburg, or the Spirit of the Prussian Army), published in 1935 by Europäischer Merkur in Paris, which had also brought out his paper entitled *Warum versagten die Marxisten?* (Why did the Marxists Fail?) in the previous year. Also in 1935, a new edition of Olden's pamphlet about Hitler was published by Querido, in Amsterdam, to be followed a year later by an English edition: *Hitler the Pawn*. In 1939, Victor Gollancz published *The History of Liberty in Germany*; another London publishing house, Allen and Unwin, brought out *Is Germany a Hopeless Case?* in 1940.

Olden, as a co-founder of the German P.E.N. Club in Exile, had taken charge of the club on his arrival in England. This meant, in effect, that he carried out virtually all the work of the London office. The development of a German P.E.N. in exile also helped to inspire the idea and formation of the Academy in Exile, although the latter of course brought together not just writers, but also other cultural figures. The Academy thus represented the 'other', free Germany more comprehensively.

The German P.E.N. Centre had previously been expelled from International P.E.N., having been immediately brought into line and 'cleansed', along with the Prussian Academy of the Arts, by the

Nazis after 1933. The new rulers, and in particular the Reich commissioner, Bernhard Rust, forced Heinrich Mann, president of the literary section, from his post as early as 15 February 1933. He emigrated a few days later. Also on 15 February, the president of German P.E.N., Alfred Kerr, received a timely warning and, despite illness and fever, escaped with a few essential belongings in his rucksack to Switzerland and thence to Paris. The P.E.N. executive and committee dissolved themselves on 7 March 1933, after the Reichstag election. They were replaced by Nazi stalwarts such as Hanns Johst, who went on to become chairman of the Reich's literary chamber (*Reichsschrifttumskammer*), Johannes von Leers and Edgar von Schmidt-Pauli.

Excluding members because of their political convictions was contrary to the principles of International P.E.N., which had been set out by John Galsworthy in 1927 and which were enshrined in the statutes and therefore binding. At the P.E.N. Congress in Ragusa, Yugoslavia, from 25–28 May 1933, chaired by the new president, H. G. Wells (one of whose books had been among the many the Nazis had just burned), the post-*Gleichschaltung* German P.E.N. delegation managed to avoid expulsion by leaving the meeting before the general debate and Ernst Toller's speech. Toller launched a passionate and well-founded attack, observing that the secretary of the new German P.E.N., a certain Herr von Leers, had dared to describe Jews as 'devils in human form' in his book *Juden sehen dich an* (Jews are Watching You):

> The portraits of Einstein, Ludwig and Lessing he labelled 'Unhanged'; the portrait of Erzberger – not, in fact, a Jew – he labelled 'Finally executed'. . . . I shall not talk of my personal fate, nor of the personal fate of all those who now have to live in exile. It is certainly hard. They are unable to set eyes again on the land in which they were born, they have been driven out, chased away, disowned. Others, however, have suffered worse.

And then Toller used practically the same words as Prince Löwenstein and Rudolf Olden:

> I oppose the methods of the men who govern Germany today, but who have no right whatsoever to equate themselves with

Germany. Millions of people in Germany cannot speak freely or write freely. I am speaking here on behalf of those millions with no voice of their own any more.[6]

In Ragusa twelve P.E.N. members voted to condemn the persecution of writers in Germany. There were two votes against and fourteen abstentions. On 8 November, the meeting of International P.E.N.'s executive committee in London took a less lenient approach. Faced with a direct question, Schmidt-Pauli was forced to admit that the German P.E.N. centre had indeed excluded members because of their political convictions. This was then unanimously declared to be incompatible with the P.E.N. statutes, and Schmidt-Pauli's was the only vote against expulsion. In January 1934, a 'Union of National Writers' (*Union nationaler Schriftsteller*) was founded in Germany, with Hanns Johst as president and Gottfried Benn as vice-president, but this then descended into oblivion as far as the rest of the world was concerned.

The idea of replacing the German group with a centre comprising those writers who had, for various reasons, left Germany was mooted at the meeting of the executive committee in November 1933 in London.[7] The exiled intellectuals responded immediately: on 15 December 1933, Lion Feuchtwanger, Ernst Toller, Rudolf Olden and Max Herrmann-Neisse wrote to Hermon Ould, general secretary of the International P.E.N.:

We the undersigned German writers living outside of Germany wish to found an autonomous group of the P.E.N. Club. We are informed that writers now living in France, Switzerland, Czechoslovakia and elsewhere share this desire. We therefore ask the Executive Committee to recognize this group, when formed as representing free German literature in the spirit of the International P.E.N. Club.[8]

The signatories informed many fellow exiles of their initiative in a circular of 28 December and urged them to participate. Rudolf Olden discussed the matter with Ould, who then confirmed in writing on 17 January 1934 that he had no doubt whatsoever that the next P.E.N. congress, meeting in June, would approve the formation of a German P.E.N. group outside Germany. He also encouraged Olden, as the acting secretary of German P.E.N. in

Exile, to try to 'find new adherents' and contact Heinrich and Thomas Mann.[9]

As noted above, it was only at the beginning of 1936 that Thomas Mann could finally bring himself to break with the regime, and he left Olden's letter unanswered. When Feuchtwanger reminded him of the matter, he replied, on 25 January 1934:

> This question once again faces me with the choice of either disappointing the German exiles or breaking with Germany, i.e. with my German public, and ending my ability to achieve anything through literature. . . . In other words, I laid Herr Olden's letter aside because I was at a loss and wanted to give myself time. I would be grateful to be granted more time still, to wait and see, before I make my decision.[10]

Olden drew Mann's attention to the significance of the forthcoming P.E.N. congress in June in Edinburgh and Glasgow and argued that this forum 'which represents the writers of the world' could and must be used to 'lodge a protest against the suppression of literary freedom in Nazi Germany'.[11] He asked Mann to participate in the congress and speak or at least send a message to the delegates, but without success.

By contrast, Heinrich Mann, who had emigrated to France in 1933, did not hesitate and joined P.E.N. in Exile as early as 20 January 1934. When, on 16 April, Olden invited him to become its president, he also accepted, although he was already president of the *Freiheitsbibliothek* (Freedom Library) in Paris and honorary chairman of the *Schutzverband deutscher Schriftsteller*. The 60-year-old writer was not, however, prepared to travel – he was working on his novel *Die Jugend des Königs Henri Quatre* (translated as *Young Henry of Navarre* and *King Wren : the Youth of Henri IV*) at the time and was also worried about possible consequences: 'Anyone who leaves this country cannot be sure that he will get back in.'[12] This ruled out his attendance as a delegate at the congress in Scotland.

In addition to Heinrich Mann, many other eminent authors agreed to join the German P.E.N. centre; a good number of them would later be admitted to the Academy in Exile. Prince Hubertus zu Löwenstein was one of those who joined, after being nominated by Heinrich Mann. In June 1934 the International P.E.N. Congress in

Edinburgh and Glasgow unanimously recognized the organization. In September *P.E.N. News* reported:

> The XIIth P.E.N. Congress, recognising that the German members of the P.E.N. outside Germany constitute the only part of German mental expression at the present time which conforms to P.E.N. ideals and being anxious to consolidate and preserve the unity of this mentality with a view to the final complete restoration of the German P.E.N. on German soil, proposes to recognise a common centre for this German P.E.N. de facto in London or Paris, and to accord that centre pro tem. all the respect due to any national P.E.N. Club.[13]

All the rights and responsibilities of the expelled German P.E.N. centre thus passed to the German P.E.N. Club in Exile. Its unusual status encouraged the international press to take a particular interest in it. There was widespread coverage when the club demanded – at the 1934 Congress in Edinburgh and Glasgow and then again, more urgently and more explicitly, at Barcelona in 1935 – the release of writers imprisoned and mistreated by the Nazis and protested against the persecution and kidnapping by Gestapo agents of authors who had emigrated.[14] When, in Barcelona, the German exiles first appeared as a united front, they showed very clearly that the overwhelming majority of literati had turned their backs on Nazi Germany.

Moreover, at the International Congress of Writers for the Defence of Culture in the same year in Paris, it became evident how close the ties were between the exiles on the one hand and the opposition and 'inner exiles' within Germany on the other. This was one of the few opportunities for both sides to appear together in public. Alfred Kantorowicz's description of their encounter betrays how moved he was. He identified two highlights in the course of the congress:

> One was Heinrich Mann's appearance on the stage of the grand hall of the Mutualité. Five thousand or six thousand people were in that hall; they all rose without any prompting. They rose in silence to honour the great German exile, Heinrich Mann; in him they honoured the Germany of the freedom fighters, the Germany that has entrusted the world with

indispensable cultural values and will continue to do so in the future. The crowd in the hall remained silent for half a minute and then began to cheer as if it would never stop.

The second highlight:

On the third day of the congress a masked man, unfamiliar to all non-German participants, appeared on the stage. He spoke only briefly in German. He said that he had arrived from that country a few days ago in order to deliver greetings to the congress from a group of anti-Fascist German writers, who continue to work there in daily fear for their lives. He hoped to return to Germany in a few days in order to tell his comrades about the intellectual solidarity with their struggle, which had manifested itself here at the congress so strongly and unmistakably. He could assure us all that in enslaved Germany, where there was currently no free literature, an underground literature was developing and eluding the clutches of the murderers. One day it would offer the best account of all the battles, all the suffering, all the willing self-sacrifice.

Kantorowicz continues: 'When the audience had recovered its breath after the translation of those brief words, the cheers, and even tears, of fraternal feeling broke out afresh.'[15]

As well as conducting all correspondence on behalf of German P.E.N. in Exile, Rudolf Olden undertook the preparations for participation in the P.E.N. congresses which took place until the outbreak of war. Heinrich Mann's function as president was more as an adviser and a figurehead. This meant that Olden, still without any secretarial or other assistance, was left to deal with all the work – although he was employed on an honorary basis. Neither was he paid as the Academy in Exile's representative in England. The true scale of his achievement is apparent in the archives of Germany's national library, the Deutsche Bibliothek in Frankfurt, which contain 1,800 items relating to P.E.N. in Exile and 14,000 from the Academy in Exile.

Olden, Heinrich Mann, Prince Löwenstein and then nearly all the more prominent members of P.E.N in Exile – about 70 in 1938 and almost 100 in 1939[16] – were also appointed to the Academy. This, however, was not the only reason Olden had taken on these two areas of responsibility. Quite apart from the way the two organizations were interwoven at a personal level, Olden was convinced that they were united by a common cause. He once described this to Löwenstein as the historic mission of the exiles in general: that of showing the world that Hitler and his regime were not synonymous with Germany.

Many other bodies in exile also shared that cause, as was manifest either in their activities or simply in their existence: the *Schutzverband Deutscher Schriftsteller*, the *Freiheitsbibliothek*, and two educational institutions – the *Freie Deutsche Hochschule* and the *Deutsche Volkshochschule* – in Paris; the University in Exile in New York and the many German leagues, organizations and political party committees there and in over 70 other countries in which exiles had found refuge; the prolific publishing houses in exile in Vienna, Prague, Amsterdam, Paris and New York; the two (three for a time) news agencies and one or two daily newspapers, the many weekly, monthly and other journals (there were 166 in France alone, including those published by leagues and parties); the exiles' theatres in London, Paris and New York.

This catalogue makes it clear that the German Academy of Arts and Sciences in Exile was just one organization among many within the diversity of life in exile, albeit one distinguished by the prominence of its members and therefore with a particularly high profile. Everything it achieved and instigated within the context of the 'historic mission' would have been virtually inconceivable without the background of exile. The German P.E.N. centre in London illustrates how effective it was possible to be in exile, despite the difficult circumstances and lack of resources. It had no staff, no offices in other countries, no sources of funding and, unlike the Academy, it was unable to sponsor its members. Yet it survived and wielded influence; under Heinrich Mann's and Rudolf Olden's leadership it enjoyed a worldwide reputation as a centre of German culture and the same status as other national P.E.N. centres.

When the XVth International P.E.N. Congress took place in Paris in 1937, several of the German delegates were already members of the Academy. The official representative was Prince Löwenstein, who announced to the congress that the Academy in Exile aimed to become a spiritual and intellectual protectorate for German culture outside Germany; it wanted to help and promote that culture and those who stood for it and, in line with its statutes, establish branch offices in Paris, London and other centres of European civilization.[17] The list of individuals supported by the Academy through scholarships or other forms of assistance soon included members of P.E.N. in Exile.

Rudolf Olden was particularly enthusiastic about his involvement as a senator in the Academy in Exile. In a letter to Richard Bermann in 1938 he wrote:

> It is becoming ever clearer to me how important the projects initiated or planned by you and the prince really are. At the moment, German literature is in fact alone in its struggle against the tyranny which has raised its bloody banner against us, and saving that literature will become the most important mission of our time.[18]

In his role as one of the five judges for the Academy's literary competition, it fell to Olden to read many of the manuscripts submitted by the deadline of 1 October 1938. He also championed the establishment of a book club, an idea which was also close to Bermann's heart and which he discussed with Arthur Greenwood, a leading Labour Member of Parliament. In February 1939 he wrote a memorandum on the subject, emphasizing the importance of German literature in exile and insisting that the influence of literature written in exile and smuggled into Germany should not be underestimated.[19] As a member of the *Senat* or Council, Olden wrote many of the reports and endorsements which were required before the Academy could approve a scholarship award. In this way he helped, among others, Elisabeth Castonier, Otto Lehmann-Russbüldt, Kurt Hiller, Paul Dreyfus, Berthold Jacob, Gerhard Hermann, Alfred Stern and Robert Musil. The number of applications increased together with the general hardship, which eventually compelled Olden himself to accept a grant.

After the invasion of Austria by German troops in March 1938, he made particular efforts on behalf of Robert Musil, who was eventually brought safely to Switzerland in August. Following the occupation of Czechoslovakia in March 1939, Olden worked with the Academy in Exile and the Arden Society to rescue those exiles who remained in Prague. The sheer number of appeals for help frequently meant that he was on the verge of exhaustion, particularly as there were so many unexpected complications. In one such incident, the British authorities sent Wieland Herzfelde back to Paris when he arrived in England, despite the fact that Olden had obtained invitations and guarantee statements for him from H. G. Wells and J. B. Priestley, among others. Eventually Olden, with Gilbert Murray's help, managed to contact Home Secretary Sir Samuel Hoare, whose intervention at least enabled Herzfelde to return to England for a limited period before continuing his journey to America. At Olden's instigation, the British P.E.N. set up a support fund for him for that period, endowed with 1,000 pounds and a starting contribution from the Lord Mayor of London.

Olden's work on behalf of friends and colleagues in danger became even more arduous when war broke out. German exiles in France were immediately interned as 'hostile aliens' along with Nazis. Wherever and whenever he could, Olden urged English friends in influential positions to intervene on behalf of internees such as Leonhard Frank, Willy Speyer, Friedrich Wolf and his own brother, Balder Olden. He did his best to make the British public realize that Germans who had been forced into exile by their opposition to Hitler were friends of Great Britain, brothers-in-arms on the side of democracy. It was to this end that he and Robert Neumann wrote an appeal published on 24 August 1939 in the *Manchester Guardian* under the headline: 'Distinguished Germans in exile. Irreconcilably opposed to the Nazi regime.'[20] On 2 October 1939, not long after the outbreak of war, Olden asked Jules Romain, president of International P.E.N., to convoke a conference of writers from all the warring countries, with the aim of creating an alliance for freedom of speech and against all forms of dictatorship, wars of aggression and hatred between peoples. No such conference ever took place, but P.E.N. did in that same month issue a 'Statement arising out of the present situation', concerning the responsibility of the writer in times of war.[21] On 1 June 1940, in some desperation, Olden finally wrote to Thomas Mann about the policy of wholesale internment which had now been adopted in Britain as well as in France. He urged Mann 'to appeal to President Roosevelt or the government to grant these German writers asylum in the United States for the duration of the war so that they can continue their important work.'[22]

England had always been Olden's country of choice as a political émigré. He regarded it as an ally in the common struggle for human rights and liberty. He had a close personal and political relationship with many Britons who shared his outlook. He was in the habit of closing his letters from Oxford to Gabriele Tergit with the words: 'Ceterum censeo: God preserve this truly humanistic England!'[23]

He was therefore particularly disappointed by inglorious British policies such as the initial effort at appeasement, which undermined opposition within Germany and weakened democratic forces throughout Europe. He was at an utter loss to understand the immediate classification of German émigrés as 'enemies'. As Olden observed to the secretary of International P.E.N., Hermon Ould, four days before the war began, the policy affected him personally, for the British Home Office had 'just declared me to be an "Enemy Alien". I deeply feel I did not deserve this.'[24] In fact he was subsequently registered in Group C, as a foreigner whose loyalty was not in doubt, but he was well aware that internment was looming even for him.

In order to save his two-and-a-half-year-old daughter Maria Elisabeth from a life behind barbed wire, Olden and his wife Ika sent her to Canada. He was interned on 25 June 1940, the day after his daughter's ship had sailed. He had just dispatched a forthright letter to the *Manchester Guardian*, which was printed on 28 June. Just as the British people had failed to recognize their enemies at the time of the Sudeten crisis, he wrote, they now appeared to be failing to recognize their friends. The government ought, if only for the sake of its own country, 'to keep on terms of the closest friendship with the men who may carry revolution one day into all those countries, especially Germany'. But how, asked Olden sarcastically, was the government going about this duty?

> By calling them 'enemy aliens', putting them under humiliating restrictions, dismissing them from their posts, hunting them out of their living places . . .? Is this the preparation for future alliance with them? Had these potential revolutionaries to come to this country to learn that only 'blood' matters? To learn that it is a British rule that everyone who takes a stand against his own government is untrustworthy, that he must be

treated like an outlaw? To learn that to fight for principles is shameful and dishonourable?[25]

Olden was first brought to an internment camp at Southampton, then to Bury in Lancashire, where he suffered his first breakdown. Finally, on 17 July, he arrived on the Isle of Man. According to his fellow sufferers, he had aged visibly and had become weary, bitter and disillusioned. When the efforts of his friend, Gilbert Murray, secured his release on 8 August, he admitted in a letter to Friedrich Burschell:

> I am in the grip of a profound disinclination for life. The doctors cannot identify any illness and call it a nervous breakdown ... I sense the cause of my illness: it is revulsion, at anything and everything, physical and mental, and it seems hard to convince oneself that the extraordinary effort required to overcome this revulsion could ever be duly rewarded again.[26]

He was released on the hurtful condition that he make preparations to leave for America as soon as possible: he had, in the meantime, received an invitation to the New School for Social Research in New York. The official who issued him his British exit visa delivered the final insult by, with Olden looking on, erasing the passage which would have permitted a return to England.[27]

On 12 September 1940, the Oldens arrived in Liverpool to board the *City of Benares* for the crossing to America. On 17 September the ship was torpedoed by a German U-boat. When the passengers were instructed to take to the lifeboats, Olden was too weak to rise. His wife refused to leave him and they perished together.

In 1941 a reorganization of the P.E.N. Club saw Friedrich Burschell become secretary on Rudolf Olden's previous recommendation, to be succeeded by Richard Friedenthal in 1942. Alfred Kerr was the new president with Thomas Mann as honorary president.

After the war, P.E.N. in Exile dissolved itself to make way for a new, democratic and thus legitimate German P.E.N.; at the XIXth International P.E.N. Congress in 1947 it secured approval in principle for re-establishing a German P.E.N. centre, and the XXth Congress a year later in Copenhagen delivered official authorization. At the constituent assembly in Göttingen in November 1948,

Hermann Friedmann, Johannes R. Becher and Ernst Penzoldt were elected to the committee with Erich Kästner and Rudolf Schneider-Schelde as secretaries. The German P.E.N. Centre, first in Munich and after 1952 in Darmstadt, promotes internationalism, tolerance in all spheres of culture and understanding between nations, as set out in the charter of the International P.E.N.

In 1948 the German P.E.N. Club in Exile was renamed the 'P.E.N. Club for German Authors Abroad', with its headquarters in London. It survives to this day in an expanded form as the 'P.E.N. Centre of German-speaking Authors Abroad' ('P.E.N.-Zentrum deutschprachiger Autoren im Ausland').

CHAPTER NINE

The Arden Society: The American Guild's Sister Organization in England

> The old world rides again to hunt its prey,
> Rattles its skeleton across the fields,
> Blasphemes the glory of the rising morn:
>
> But life is stronger than the world's decay,
> And now to Truth which neither dies nor yields
> She sounds her last and all-compelling horn.
>
> Stanley Richardson, Poems on Spain

In his plans for an organization in England parallel to the American Guild, Prince Hubertus zu Löwenstein had to take into account the different circumstances there. America, as a country of immigrants, is generally open and sympathetic to newcomers. At many levels of English society there is a rather more distant attitude towards foreigners. This should not be confused with unfriendliness; it is rather, as Arthur Koestler – who was fond of England and returned there repeatedly – ironically noted, a kind of benevolence summed up in the maxim: 'Be kind to the foreigner, the poor chap can't help it.'[1]

There were also specifically cultural problems. German and Austrian painters and sculptors were at a disadvantage because the styles they imported with them – such as *Neue Sachlichkeit* or the Expressionism of the *Die Brücke* movement – did not go down well in the conservative climate then prevailing in British art. Architects

of international renown, such as Erich Mendelsohn or Walter Gropius, received a warm welcome from the progressive members of
the Royal Institute of British Architects, but the differences between
the British tradition and modern, continental architecture were so
great that Mendelsohn, for example, despite becoming naturalized
as early as 1938 and enjoying success in a competition with his
English partner, opted to move on, via Palestine, to the United
States.

The most daunting hurdle facing writers, poets and actors was, of
course, the language. This was a particular problem for actors, as
audiences in England (unlike those in America) are sensitive to foreign accents and tend to accept them only if they are appropriate to
a particular role. Moreover, unlike many of the other countries
where Germans sought refuge, Britain had no German-language
theatres. It was not until 1939 that émigrés in London in the *Freier
Deutscher Kulturbund* (Free German League of Culture in Great Britain) founded the 'Kleine Bühne', which was so small (the stage
measured just six square metres) that it also became known as 'Das
Nudelbrett' ('the pastry-board'). In 1940, Austrians in London
founded 'Das Laterndl' ('The Lantern'). Apart from international
stars such as Elisabeth Bergner, Conrad Veidt and Lucie Mannheim,
very few émigré German actors were able to make names for themselves in England. Those who did included Adolf Wohlbrück (who
called himself Anton Walbrook), Friedrich Valk, Martin Miller, Amy
Frank and Friedrich Richter. For most others, however, England
was simply a stopover *en route* to the United States.

Elisabeth Bergner, via Richard Bermann, volunteered to do whatever she could for the German Academy in Exile. She enjoyed
exceptional success soon after arriving in London. In his essay on
'The Emigration and the Arts', John Willet notes that

> the English public took to its heart the waif-like Elisabeth
> Bergner, whom the leading impresario of the day, C. B.
> Cochrane, immediately treated as a star. Basil Dean having
> been impressed with her success in the German dramatisation
> of Margaret Kennedy's immensely popular novel *The Constant
> Nymph*, Cochrane accordingly decided to produce her in a
> play by the same author. This was *Escape Me Never*, which
> instantly put her at the top of the West End social-theatrical

tree. Queen Mary told her she made her cry; Noel Coward wrote 'You are fantastic!'. . . Bernard Shaw received her with . . . a private performance of 'Deutschland über alles' to his own accompaniment. It was a multiple accolade from the high British establishment.[2]

For all that, even Elisabeth Bergner was let down by her accent, which caused her to be judged a complete flop when she appeared alongside the young Laurence Olivier in a film version of *As You Like It*. She fared no better in the title-role of *The Boy David*, vanquisher of Goliath, in a play written especially for her by James M. Barrie, author of *Peter Pan*.

Writers such as Arthur Koestler, Robert Neumann, Rudolf Olden, Peter de Mendelssohn and Hans Flesch von Brunningen, who managed to master English idiom, were exceptions to the general rule. The rest were often unable to afford a competent translator. On the other hand, the English P.E.N. Centre, frequented by the likes of H. G. Wells and J. B. Priestley, was receptive and helpful to German émigré writers, as Hilde Spiel discovered. The Club, she recalls, was 'a link with English intellectuals and was vitally important . . . The English are, of course, generally rather distant. They are helpful, but not to the extent that they will really look after a foreigner. In P.E.N., however, they did.'[3]

Prince Löwenstein was fortunate enough to be spared the special problems of life in exile in England. His mother was English, and his relatives there included his elder brother Prince Leopold, like Hubertus a resolute opponent of National Socialism. Having lived in England since the 1920s, he had good connections and was able to smooth the way for his brother Hubertus. He introduced him not just to people with political influence, but also to literary figures. He was a well-read connoisseur of German and English literature, and English publishers valued his advice on German texts. After the seizure of power he had taken a particular interest in literature written in exile, and his expertise was of considerable help when the English equivalent to the Guild was founded.

On Hubertus's first visit to England in July 1933, Prince Leopold had introduced him to Viscount Cecil of Chelwood, who had drafted the League of Nations Covenant with Woodrow Wilson and the South African, Jan Smuts. Chelwood had recalled that the

Löwensteins' grandfather, Lord Pirbright of Pirbright, had been under-secretary of state for the colonies in the cabinet headed by his own father, the Marquess of Salisbury. Sir Austen Chamberlain's father had also worked with Pirbright at the Board of Trade.

These good connections in England had also been useful during the Saar plebiscite campaign of 1934–5: Sir Victor Schuster, a director of the National Provincial Bank, provided Löwenstein with a generous donation which enabled him to publish the weekly paper *Das Reich*. When it then became apparent that there was a danger of Hitler's employing direct or indirect force in the Saarland, Löwenstein was able to persuade Sir Reginald Wingate – who had served under Kitchener in the Egyptian army at the celebrated victory over the Mahdi's successor and took over from Kitchener as army commander and governor-general of the Sudan – to use his influence over the government to get a contingent of troops deployed to the Saar.

The value of such connections was demonstrated again when, as soon as Löwenstein arrived in England, Reginald Harris, editor-in-chief of the highly regarded monthly review, *The Nineteenth Century and After*, asked him for an article about 'The Real Germany'. Löwenstein obliged, closing his contribution with the prediction: 'And as already the outer foundation exists, we need not feel too pessimistic when thinking of Germany's future. Its real image will live when in works of history Hitler's name will hardly be mentioned.'[4] Viscount Cecil, moreover, encouraged him to speak about Germany at the Royal Institute for International Affairs. Sir Austen Chamberlain was so impressed by the lecture, delivered on 20 October 1933, that Löwenstein had to repeat it shortly afterwards at the League of Nations Union.

The prince's growing reputation led Richard de la Mare of Faber & Faber to suggest he write a book about the fate of the Weimar Republic. *The Tragedy of a Nation* was published only a few months later, early in 1934; Steenuil went on to bring out German and Dutch editions in Amsterdam. In the same year, Faber also published Löwenstein's *After Hitler's Fall – Germany's Coming Reich*. These two books gave him an international reputation almost overnight. They, along with his dissertation, were instrumental in securing him a visiting professorship from the Carnegie Endowment for International Peace, for which he was nominated by the English historian, George P. Gooch.

All this was of considerable assistance in laying the groundwork for an English fundraising organization allied to the Academy. In June 1938, on his return to London, Löwenstein persuaded the English poet Stanley Richardson to organize the establishment of a sister organization to the Guild. This organization, explained Löwenstein in a lengthy memorandum to Richardson, was 'by assisting German culture in exile . . . to serve the cause of peace and international understanding'. It 'might be called upon to preserve those forces which one day will be . . . responsible for a peaceful settlement of European and world affairs'.[5]

Richardson, the author of the verse collections *Dark Blue Sunlight, The Road to Emmaus, The Heart's Renewal* and *Poems on Spain* (about the Spanish Civil War), had studied in Madrid after completing his Cambridge examinations and had translated the poems of his friend Garcia Lorca into English. Löwenstein described him as 'a "Shelley-like nature." With his fair wavy hair, light complexion, and blue eyes, Stanley was very much the Anglo-Saxon type of Englishman. He liked the idea that there was no Norman blood in his family.'[6] We regarded him as one of the great emerging talents in English literature. Like Shelley, however, he died young, early in 1941. He had volunteered for the Royal Navy when war broke out, but fell victim to one of Hitler's bombs in the London blitz during a spell of shore leave.

In 1936, Richardson's anti-Franco sympathies had led him to offer his services as press attaché to the Spanish embassy in London. When Löwenstein chose, as *A Catholic in Republican Spain* (the telling title of his published account), to characterize Franco as an ally of Hitler rather than a defender of his religion,[7] Richardson introduced him to the ambassador, Don Pablo de Ascárate.

The two shared many fundamental convictions, and they also agreed that the organization planned for Britain needed, like the American Guild, to be more than just an aid organization for needy artists. Rather, it had to be distinctly political: a forum for debate, a meeting place for German exiles in Europe and a voice for the culture of the other Germany.

Just as in founding the American Guild, it was important to enlist the help of eminent, respected figures, whose influence would be needed – even more in England than in America – to persuade the general public to accept and support the German exiles. Richardson played an important part in this regard. Like Löwenstein's brother he had connections in high places, and he introduced Prince Hubertus to, among others, Emperor Haile Selassie of Ethiopia. He was also a friend of the Archbishop of York, William Temple, whom he prevailed upon to accept a leading role as one of the British guild's patrons.

Another factor in Richardson's success in recruiting prominent members was his sage and pragmatic approach. On 7 July 1938 he wrote to Prince Löwenstein:

> One of the key persons to be got is the Dowager Marchioness of Reading. I understand from Dr Berman [*sic*] that you know her well, and that she is likely to do all you ask. Could you write to her winningly, and get her to communicate with me, or to let you have an answer 'Yes' or 'No'. Don't frighten her that she will have to work hard: we only want her name . . .
>
> Once I have a list of some dozen notabilities who are in support, I shall send out a typed statement with this pro-visional list, and a more or less confidential and personal let-ter. Then, having got about forty acceptances, send out a *printed* form, with a tag for cheques to be paid to the Treasurer (I think Lord Faringdon?? rich and safe). By this time, September will be here, we can call the most important people together, elect Chairman etc. and get going to collect money, get up a public meeting, arrange for speakers in the Universities, etc.[8]

In Löwenstein's letter to Lady Reading, he assumed from the start that she would understand the political significance of found-ing such an organization, for her husband (who had died in 1935) had been Lord Chief Justice and then viceroy of India when Mahatma Gandhi's freedom movement was starting to rear its head. He had been on friendly terms with Löwenstein's older brother, Prince Leopold. Löwenstein told her that there was a spir-itual and intellectual obligation at stake, one which educated people abroad would doubtless be ready to recognize in view of the Western world's common cultural heritage and Germany's contri-bution to it. He looked forward to Germany resuming her place among the civilized nations when peace arrived – but warned that this would be impossible unless free German culture, currently languishing in exile, was still alive. The greatest challenge, he went on, consisted of securing the survival of this international community of Germans and non-Germans, Jews and Christians, of benevolent, peace-loving, civilized people.[9]

On 4 July 1938, Richard Bermann, who was in close contact with Richardson and took a very active interest in the founding of the English guild, made a similar appeal to the Archbishop of Canterbury, Cosmo Gordon Lang, whom he knew personally: 'To save not only the persons but also the work of European intellectuals is, after all, a concern of all the European nations who kept themselves free from a totalitarian spirit.'[10] Lang agreed, after Löwenstein had also spoken to him, to join the Archbishop of York as a patron of the English guild.

Along with the archbishops and Lady Reading, the Duchess of Atholl, who had been a member of parliament since 1923 and held several honorary doctorates, declared herself ready to support the aid organization. Like Löwenstein, she had involved herself in the Spanish Civil War on behalf of the Republican government, and in 1937 the prince and Bermann had arranged her democratic mission to Austria, then under the semi-Fascist Schuschnigg regime, to encourage and help the forces of freedom. Bermann was her guest when he fled to England from Austria, and she was the dedicatee of his last book, *Home from the Sea*, about Robert Louis Stevenson.

She was joined as a patron by the liberal Dean of Chichester, Duncan Jones, who took a particular interest in events in Germany and in 1938 had just published *The Struggle for Religious Freedom in Germany* and, together with the German pastor, Martin Niemöller, *From U-Boat to Concentration Camp*. Later, during the war, he encouraged Bishop Bell of Chichester to establish contact, via Sweden, with Pastor Dietrich Bonhoeffer and other resolute figures in the resistance and to make representations to the British government on their behalf. These efforts, unfortunately, turned out to be in vain.

Other patrons included the president of the Women's Liberal Federation, Lady Violet Bonham Carter; Randall John, the Earl of Antrim; the Master of Balliol College, Oxford; the Provost of King's College, Cambridge; Professors Ernest Barker and John Hilton; the poet and writer, Walter de la Mare; the painter and graphic artist, Augustus John (famous for his portraits of Lloyd George, Lawrence of Arabia and Queen Elizabeth); Dame Marie Tempest, who was then well known as a singer and had just made an early British sound-film, *The Moonlight Sonata*, with the Polish composer, Jan Paderewski (she went on to become a choreographer and producer); and Elisabeth Bergner.

The elected committee, to which most of the day-to-day work fell, consisted of Sir Nevill Coghill, Provost of King's College, Cambridge; the Spanish scholar, Professor John Braden Trend; the writer and publisher, Herbert Read; Evan John; and Helen Simpson. The treasurer was Christopher Holland Martin, a director of the Bank of England, and Stanley Richardson was the honorary secretary.

Richardson had come up with a far more poetic name for the British guild: 'The Arden Society for Artists and Writers Exiled in England' – in allusion to Shakespeare's *As You Like It*, in which the duke unseated by his young brother dedicates himself to the arts in the Forest of Arden, until goodness triumphs and he can return from exile as the legitimate ruler.

The statement issued by the Arden Society to introduce itself to the public referred to the German Academy of Arts and Sciences as an 'allied society' in the United States and explained:

> The Arden Society exists for the purpose of securing to exiled artists and writers living amongst us some chance of self-expression in their own medium. By co-operation and sympathy it should be possible for works to be translated, small anthologies of poetry and prose published, pictures exhibited, and useful individual contacts brought about.
>
> The Committee intends to establish a Centre in London, to be opened in the autumn, where meetings for discussion and reading can be held. This Centre will contain a valuable Library; it will also provide newspapers and magazines which are not always obtainable by the individual. Exiled artists will be invited to use its rooms for the exhibition of their works, and we hope that it will offer both quiet and recreation for those who have been forced to abandon so much in the countries they have left.[11]

The Society launched itself by holding a dinner on 10 February 1939. It was a memorable event and received extensive coverage in the press. *Tatler*, for example, reported:

The Arden Society, newly formed to help artists and writers exiled in England as the result of persecution in their native lands, gave a dinner at Claridge's not long ago. His Grace the Archbishop of York and Mrs. Temple received guests, and speechmakers included the Archbishop and Sir Muirhead Bone, the distinguished etcher and painter. Lady Bone, was amongst literary lights present; these also included poet Mr. Humbert Wolfe, novelist Miss Rose Macaulay, and that noted patron of the arts, Sir Edward Marsh. Frau Elizabeth Gundolf, whose late husband was famed throughout the literary world as the last humanist, sat next to Professor Ernest Barker, Professor of Political Science at Cambridge since 1927 and the author of many very erudite works.[12]

The foundation of the Arden Society represented a welcome beacon of hope, for the position of the émigrés had become increasingly difficult in recent years. Rudolf Olden, who was as unstinting in his efforts on behalf of the Arden Society as he had been in virtually single-handedly creating the P.E.N. Club in Exile, wrote to Löwenstein from England:

> The hardship faced by our German authors in England is far from negligible. Depending on the circumstances, the grants from the *grand comité* can even be insufficient to guarantee their ability to work. Something should be done. The English P.E.N. Club has achieved wonders given its own circumstances and attitudes, but now, it appears, its funds are exhausted and it is gradually pulling out. There are more or less vague plans for the foundation of a new society which would try to get closer to the pockets of those Englishmen well disposed towards literature. But then there is the Arden Society! ... Please be kind enough to inform me. Overorganization is not good either; maybe I can help to avoid it.
>
> I write to you on the eve of war – which is every evening, so to speak. One day, however, the war itself may well arrive unexpectedly, and then it would be necessary to do more with the German writers than just keep them barely fed.[13]

In fact, prompted by our letter from France in July 1938, Stanley Richardson had already put together a plan for offering scholarships

and subsidies. The plan was dated 2 August and based on the provisional annual budget for the Arden Society. It involved 50 scholarships worth from 10 to 30 pounds a month and valid for half a
year, with the possibility of renewal. There would also be translation fees, competition prizes, lecture fees, subsidies towards printing costs and an emergency fund, amounting in total to 14,000
pounds. Added to this would be the relatively modest sum of 2,160
pounds for administrative costs.[14]

Today, over half a century later, it is unfortunately impossible to
determine exactly how much of this scheme could be implemented,
what was spent and how many of the planned scholarships and
subsidies were actually awarded. Unlike the archive of the
American Guild and Academy in Exile, which survives intact, that
of the Arden Society was lost due to wartime occurrences and
Richardson's early death. It is clear, however, that the Arden Society
was also invaluable in affording another form of assistance:
assistance which, as Olden had predicted, became necessary very
soon – even before the outbreak of war – when Hitler invaded
Czechoslovakia on 15 March 1939. It helped organize the rescue of
German émigrés from Prague, just as Hubertus Löwenstein and
Oswald Garrison Villard had done in America when Austria was
annexed.

To support these rescue efforts, the American Guild made an
emergency contribution of 600 dollars to the Arden Society on the
day of the invasion, earmarked for the ten individuals in Czechoslovakia who had been awarded scholarships or had applied for
them. Eight of the ten were successfully brought to safety in
England, where the Arden Society immediately made the Guild's
money available to them to help with their initial outgoings and
give them something to fall back on.[15] One of those eight was the
brilliant young working-class poet, Jesse Thoor, one of the great
literary discoveries of the exile era.

CHAPTER TEN

Jesse Thoor: A Poet Discovered in Exile

In Nürnberg haben sie bei Sturm und Hagelschlag mich ausgestossen.
In Hamburg löschten sie mir niederträchtig beide Augen aus.
Mit Lüge haben sie in München meine Seele übergossen. –
Den letzten Rest Vernunft, den schlugen sie mir in Berlin heraus.

So habe ich das Sterben fürchterlich und tausendfach erlitten,
Da ich – nicht Mensch noch Tier mehr – stöhnend aufgeschrien,
Als sie, die Tollen, mir das Herz in meiner Brust entzweigeschnitten.
War es an jenem Tage der Gewalt im März, war es in Wien?

In Nuremberg they cast me out amid the hailstorms fiercely
   raging,
In Hamburg their malevolence moved them to put out both my
   eyes.
In Munich then they took my soul to saturate it with their
   falsehood. –
Berlin was where they bludgeoned out what little sense remained
   in me.

And so I suffered death unspeakably, a thousand times repeated,
When I – no longer man nor even beast – cried out.
When they, the madmen, tore my breast apart and cut my heart in
   two there.
Was it upon that violent day in March? Was it in Vienna?

Jesse Thoor, from 'Sonett vom guten Willen'
('Sonnet of Goodwill')[1]

The further the Nazis extended their sphere of power and influence in Europe, the greater became the number of those émigrés – artists, writers and scholars – who turned to the Academy for help. As Hitler's apparatus of terror engulfed one country of asylum after another, those who had managed to escape from Germany found that their very lives were once again in danger. These were the people who now urgently needed help in the form of money, papers and residence permits. The most difficult, and often dramatic, rescue operations were the ones which highlighted the role and importance of the Academy for us and our sponsors most clearly, and which lent us the strength we needed for our work.

One such operation, on which I still look back with pleasure and satisfaction, was the physical, spiritual and artistic rescue of Jesse Thoor, a poet of the working-classes whom the Gestapo had harried from country to country. His first letter, characterized by exhaustion and desperation, reached us in mid-August 1938 at the Academy's European office in Paris. This was where most such letters arrived after the abrupt demise of the office in Vienna when Hitler invaded Austria in March 1938. Jesse Thoor wrote from Brno, shortly before Germany launched its attack on Czechoslovakia, requesting a scholarship to help him complete a cycle of poems. His letter, addressed to Löwenstein, was moving in its simplicity:

> Dear Sir,
>
> To date I have thrown away every letter I have written you. I wished (and still wish) to present you with a complete work consisting of 46 sonnets. The road, however, is too hard for me, and I no longer believe I can manage it alone. Please help me. I am a working man, a Berliner, an émigré, 33 years old. More-over, sonnets ought not only to be bitter. And I am convinced that this does not depend on me alone. The 21 sonnets enclosed are the cream of the crop and all I possess. My prose works were lost when I left my homeland. And please, would you be good enough to reply soon?
> Yours faithfully, Jesse Thoor.[2]

The poems he enclosed were unforgettable. Jesse Thoor was completely unknown at this point. Nothing he had written had ever appeared in print in Germany, and although he had apparently published the occasional poem in Vienna after 1933, his work had not attracted any notice. The examples he sent were, however, more than just the efforts of an emerging talent. They were powerful lyric poetry, fully formed sonnets of breathtaking beauty and couched in mature, potent language. We returned to 'Sonett im Herbst' ('Sonnet in Autumn'), for example, over and over again:

Wie oft wohl muss ich noch, dass Gott erbarm – ein stiller Gast
An fremden Tischen dankbar meinen kahlen Schädel neigen?
Ich lege ihn am Abend hin – auf Federn, Strohsack, oder Bast,
wie ich ihn schon am Morgen hob; zum Trauern nur und Schweigen.

Denn wieder blühn in Deutschland Wicken, Astern und Zyklamen.
Ich weiss, da gehn die Alten schweren Schrittes vor das Haus.
Und wieder pocht der Herbst an Tür und Fensterrahmen,
und bläst die Lampe flackernd in den engen Stuben aus.

In diesen Nächten werden viele einsam durch die Strassen gehn.
Und wird es nur der Wind, ein Frösteln sein in Baum und Strauch?
"Vielleicht – viellecht bringt uns der März ein Wiedersehn?"

Und allen wünsch ich und auch mir die Kraft, nach altem Brauch,
dass wir den Frost, die Kälte und den Hunger überstehn. –
Und alles Unheil und die tiefe Schande der Tyrannen auch.[3]

How often, God of mercy, must I as a quiet guest
at other tables, bow my hairless head in gratitude still?
I lay it down when evening ends – on feathers, on palliasse or bast –
just as I raised it with the dawn: in silence and in sorrow.

For Germany blooms once again with cyclamen, vetch, aster.
I know the elderly will tiredly step before the house.
And once again the autumn knocks at doors and windows,
extinguishes the flickering lamps within the narrow rooms.

During the nights now many lonely folk shall wander through the
   streets.
And will it be just wind, a shiver in the trees and shrubs?
'Perhaps – perhaps this March will bring us our reunion?'

And, following tradition, I wish all of us the strength,
which we shall need to stand up to the hunger, frost and cold. –
As well as all disaster and the deep disgrace of tyranny.

The first person to whom we showed the poems was Richard Bermann. He had just been plucked to safety from Vienna and was with us on the Isle aux Moines in Brittany. Severe critic though he was, he shared our enthusiasm. The ensuing rescue operation gave us particular pleasure because only the formation of the German Academy and the Guild made it possible to offer a young poetic genius, who had matured and been discovered in exile, the chance and wherewithal to survive. This was welcome proof that an umbrella organization designed to offer hope and encouragement really was capable of not just preserving, but also nurturing and developing the cultural and intellectual life of Germany, even in the circumstances of life in exile.

Löwenstein wasted no time in responding warmly to Thoor's letter, promising to apply immediately for a scholarship on his behalf. For this purpose he enclosed a questionnaire we had drafted, requesting further information. Thoor's reply from Brno, which reached us on 24 August 1938, told us a little more about him:

Dear Prince Hubertus zu Löwenstein,

I received your letter today. I am now completely mortified, for I did not really expect a reply. I was already utterly disheartened . . . I have, however, never written for money or any other reward. Nor shall I ever do so. I had to think long and hard before appealing to you for help, because I want to earn my own discoveries and because I wanted to prove that I deserved assistance by producing a work complete in itself . . . If I survive this winter, that will be fine. And in fact I do not even want any money. (I need it with rare urgency: I am unwell and I am more ragged than I ever have been before.) What I wish: to be able to spend some time somewhere writing and thinking without interruption. That is the age-old wish. And it is possible, after all, that this wish could be fulfilled directly. . . . My name is Karl Höfler, I am known as Peter, and I call myself Jesse Thoor, as I want to avoid the poet's private experiences being affected by any particular external circumstance. I am thirty-three years old, single, Austrian. I was born in Berlin and emigrated in March 1933 to Vienna as a Communist. I never placed any importance on getting into print because my self-criticism rejected the idea in the course of my inner development. Apart from that, in those days my poems were passed on to the public by radio, at events organized by certain district education authorities, [and in] 'Die Jugend' and 'Der Sturm' magazines. Today I possess nothing, but I stand by what there is.

A volume of short stories was unfortunately lost on the journey to Brno. Yes, I work; that is – I attempt to. But it is and was ever thus: four weeks of work, two years of worry. I wrote to you because I wanted to work for a whole year for once. Extent? Theme: anti-Fascism. Truth. Yes, that's right: I want to serve the truth. (That sounds funny, but it is impossible to explain any other way.) And I want to and shall confront untruthfulness wherever possible. Even if many people believe (alas even today) that it is simply always somewhere other than where they themselves are. (Brrr – very awkward.) How much time I need? – What referees? Please do the refereeing yourselves, for I was never centre stage, and whom should I name? Maybe Th. Mann can remember a few sonnets? I once sent them to him at Küssnacht. Wolfgang Langhoff helped me for a while, Arno Holz encouraged me years ago, Paul Wiegler sent me a message which cheered me. H. H. Ebers [Ewers] (the *Alraune* monk) threw me out. Frau E. Ludwig once let me tap her for some cash and wrote to tell me to keep my chin up. . . . I receive a small sum [in Czech crowns] from the League for Human Rights. But from payday to payday and between there is the great anxiety: when will it be over. And that will probably be soon . . . If I had a passport I would be considerably more confident, for I would take to the road once again. Yes – if I could still endure it . . . May I hope for a prompt answer? That knowledge is a comfort to me in this abominable predicament.[4]

Bermann had nominated Alfred Neumann as one of the referees or appraisers to be consulted before a scholarship could be awarded. When we sent him the poems, we received his emphatic approval by return of post:

I have received and read the sonnets by Jesse Thoor: they made a powerful impression on me. They are indebted to Villon and Rimbaud, but with the nihilism quadrupled by the horror of our age. This is a poet of horror, but emphatically a poet. There are sonnets ('Von der endgültigen Frage', 'In Graz' and the best two: 'Am Totenbett der Mutter' and 'Vom Manne, der krank am Wege lag') which are, without a doubt, among the most extraordinary lyric poems I have read in the last ten years. I can say with certainty that, except for young Politzer, who is actually more or less the antipode to this Thoor, I have come across nothing more powerful in post-Hitler poetry. (Anyone who comes up with lines such as: 'At night I saw the solar sphere extinguished in its orbit / akin to a black crow that falls in winter from the boughs' – is already almost a great poet even if, here too, one hears very clearly the overtones of Rimbaud.) I therefore wholeheartedly support the award of a scholarship to allow this man to complete his cycle.[5]

We advised Jesse Thoor to contact somebody such as Max Brod in order to obtain a second endorsement. Brod was a member of the Academy and would have been the easiest person for Thoor to reach, as he lived in Prague. Thoor, however, was unwilling to do this, even if that attitude 'might turn out not to be good' for him, as he put it in a letter after a considerable delay. 'I have already written that kind of letter too often. Now I cannot and will not do so any more.'[6]

I therefore stepped in on his behalf. Instead of writing to Max Brod I decided to turn to Franz Werfel, whom Richard Bermann had also suggested as an assessor for Jesse Thoor. I asked Alfred Neumann to help me contact Werfel. It was not long before I heard back from Neumann:

> Today I received Franz Werfel's evaluation of Jesse Thoor's sonnets, and I am now passing it on to you. As you will see, he shares my view completely. Do give Herr Thoor the pleasure of hearing Werfel's opinion. I am convinced that we have discovered the great German poet of these evil times.[7]

Werfel's appraisal was brief and to the point:

Dear Prince Löwenstein,

I fervently recommend the poet *Jesse Thoor* for a scholarship. His sonnets are, without a doubt, the most astonishing achievement I have encountered in German lyric poetry for many years. They not only demonstrate a high level of poetic language and imagery, but also give form to a condition of the soul that will perhaps come to have documentary value as being characteristic of our age. This is the dawn of a literary phenomenon which we are obliged and honoured to help on its way.[8]

The application for a scholarship, supported by the two appraisals, was approved at the next meeting of the Guild's Council in December 1938 and payments began in January 1939. In the meantime, however, it had become clear in the light of political developments that this assistance would, in itself, be insufficient. We had no doubt that the seizure of the Sudeten region agreed in the Munich Pact would be no more than a first step on Hitler's path towards the complete subjugation of the peoples of Eastern Europe, and that the émigrés would be among the earliest victims. As early as November 1938 came Jesse Thoor's urgent appeal:

Dear Prince Hubertus zu Löwenstein,

After some failed attempts to leave this country, I now find myself back in Brno. I found a letter from your secretary, Herr von Zühlsdorff, and another with two appraisals of my work. Thank you for these. I have written five more sonnets, but I cannot send them to you. My situation is simply hopeless. But how can I begin to explain it all? I have neither accommodation nor money, and my Austrian passport does not contain the exit permit, and it will automatically expire at the end of December. Legality is not even an issue any more ... And in short: is it perhaps possible for you to help me somehow. Maybe you know somebody who could send for me from England, for example. There is no other way for me to obtain a visa. And please: excuse this clearly stated request. But I am simply stuck as never before and have to make every word and every minute count.[9]

This letter does no more than hint at a further reason for Jesse Thoor's keenness to leave Czechoslovakia. He only told me of it later. His hatred of Hitler and his ingenuous idealism had made him a Communist, but he had subsequently changed his mind, 'repelled by the party inquisitors', as Gerdamaria Thom, herself an émigré and a long-time friend of Thoor's, puts it in her biography of him.[10] Such a defection was something of a risk, given the growing fanaticism of the Communist Party members.

Prince Löwenstein and I were already in America when Thoor's letter arrived. It therefore fell to Löwenstein's wife, Princess Helga, who had stayed behind in London, to pursue an entry visa for Jesse Thoor. She was assisted by Stanley Richardson in his capacity as secretary of the Arden Society, and achieved her object faster than she might have expected. After the Munich Pact, for which Prime Minister Neville Chamberlain was largely responsible, the British authorities adopted a much more welcoming attitude than previously to the émigrés trapped in Czechoslovakia. After only a few days the princess was able to inform Jesse Thoor that the necessary arrangements had been made. Thoor's reply, thanking her for her help, makes it clear just how hopeless his situation had appeared to him:

> I really cannot express it. But I feel warm inside for the first time in a long while. It all seems like a fairytale to me . . . – you see: I really thought logic dictated that my next step would have to be back to Berlin. That was how it looked. I thank you from the bottom of my heart.[11]

Since everything now depended simply on our ability to pay for Jesse Thoor's flight (the only way for German émigrés to leave Prague was by air), I urged the American Guild's treasurer in New York, Oswald Garrison Villard, to approve the wiring of the necessary sum to Brno before Christmas. This he did, and not long afterwards, Jesse Thoor arrived in London. He did not yet speak a word of English; Stanley Richardson greeted him at the airport in Croydon, took him to a small hotel in London's West End, and ensured that the Arden Society looked after him. The scholarship from the Academy in Exile was enough for him to live on initially.

When I returned to Europe with the Löwensteins in May 1939, visiting England in June and July, I finally met Jesse Thoor in person. He was an impressive individual, small but strong and well proportioned, with a high, domed forehead, a powerful gaze and an aura of self-confidence, particularly when he began to talk. He had been born and brought up in 1905 in Berlin-Weissensee, although his parents were originally from Upper Austria. His father was a cabinetmaker by profession, but appears to have been unable to establish himself in Berlin. He became a disillusioned factory worker, began to drink and to beat his wife when he was under the influence. Jesse Thoor's childhood was poor, grim and oppressive. After leaving school he trained as a dental technician, but never worked as one. Instead, almost like the journeymen of centuries gone by, he took to the road, travelling through Germany and to Switzerland, France and Spain.

His one desire had always been to write, and – unusual for a working-class youngster – he did just that even as a schoolboy. He returned to Berlin in the late 1920s, when the city was not just a turbulent political hotbed, but also a stimulating and fertile intellectual centre. His opposition to Hitler moved him to become a Communist – or rather an anarchist. Whenever Kurt Tucholsky, Erich Mühsam, Joachim Ringelnatz and the like met for readings and for their heated debates, Thoor was there too.

In London he also told me that before 1933 he had engaged in scuffles with the SA and SS, just as we had in the democratic *Reichsbanner Schwarz-Rot-Gold*. After the seizure of power on 30 January 1933 he had hoisted the Red Flag atop roofs and factory chimneys. He left the country at about the same time we did, heading first for Vienna. It was in exile, he once told me, that his creative life as a poet really began.

Friends who had known him for years, such as fellow emigrants Gerdamaria Thom and Alfred Marnau, and his devoted, altruistic companion during the difficult years of the war, Wilhelm Sternfeld, testified to Jesse Thoor's unusual personality. Sternfeld wrote of him:

> There can hardly have been another artist in our time who was so determined a perfectionist as Jesse Thoor. He was relentless towards others, but in his art he was equally relentless towards himself. His poems are not sudden impulses; they are the results of periods of reflection lasting for days and nights and even weeks. He tweaked them this way and that, tore them up and then began to form his ideas anew simply because he did not like a particular word, because a sound bothered him or an expression seemed insufficiently succinct. His social conscience was as strong as his sense of artistic responsibility. None of his sonnets, none of his poems, fail to

reflect his humanity and his sense of justice. What manifests itself is not a sense of pity, but rather a real empathy with the abused creature.[12]

Gerdamaria Thom called it a phenomenon, a 'mystery', a 'miracle' that 'the elementary school pupil from a sad environment should grow into a man who expressed himself like an academic, who was never vain, whose formulations were always crystal clear, who often came across to others as otherworldly'. Thoor also possessed the almost uncanny ability to work brilliantly at crafts he had never learned,

> . . . for example, to produce furniture which was properly jointed rather than glued or nailed, as if he were an old-fashioned cabinetmaker. And he portrayed his mother, Churchill, Beneš and his wife Friederike in stone. The way he created busts with his hammer and burin – patiently, with his characteristic lack of haste – resulted in really outstanding works.[13]

He worked, moreover, from memory, without a model.

When I was in London he showed me a small sculpture, an Ecce Homo, of exceptional beauty. With almost oriental generosity, he immediately wanted to give it to me when he saw how greatly I admired it. He was also a skilled goldsmith, and earned his living as such for a while during the war. When peace returned he visited us in Germany and presented Löwenstein with a fine silver goblet. This too was a generous expression of gratitude: in 1939 the prince had encouraged Golo Mann to publish six of Jesse Thoor's sonnets, including 'Sonett im Herbst' and 'Am Totenbett meiner Mutter' in the journal *Mass und Wert*.[14]

Jesse Thoor became increasingly devout in the course of his life. His faith was idiosyncratic, his deep reverence for the Virgin Mary being accompanied by a certain esotericism and a great openness to mysticism. Alfred Marnau wrote of Thoor in wartime London:

> The sea of houses – subject at that time to frequent, alarming upheavals – beneath Primrose Hill (where Jesse Thoor lived) was also adjacent to that hilly place where William Blake had observed Jerusalem's pillars of gold – and it was here that Jesse Thoor consorted with angels and archangels.

On one occasion he shouted to Marnau: 'It was an angel, I spoke to an angel. It was dreadful.'[15] (It was hard not to hear overtones of Rainer Maria Rilke – whom Jesse Thoor had probably never read – and the first of his *Duineser Elegien*: 'Who, if I cried, would hear me from the orders of angels?' and 'Every single angel is terrible'.) In conversation he did indeed have a tendency to veer towards religion and transcendence. In a letter to me from London of 19 August 1939, when I was in Paris, he asked: 'Do you still remember our talks in London? No doubt, for in your letter to me you say that matter yearns for redemption.' And then one day I received a sonnet from him which reads like a canon of the Beatitudes:

Selig ist . . .

Selig ist der allmächtige Vater, Schöpfer des Himmels und der Erde.
Selig ist der einzige Sohn, denn er sitzet zur rechten Hand Gottes.
Selig ist die verklärte Mutter . . . sie kommt und bittet für uns.
Selig ist das Licht über allen Dingen ohne Anfang und ohne Ende.
Selig sind die Hügel, die Berge . . . und die verschiedenen Schluchten.
Selig sind die Bäche, die Wiesen, die Sträucher und die Bäume.
Selig sind die Steine und die Metalle, die Strassen und die Wege.
Selig sind die Töpfe, die Geräte, die Scheunen, die Häuser.
Selig sind die gewaltigen Ströme, die aus den Tälern hervorbrechen.
Selig sind die Wolken, die sich öffnen und die herabfallen.
Selig sind die Dächer und die Türme, die im Winde einstürzen.
Selig sind die trocknen Bretter und Balken, die lichterloh brennen.
Selig sind die geborstenen Wände, die der Sturm ganz niederreisst.
Selig sind die Propheten . . . die schweigen und ausruhen dürfen.[16]

Blessed is . . .

Blessed is the almighty Father, creator of heaven and earth.
Blessed is the only Son, because he sits at God's right hand.
Blessed is the transfigured Mother . . . she comes and pleads for us.
Blessed is the light above, without beginning and without end.
Blessed are the hills, the mountains . . . and all the ravines.
Blessed are the streams, the meadows, the shrubs and the trees.
Blessed are the stones and the metals, the roads and the paths.
Blessed are the pots, the tools, the barn, the homes.
Blessed are the mighty rivers which break forth from the vales.
Blessed are the clouds which part and then descend to earth.

Blessed are the roofs and spires which cave in to the wind.
Blessed are the dry planks and beams which burn to cinders.
Blessed are the fractured walls demolished by the storm.
Blessed are the prophets . . . who may hold their tongues and rest.

He probably had himself in mind when he wrote the last line.

When war broke out, Jesse Thoor was arrested as an 'Enemy Alien'. It soon turned out that this was due to a libellous denunciation of him. We immediately sprang into action in America on his behalf. In England, Stanley Richardson persuaded the Archbishop of Canterbury, the Dean of Chichester and other leading members of the Arden Society to intervene, and he was released.

'I was interned for nine weeks', he wrote in a letter of February 1940, which we only received months later on account of the censorship process. 'My dear friends [the Communists] from the old days probably attached a warning footnote to my name somewhere.'[17]

Gerdamaria Thom, who also spent those years in England, was able to confirm his suspicion: 'His name was included in a list of 72 alleged Gestapo agents.' Thom saw the list herself. It was an attempt at revenge on the part of 'apparatchiks', directed at 'former fellow-Communists' and at a few 'intellectuals who had spoken out, orally and in print, against that dictatorship as well as the Nazi one'.[18]

When the second, general round of internments took place, Jesse Thoor was again detained, this time – like Rudolf Olden – on the Isle of Man. We again managed to secure his release with the help of the Archbishop and the Arden Society, but more than half a year later, at the end of 1940.

Jesse Thoor found the restriction of his freedom the hardest thing of all to bear. This was why he now made a serious effort to be allowed to come to America. He knew himself, however, that it was too late for that by then. As he said in his letter to me of June 1941, in Germany and Austria he had 'a whole pack of relations, father, brother, aunt, uncle, nephew and who knows what else! That means, therefore, that I simply cannot get to America. (According to the latest regulations.)'[19]

Jesse Thoor did not in fact leave England even after the war, despite the publication in Germany of a selection of his sonnets by Nest, of Nuremberg, in 1948. In 1956 this was followed by *Die*

Sonette und Lieder (The Sonnets and Songs), edited and with an afterword by Alfred Marnau and published by Lambert Schneider of Heidelberg and Darmstadt in the series of *Deutsche Akademie für Sprache und Dichtung* (German Academy for Language and Literature) publications. The Eremitenpresse in Stierstadt, Taunus, published *Dreizehn Sonette* (Thirteen Sonnets) with an afterword by the editor, Wilhelm Sternfeld, in 1958. In 1965 the Europäische Verlagsanstalt in Frankfurt am Main published *Sonette, Lieder, Erzählungen* (Sonnets, Songs, Stories) edited and with a foreword by Michael Hamburger, and in 1975, also in Frankfurt, Suhrkamp brought out Thoor's *Gedichte* (Poems), edited and with an afterword by Peter Hamm.

These volumes appeared posthumously. In 1940 Jesse Thoor had married another exile, Friederike Blumenfeld, who took devoted care of him and worked to keep the wolf from the door. The years had taken their toll on him. We urged him to return to Germany, but he came only for occasional visits. In 1949, while we were living at Amorbach in the Odenwald, he came to stay with us and Prince Löwenstein attempted to persuade him to remain by obtaining for him an offer of employment as a librarian. Later, friends in Hamburg tried to organize a job for him in radio. He turned down these offers, however; regular employment had never suited him, and he probably felt too weak by then in any case.

In 1952 he travelled to Switzerland again, and the following spring he broke down in London. According to his biographer, he had suffered a heart attack. Friends invited him to recuperate at Matrei in the Tyrol and he went there immediately, in a state of euphoria, even embarking on a 'gentle' walking tour in the mountains, quite against the emphatic advice of his doctors. This led to a second breakdown. Four days later, on 15 August 1952, the day of the Assumption of the Virgin Mary, he died in the arms of his beloved Aunt Josefin. The inscription on his gravestone at Lienz in the Eastern Tyrol reads: 'For now I see more clearly than before that love will never end.'

In his 'Auferstehungssonett' (Resurrection Sonnet), Jesse Thoor had written:

Die Wolken ziehn am Horizont wie weisse Vögel schon gelassen hin.
Doch traumverwirrt noch schläft der Glockenblume blauer Schlag.

Es liegen staunend Dachs und Hund und Hamster auf den Knien.
Und wundersam von zarter Röte überhaucht erwacht der jüngste Tag.

Dies ist der milde Atem wohl, der tröstend in den Lüften schwebt.
Schon regt es sich in allen Zweigen, und die Bäche raunen.
Von allen Gipfeln zittert es beglückt und drängt und bebt,
dem Sphärenjubel ähnlich und den Liedern himmlischer Posaunen.

Wer spricht hier noch, wie fern ich war im Strome wesenloser Dinge?
Nun blühe ich empor aus jedem Tropfen und aus jedem Blatt,
und trinke mich mit tausend Mündern an der frühen Klarheit satt.

Aus Zedernholz sind meine Flügel, die ich rauschend schwinge.
Aus Meerschaum ist mein Leib, und meine Füsse sind Kristall.
Und Sonnenstaub ist alles, was ich schuf aus meinem tiefsten Fall.[20]

Already clouds are gliding calmly like white birds on the horizon's
    line.
Yet still bemused by dreams the bluebell blossoms slumber on.
The badger, dog and hamster lie amazed upon their knees.
And eerily and slow, suffused as by a blush, the day of doom
    awakes.

This is, no doubt, the mildest breath consolingly imbuing the air.
It stirs already all the twigs and makes the brooklets murmur.
From all the mountain peaks it shivers gladly, urges, quakes,
recalls triumphant music of the spheres, the songs of heaven's
    trumpets.

Who still remarks my past remoteness midst the flow of things
    ethereal?
For now I blossom forth from every shining drop and every leaf,
and drink my fill of early clarity with all my thousand mouths.

My wings are made of cedarwood; they roar each time I flex them.
My body is of meerschaum made, of crystal are my feet.
And sundust is the whole of my creation from my deepest fall.

MANN ARRIVES; TO ASSAIL NAZIS

Exiled German Author Hopes to See Hitler Fall—Will Speak Here

By DAVID DAVIDSON

Thomas Mann, who is Germany's greatest living novelist but who may not be read in Germany under pain of prison, arrived today on the Normandie glad to be freed of a burden of silence.

Two years ago, when he came here to receive an honorary degree from Harvard, it was a sad, enchained genius who landed.

To keep in contact with his great German audience, to keep his writings from being barred, he had undertaken to remain quiet on the subject of Hitler and Nazism, though his brother and his children were fighting the Nazis without restraint.

Hopes to Return to Germany

Today, deprived of his citizenship and his German degrees, but with a flash in his eyes and a lift to his shoulders, he said:

"Now there is no reason to be silent. I feel much better, though still bitter, of course.

"I fear that Hitler will not go out so quickly, but I hope very much that I'll see other times in Germany. I am sixty-two, but I hope before I die that I will return to Germany."

He is here as guest of honor at the celebration of the fourth anniversary of the University in Exile, the group of German fellow intellectuals for whom there is no place in Germany and who have found asylum here.

Among the addresses he will deliver, two will, quite frankly, be a "little political."

It was with a Czechoslovakian passport in hand that Dr. Mann landed. Though Nazi Germany would not have him, the tiny market town of Prosec, in Czechoslovakia, did itself honor a month ago by making him a Czech national.

Speaking in English, but appealing for help intermittently from bright-eyed, vivacious Mrs. Mann, who accompanied him, the Nobel Prize novelist said:

"They are learning now what is freedom and democracy. They are learning the value of these goods in Germany. Literary life there is very quiet, not very much alive. Fascism, it woul dseem, has passed its peak.

Hails Belgian News

"The news from Belgium today, the news of the defeat of the Fascists there, is very good. Altogether it seems that Fascism has not the future. There are changes. Youth, for instance, does not care so much for it.

"There are changes in Germany, too. The regime has disappointed so many people. One of the signs is the hunger for literature smuggled in from abroad. The letter I wrote to the dean of Bonn University when my degree was taken away has been reprinted and ten thousand copies smuggled into Germany."

But even before the Nazis suppressed his books and deprived him of his citizenship last December, Dr. Mann had decided that he could no longer maintain an "above-the-battle" attitude and had begun to speak out.

"I found that although the artist is supposed to be concerned only with the spiritual things, it was not possible to keep quiet and apart from the issues in the world today."

A member of a Hanseatic patrician merchant family of Luebeck and a novelist for more than forty years, Dr. Mann looks like nothing so much as a shy provincial university professor, even down to the quiet and baggy tweeds he always wears. And on a finger of his left hand is a broad gold wedding band.

He is working at present, he said, on a novel about Goethe, his hero, and on the last book of his Biblical tetralogy on Joseph.

He will attend sessions of the celebration of the University in Exile at the quarters of its parent body, the New School for Social Research, 66 West Twelfth Street, tomorrow, Wednesday and Thursday.

He will lecture there April 19, 21 and 22 on Wagner, Freud and Goethe, respectively—the latter lecture being in English.

Thursday night at a dinner at Sherry's he will speak on "Liberty and Freedom of Science and the Spirit as It Exists Today in Germany"—one of the two political talks.

The second will be at a dinner of the American Guild for German Cultural Freedom April 20. He heads the world council of this organization whose purpose is to encourage German writers, artists and musicians to continue their work in exile.

Among Dr. Mann's best known works in America are "The Magic Mountain," "Buddenbrooks," "Death in Venice" and the "Joseph" series.

Post Photo

MR. AND MRS. THOMAS MANN
Deprived of his German citizenship and shorn of his German university degrees, the writer arrived on the Normandie today, to be an honored guest of the University in Exile. He was outspoken on the subject of Nazism and said it was on the decline in Germany.

Press clipping: Mann arrives to assail Nazis

Prince and Princess zu Löwenstein in New York

Volkmar Zühlsdorff

39 Elsworthy Rd
NW 3

7.8.1938

Letter to Prince Löwenstein from Freud

Prof. Dr Freud   39 Elsworthy Road NW3

                                                         7 August 1938
Dear Prince

Going over your letter of July 26 once again I was struck, more forcefully than when
I first read it, by our contrasting emotional reactions concerning this little difference
of opinion. If this matter means so much to you and if you feel it is so important, I
must give in and let you proceed in accordance with your wishes. This is precisely
because I am by no means keen on the idea, being convinced that there is nothing I
could do for the cause – and also having nothing to lose but some personal
sensitivity. But please do not forget that I can only play the role of a dummy in all
this, that you will have to dictate to me everything to which I must lend my name.

I am sorry to hear that Einstein is so badly afflicted. Th. Mann, so I read in a
newspaper, is said to be coming to London for an extended period and I hope to see
him then after all. Once Dr Kurt Hiller with whom I was in touch occasionally
complained to me, from Prague, how badly off he was. He has already approached
you. Isn't there something you could do for him?

My most cordial greetings; I hope to hear from you soon.

Your old friend

Freud

AMERICAN GUILD FOR GERMAN CULTURAL FREEDOM.   *January 9, 39.*

LIST OF 20 URGENT CASES OF APPLICANTS FOR SUBSIDIES.
FULLY INVESTIGATED.

$ 30 each.

#25   1. Oskar Baum,
          Prague.
          Recommended by Bruno Frank, Arnold Höllriegel.

#26   2. Ferdinand Hardekopf,
          Paris
          Recommended by René Schickele, Arnold Höllriegel.

#27   3. Dr.Fritz Bruegel,
          Prague
          Recommended by Oskar Maria Graf, Max Hermann-Neisse.

#28   4. Dr.Kurt Hiller,
          Prague
          Recommended by Thomas Mann, Rudolf Olden.

#29   5. Dr.Heinz Paechter,
          Paris
          Recommended by Stefan Zweig, Veit Valentin, Bert Brecht.

#30   6. Victor Wittkowski,
          Rome
          Recommended by Alfred Neumann, Annette Kolb.

#31   7. Dr.Artur Neisser,
          Milano
          Recommended by Alfred Neumann, Franz Werfel

#9   8. Herbert Schlüter,
          Naples
          Recommended by Thomas Mann, Klaus Mann.

#32   9. Richard Duschinski,
          Prague
          Recommended by Max Hermann-Neisse, Arnold Höllriegel.

#6   +10. Uriel Birnbaum,
           Holland.
           Recommended by Alfred Neumann, Arnold Höllriegel.

#33 11. Prof.Max Hochdorf,
          Ascona
          Recommended by Thomas Mann, René Schickele.

#1   +12. A.M.Frey, Basel
           Recommended by Thomas Mann, ~~Arnold Höllriegel.~~ *Toller*

List of 20 urgent cases of applicants for subsidies

#17   +13.   Dr.Hans Sahl
             Paris
             Recommended by Joseph Roth, Erika Mann

#34   14.   Maria Leitner
             Paris
             Recommended by Oskar Maria Graf, Anna Seghers

#35   15.   Alexander Maass
             Paris
             Recommended by Ernst Toller, Erika Mann.

#36   16.   Dr.Rudolf Frank
             Zuerich
             Recommended by Lion Feuchtwanger, Arnold Höllriegel

#22   17.   Renato Mondo
 +   France
             Recommended by Joseph Roth, Ernst Leonhard.

#20   +18.   Dr.Paul Dreyfus
             Paris
             Recommended by Rudolf Olden, Arnold Höllriegel

#21   +19.   Berthold Jacob
             Paris
             Recommended by Rudolf Olden, Arnold Höllriegel.

#44   20.   Dr.Otto Mainzer
             Paris
             Heinrich Mann, Erik Wolf, Alfred Neumann.

$30 each.

+ These are renewals.

Approved & authorized

Oswald G. Villard

January 9, 1939.

Payments completed

AMERICAN GUILD
FOR GERMAN CULTURAL FREEDOM, Inc.
20 VESEY STREET   NEW YORK, N. Y.

HON. WILBUR L. CROSS, *President*

March 7, 1940.

Allan Weke, Esq.
14 East 90th Street
New York City

Dear Mr. Weke:

The struggle to maintain the creative sources of culture cannot be suspended because of the outbreak of the war. Now, even more actively than in times of peace, those of us who care about the things of the mind and the spirit must stand ready to support the men and women who give these their most excellent expression.

For the group of German writers in exile, these are days black even beyond the days preceding the war. The American Guild feels therefore that it is unusually strategic at this time to renew its appeal for help for these authors and artists. Many of them have been segregated into camps in France. Some of them of proved position have been set free. All of them are in need of encouragement. It is in them that we must keep alive the spirit that will lead a free Germany when Hitlerism has passed away.

Please send us your check that we may sustain them.

Sincerely yours,

Dorothy Thompson

Wilbur L. Cross

Thomas Mann

P.S.   Contributions to the American Guild are deductible for income tax purposes.

A letter of appeal from the American Guild

CHAPTER ELEVEN

The Academy in Exile's Public Relations Work and its Influence

The noble message of the old creative Germany is still listened to, here and elsewhere . . . We pay homage to it now and will rejoice when it again frees itself within the German borders.

New York Times, *19 February 1939*

One of the German Academy in Exile's most important tasks was to keep reminding the world that Hitler was not identical with Germany. People had to understand that, even while the Nazi regime was carrying out its most infamous and bloody crimes, there was still another Germany which remained loyal to the historical tradition of that country in the heart of Europe whose spiritual and artistic creativity had contributed so fundamentally to Europe's common culture. Despite all the counterpropaganda from the Hitler regime, this message did get through, and Germany was able to resume its rightful place in the community of free nations after the dictator met his end. That success was due in no small measure to the writers, artists, architects, scholars and scientists who belonged to the German Academy of Arts and Sciences and who had gone into exile on all four continents. It is testimony to just how effective spiritual and intellectual forces can be, even in the political sphere, when they confront violent power or the sheer opulence of material resources.

The emigration of so many famous figures from Germany and their declared opposition to the regime had already impressed the international public. The fact that the exiles were distributed among more than 70 countries may have limited their influence at first, but this changed when they united to form the Academy. Its numerous prominent members showed the world that from 1933 most of Germany's cultural and scientific élite was in exile, in tacit solidarity with those intellectuals still in the country who were condemned to remain silent and forced into 'inner exile'.

The Academy soon found that the benefits of having its members scattered across the globe outweighed the inconveniences. Eventually there were over 100 senators and members, 163 recipients of grants, and numerous émigrés who worked with or for the organization. Their connection with the Academy boosted their status and helped them in their work whilst they and their activities, in their turn, augmented the Academy's reputation and prestige in their particular host countries.

One particularly effective element in the Academy's public relations work turned out to be the large-scale events which took place mostly in America, where the Academy had its headquarters and focal point, but also in England under the aegis of the American Guild's sister organization, the Arden Society for Artists and Writers Exiled in England. The competition launched by the Academy early in 1937 for works of literature written in exile showed just how well known the organization had become only a few months into its existence. At first the American publisher Little, Brown & Company was the only partner involved, having contributed the substantial sum of 2,500 dollars. When the Academy announced the competition internationally, however, major publishing houses from seven other countries – England, France, the Netherlands, Denmark, Sweden, Norway and Poland, along with the émigré press Querido, of Amsterdam – quickly agreed to participate.

Indeed, as noted above, the American Guild's very first public event, the glittering dinner in honour of Prince Löwenstein presided over by Archbishop John Joseph Cantwell of Los Angeles on 26 April 1936, had caused a stir both in America and abroad. The 300 guests included nearly all the top names in Hollywood at that time. The media's interest only quickened when the Hitler regime instructed its consulates to attempt to obstruct such events, as they had previously when Löwenstein was lecturing in Chicago and elsewhere. None of these attempts was successful, and they could be relied upon to create headlines along the lines of 'German Prince

Speaks – Nazi Consul Protests'.[1] Later we heard a rumour that Goebbels was so furious about such failures that he had threatened to ban the import and screening of all American films.

There was similarly widespread interest in the concert of 23 September 1936 at the Philharmonic auditorium in Los Angeles, the 'foundation concert' of the American Guild and the Academy, at which Otto Klemperer conducted works by Wolfgang Amadeus Mozart, Ludwig van Beethoven, Arnold Schönberg and Ernst Toch. Further events on the West Coast followed. The press coverage made it clear that the exiled artists were welcomed as representatives of a living German culture, whose achievements were a valuable addition to the cultural life of the host country. This review of a production of *William Tell* in Hollywood is typical:

> If America's finest actors and cleverest directors; her most imaginative set designers and brainiest producers, were all suddenly uprooted from their native soil and transplanted to a new clime, the loss to Broadway and Hollywood would, naturally, be as great as the gain to the land of their resettlement. An analogous state of affairs today finds Hollywood and Broadway as the gainers, while Nazi Germany finds itself bereft of the cream of its stage and cinema artists and craftsmen. Transplanted to the nourishing soil and free order of Democratic America, these top-ranking professionals, Jewish and non-Jewish, are now beginning to contribute to the cultural life of the American community.[2]

The Academy and Guild also made public relations capital out of their congresses and general meetings in New York, sometimes with the help of a professional agency. As was usual in America, public events such as these were organized as formal dinners, with well-known guests helping attract the attention of the press and radio stations. The annual general meeting of 20 April 1937 at the Ritz Carlton and of 11 May 1938 in the Town Hall Club, at which Thomas Mann spoke on behalf of the Academy, were particularly successful in this regard. In order to secure and maximize media coverage, journalists were always informed in advance of the order of events and of the organization's work and aims. Erika Mann was one of those involved in the annual general meeting of 1937, announcing shortly before her father's arrival that he had travelled from Europe to the United States especially for the occasion.[3]

When Thomas Mann arrived in America with his wife, Katia, on 12 April 1937, New York's pressmen, including representatives of the main news agencies, were out in force on the pier to greet him. His statements and interviews concerning the Academy and the University in Exile at the New School for Social Research in New York (which had also invited him) were immediately reported across the continent and beyond. The *Citizen* noted:

> Renaissance of German culture, to take place outside of Germany because it cannot take place within the Reich, is the aim of Thomas Mann, the outstanding German author, who is now visiting us. His is a noble purpose, for it is essential, not only for the culture itself but for all of us, that the inheritance of Goethe and Schiller, of the great German composers and artists, should not be allowed to die just because of a political upheaval within the Reich.[4]

Such reports left no doubt about the political character of the Academy's aims. The *Evening Sun*, for example, pointed out that Thomas Mann's address at the Guild's event would – unlike his three lectures on Sigmund Freud, Richard Wagner and Johann Wolfgang Goethe and his talk at the University in Exile – be an 'out-and-out political speech' about Germany.[5] 'That great nation', *The State* quoted him as saying, 'feels already betrayed. It feels humiliated and ashamed before the world.'[6] The *Evening Sun* also mentioned Mann's belief that there would be armed revolt in Germany if Hitler were to spark a war.[7] The following year, when Hitler decided to invade the Sudeten region, the chief of the general staff, Ludwig Beck, and his co-conspirators did indeed plan such a revolt. Beck was only prevented from carrying it out by British Prime Minister Neville Chamberlain's kowtowing concession in the Munich Pact of 29 September 1938, which obviated the invasion by making Hitler a present of the Sudeten region.

The advance publicity for Mann's address to the New School for Social Research in New York on 15 April 1937 indicated that it would be 'semi-political'. Many newspapers carried reports and the *New York Herald Tribune* reprinted it in its entirety. Mann described how, having tried for so long to defend his creative autonomy and activities against all external pressures, he finally concluded that he had a political duty. Since the fate of humanity was currently above all a political issue, nobody – least of all a writer – was entitled to shirk his responsibility by failing to state his position. To do so would be to betray the human spirit.[8]

This and other statements at the New School were ideal advance publicity for the Academy's annual gathering, chaired by the president of the American Guild and governor of Connecticut, Wilber L. Cross. As noted in the chapter on Thomas Mann, the many telegrams of greeting sent to the meeting included those from the governors of 27 of the then 48 states of the USA, and the ripples created by the event were felt even in Germany.

The second annual general meeting of the Academy and Guild, on 1 May 1938 at the Town Hall Club in New York, was equally effective in raising public awareness. Löwenstein was unable to be there; after successfully extricating Richard Bermann from Austria, we had returned to Europe on 23 March to continue the work of the Academy's European office in Paris. In advance of the meeting, Thomas Mann spoke fervently against the Nazis at an event organized by the American Committee for Christian German Refugees at the Hotel Astor in New York on 9 May 1938. Since many of the members and guests attended only one of the two gatherings, the Guild's dinner was less well attended than it had been the previous year, but the publicity was all the greater since both events were reported in the media.

This time it was Ernst Toller – the main speaker apart from Thomas Mann – who talked of the political duty of poets and artists to fly the flag of truth, justice and liberty:

> When the yoke of barbarism oppresses, one must fight and not be silent. Whoever is silent at such a time, betrays his human mission . . . But it is not the task of the true artist to portray a happy ending which is nowhere visible in the world today. On the contrary, he must correct his age when it betrays the spirit. That is what all true writers have done, that was what Sophocles and Aristophanes did, and Dante and Shakespeare, Lessing and Buechner, Goethe and Schiller, Swift and Dickens, Byron and Shelley.[9]

Toller described the fight on behalf of humanity within the Third

Reich and mentioned the poet, Erich Mühsam, and the Nobel Prize-winner, Carl von Ossietzky, as examples of individuals whose ability to overcome fear and thus death itself had prepared them to face torture and martyrdom in the concentration camps. He highlighted the fate of thousands of Christians under Hitler and concluded confidently: 'Dictatorship and terror may triumph a short while. In the end they are powerless before the might of the spirit.'[10]

Thomas Mann began his speech by announcing his own, changed circumstances: he was now a resident of, not just a visitor to, America. Then he pointed out how much had already been achieved, above all in the form of the many scholarships and other grants which had helped alleviate the 'hard fate' of, among others, Annette Kolb, Bert Brecht and René Schickele. A number of Austrian emigrants would now be able to enjoy similar assistance. Also in need of help, however, were other individuals: those who had responded to events by exchanging their pens for weapons:

> I mean such writers as Ludwig Renn, Gustav Regler, Bodo Uhse . . . These have transitorily laid down their pens to bear arms and to have staked their lives, their physical bodies, for the threatened ideals. They are by no means unfaithful to their original vocation by such behaviour, nor ever lose sight of it, for by this mode of acting they will collect the greatest and most terrible poetical matter which our time has to offer, aside from the fact that their personal heroism will, one day, be fruitful in the cause of literature. And so we have every reason, in such cases where artistic production is temporarily overcome by personal heroism, to prove our sense of honour and be ready to help.[11]

He insisted, however, that 'deeds of spiritual charity' were not the main mission of the Academy in exile and its aid organization, the American Guild. Rather,

> it must become a forum of the whole of the German-speaking emigration, worthy of the confidence of every group of exiles and recognized by all as representative. It must in future become a decisive voice for German exiled culture in all political as well as cultural matters . . .[12]

Turning to America, Thomas Mann said: 'I know of no other land in the world where there lives so honest an aversion to evil, ready for action – the evil disfiguring the face of Europe today.' And he added: 'So America can, through our "Guild", protect the creative works of German culture and in return perhaps gain the enrichment that the German-European spirit perhaps has to offer it.'[13]

Mann had previously suggested publicly that Germany's exile community, in the form of the Academy and the Guild, should take part in the New York World Fair of 1939 in place of the Nazi regime, which had just pulled out. This would be a chance to present the other Germany to an international public. When he repeated that suggestion in his speech it created particular interest and gained a great deal of support. It was widely and sympathetically reported in the American press, even in many provincial newspapers which otherwise tended to neglect foreign affairs. This was very encouraging for us, as it demonstrated that the American public understood and backed the Academy's goals.

In order to maintain and bolster such support, the Academy exploited the airwaves as well as the press (television, of course, had yet to arrive). On 29 December 1938, for example, Radio WMCA broadcast a talk between Prince Löwenstein and Emil Lengyel, a founding member of the Academy and of the Guild, about the Academy's structure and aims. A week later, on 4 January 1939, treasurer Oswald Garrison Villard spoke on WOR about 'Shall German Culture Perish?', and on 14 January Henry Seidel Canby, editor-in-chief of the *Saturday Review of Literature* and a member of the Guild's Board of Directors, discussed the enriching influence of German émigrés on American culture.

One of the reasons public relations work mattered so much was that the American Guild was responsible for funding its sister organization, the Academy. At this time there was no state funding available for such bodies in the United States, and neither was there any help from the many private foundations. This meant that the main source of income consisted of donations from ordinary Americans who were prepared to lend their moral and financial support to a good cause. The office shared by the Guild and the Academy launched regular fundraising campaigns, sending out thousands of personally addressed letters. The better the public was acquainted with the importance, goals, activities and sponsors of the organization, the better the results of these campaigns tended to be.

One fundraising function on behalf of the Academy that caused a particular stir was the Guild's auction of manuscripts on 19 February 1939 at the Hotel Delmonico in New York. We managed to enlist the League of American Writers and the Booksellers' Guild of America for a joint event. The organizing committee was chaired by Princess Helga zu Löwenstein and also included Hubertus Löwenstein; the Guild's American secretary, Maria Heinemann; and me. Our task was to obtain at least 50 manuscripts to contribute to the total of 150 which the three organizations intended to offer for sale at auction. In our search for suitable sale items we did not confine ourselves to members of the Academy; prominent American authors also turned out to be keen to help their persecuted German counterparts. Stuart Chase, Lewis Mumford and John Erskine all contributed manuscripts – the latter that of his *The Influence of Women*. Some of the literary figures among the Guild's directors also gave us texts; Henry Seidel Canby, for example, donated the draft of his *The Age of Confidence*.

From Thomas Mann we received the manuscript of his essay about the Munich Pact of 1938, *Dieser Friede* (*This Peace*), from Albert Einstein a Commencement Speech (delivered at Swarthmore College on 6 June 1938), from Sigmund Freud's American translator the manuscript of *Der Prometheus-Komplex*. Franz Werfel also gave us a manuscript, as did Bert Brecht (his collection of sonnets, *Studien*) and Ernst Toller (the last scene of his play, *Pastor Hall*). Rudolf Olden sent us his biography of Hitler, Alfred Neumann the first two acts of his play, *Krieg und Frieden* (based on Tolstoy's novel, *War and Peace*), Klaus Mann a chapter from his novel, *Der Vulkan*, Löwenstein a letter from the former Austrian federal chancellor, Kurt von Schuschnigg.

The musical world was also represented, with scripts from the composers Arnold Schönberg, Kurt Weill, Ernst Toch, George Gershwin and Erich Wolfgang Korngold. We also received original scores written by Franz Liszt, Richard Wagner, Vincenzo Bellini, Richard Strauss and Johann Nepomuk Hummel. The buyers at the auction, unfortunately, were interested mainly in literary items, and Löwenstein withdrew the scores in the absence of acceptable offers during the auction. They were later sold more satisfactorily at a further benefit auction organized by the League of American Writers on 14 January 1940.

As usual, we did our best to alert the press and radio in advance of the event. On 12 February 1939, a week before the auction, the *New York Times* reported that the event was creating unprecedented interest. It described 'a rather wonderful assortment of literary and historical manuscripts, drawings, musical scores and inscribed books' which had been 'contributed mainly by the authors, composers and artists themselves to make the sale the dramatic highlight of the season.'[14] The *Daily Worker*, the *New York Post*, the *Evening Sun*, the *World Telegram* and the *Herald Tribune* featured similar pieces. In San Francisco the *Chronicle* noted that the manuscript contributed by Thomas Mann was the only one by that author not yet in the possession of a public institution.[15]

On the day of the auction itself, the Sunday edition of the *New York Times* published a leading article that confirmed once again that the Germany represented by the Academy in Exile was indeed regarded as the real Germany:

> With some reservations it is impossible to disagree with Count Baldur von Schirach's recent observation that 'no achievement of German cultural life could be eliminated from the world without mankind's suffering thereby.' ... Naturally, we would not agree that our own 'creative achievements' are of no importance; but most of us would concede that we have not yet produced a genius in any of the arts who has reached as high as did some of the great writers and musicians whose native tongue was German.
>
> In music we gladly and gratefully acknowledge Johann Sebastian Bach, Handel, Mozart, Pap Haydn, Beethoven, Schubert, Mendelssohn, Schumann, Wagner, Brahms, Richard Strauss and many another who was in the mainstream of the majestic and beautiful musical tradition of Germany. Our concerts would be poor without them. We have our own music which we love, but with the exception of the two popular strains for which the Negro is largely responsible – spirituals and jazz or swing – we have relatively little that is truly native. We have been more colonial in our serious music than in literature. Time will remedy – perhaps already is remedying – that lack, but we should be starved indeed if we boycotted the music of those countries with whose politics most of us do not at the moment agree.

The written word loses in the process of translation. We have certainly been influenced, whether we know it or not, by the philosophy of Kant and Hegel; by the many-sided Goethe; by Schiller and Heine; by those who gave words to many a song we still love to sing. The German spirit has soared high. It has been grandly interpreted by many who would not be recognized in Germany today as belonging to the 'pure' race. We find it clear and brave in the work of German exiles, such as Thomas Mann. It was perfectly understood by Emerson and Thoreau, Hawthorne and Alcott. It was not alien to Melville and Whitman; and Mark Twain found much in the old German culture that warmed the cockles of his heart. We have the warmest fellowship of the best that is in German civilization. Unfortunately, the Hitler Government has made that best an outlaw in its own country.

We have faith ... that nothing good, true or beautiful in civilization ever dies. It may be exiled or driven underground, but it does not die. It does not belong to any one country or any one race. It is not competitive. The noble message of the old creative Germany is still listened to, here and elsewhere. It is not drowned out by the vulgar and brutal note which we often hear when we tune in on an oversea broadcast. We pay homage to it now and will rejoice when it again frees itself within the German borders.[16]

The auction did a great deal for the reputation of the Guild and the Academy, although the income it generated did not exceed the modest standards of the time. The bulky manuscript of the bestseller *Look Homeward, Angel* by the recently deceased American author Thomas Wolfe commanded the highest bid of 1,700 dollars. Thomas Mann's short essay earned 300 dollars, Sigmund Freud's manuscript 200 dollars and the script of Einstein's speech 100 dollars. The total revenue from the 50 or 60 items sold was about 5,000 dollars.

This encouraging cultural acknowledgement of the other Germany in exile was soon followed by political recognition at a high level. The US secretary of the interior, Harold C. Ickes, made the gesture of travelling to New York from Washington to deliver a formal address as guest of honour at the Academy's next annual congress, on 26 April 1939 at the Waldorf-Astoria. In his speech, Ickes recalled that hundreds of Germany's cultural representatives had fled the country not for reasons of race or religion, but rather because they could not tolerate life in a totalitarian state where they would have been unable to keep faith with their ideals or go on with their work:

> They have preferred even to make precarious livelihoods as factory workers, porters and laborers rather than submit to political oppression and be forced to function by censorial dictate. The American Guild for German Cultural Freedom is aiding hundreds of men and women eminent in the literature of a country which, during the centuries when its culture was free, enriched the civilization of the world, as it will do again in the future.
>
> Happy as we are to know that these builders of cultural values are being given help and encouragement, our pleasure is not entirely unselfish. For in aiding creative minds, no matter what their origin, we are accumulating treasures for ourselves . . .
>
> . . . Professor Einstein's religion is a bar to his being a great scientist in his native country, but his religion has nothing to do with our judgment in considering him one of the world's luminaries. Dr Thomas Mann and his books may be proscribed in the land where he was born, but here in free America he is welcomed and encouraged to continue his distinguished career.[17]

The reports in nearly all the main newspapers reflect just how clearly the government minister's presence at the congress and the speech he made there were understood.[18] They quoted precisely those passages in which he paid homage to the Germany represented by the Academy. Some of the newspapers also published a photograph showing the minister during his speech, on the podium, above which the Star-Spangled Banner hung alongside a black, red and gold flag bearing the German eagle. This was the same flag beneath which, back in Germany, we had fought the Nazis and Communists with our comrades in the *Reichsbanner*. Prince Löwenstein had brought it into exile with him; today it is in the *Historisches Museum* in Berlin.

Not long afterwards, at the end of June 1939, the League of American Writers invited members of the Academy to address the delegates at their three-day federal congress. The closing session was to be devoted entirely to the German guests. The *New York Times* carried a report on the individual speeches[19] by, among others, Ludwig Renn, Oskar Maria Graf, Ernst Bloch, Klaus Mann, Walter Schoenstedt, Bodo Uhse, Erich Franzen and Manfred George. George declared: 'Within one year Germany lost the overwhelming spiritual influence its famous thinkers and writers had exerted over the whole world. It was a kind of death – the body stayed where it was, the soul was spread all over the world.'[20] Finally the League of American Writers resolved that it would offer as much moral and material help as it could to the exiled writers and support all attempts to make their particular host country a second home for them.[21]

The extent to which the other Germany was recognized in America was clearly evident in the public's reaction to the Morgenthau Plan for post-war Germany, which advocated dismantling the country's industry and reducing it to an agrarian economy. When it was made public in September 1944, at the height of the war and at a time when Nazi atrocities were causing passions to run particularly high, it provoked outraged protests throughout America. In England, too, there were many who never identified Hitler with the German people and objected vigorously when Sir Robert Vansittart did so in his vitriolic 'Black Record' of 1939.

Secretary of the Interior Ickes had closed his address to the Academy's annual gathering by affirming:

> These scientists and artists and men of letters are living reminders of the ancient truth that even the most powerful tyrant can not kill the soul of man. The tyrant represents only the nether spirit of his country. Under a tyranny the best and noblest of a people submerge or go into exile. Those in retirement bide their time until the bright ray of freedom again breaks through the lowering clouds, as in due course it will do even in the totalitarian states of Europe. Those in exile carry on, despite privations and obstacles, as true soldiers of the spirit. They keep alive the sacred fire of their culture on foreign shores and wait for the day of liberation to come.[22]

CHAPTER TWELVE

Academy Scholarships

If it had not been for this help . . . who knows whether I would still exist.
Paul Zech to Prince Hubertus zu Löwenstein,
Buenos Aires, 26 July 1938

If the Academy's main aim was that of representing the other Germany – and in particular that other Germany's cultural and political opposition to the Hitler regime – its efforts to help needy exiled writers, artists and scholars to continue their work or, in many cases, simply to survive, were hardly of lesser importance. Such efforts were of course limited by the resources available to us, which amounted to whatever funds the Guild could raise in its capacity as an aid organization.

Thanks to the vigour of the Guild's treasurer, Oswald Garrison Villard, the first funds for scholarships, contributions to printing expenses and a wide variety of other subsidies were available to the Academy by the end of 1937. We had already been through the applications received by the Academy's European office, each of which included a detailed questionnaire, so that many of them were ready for consideration along with the necessary report or recommendation from a member of the Academy (later two were required).

On 26 January 1938 the Guild's Board of Directors released the first monthly payments to fourteen individuals – those we regarded as the most urgent cases. Five of the recipients were in Czechoslovakia when they made their applications, three in France, two in Austria and one each in England, the Netherlands, South America and South Africa. On 28 February 1938 scholarships for

eleven further exiles were approved, followed by a third list on
13 April.

In drafting the questionnaire, the Academy had allowed for the
possibility of exiles who were neither German nor Austrian receiving a scholarship if they could prove that they had been affected
spiritually or materially by the upheaval in Germany or that specific events or personal beliefs meant that they should be regarded
as German émigrés.

One candidate to whom all this applied was Ernst Weiss, whom
Thomas Mann recommended for a scholarship. He had won the
literary prize at the Amsterdam Olympics of 1928 and the City of
Prague's Stifter Prize in 1930, being the author of numerous novels
such as *Die Galeere, Franziska, Hodin, Tiere in Ketten, Stern der Dämo-
nen, Die Feuerprobe, George Letham – Arzt und Mörder*. Born a Czech,
he had lived in Germany from 1910 until his expulsion in 1933. The
Nazis had banned his books – previously published by Ullstein,
Propyläen, Rowohlt and Fischer – on account of his being a
liberal-minded Jew. The scholarship he was awarded in April 1938
was renewed several times. Driven first from Germany, then from
Austria and not long afterwards from Czechoslovakia as well,
Ernst Weiss – who had been awarded a medal for bravery in
the First World War and tried unsuccessfully to enlist in the Czech
Legion in 1940 – finally sought refuge in France. When Hitler's
troops marched into Paris on 13 June 1940, he elected to take his
own life.

The recipients of the Academy's scholarships came from a wide
artistic spectrum. Some of their names, such as those of Bertolt
Brecht, Ernst Bloch, Hanns Eisler, Oskar Maria Graf, John Heartfield, Kurt Hiller, Lotte Jacobi, Hermann Kesten, Egon Erwin Kisch,
Annette Kolb, Siegfried Kracauer, Ludwig Marcuse, Walter
Mehring, Robert Musil, Alfred Polgar, Joseph Roth, Anna Seghers
and Arnold Zweig, remain familiar today. Others have, in most
cases unjustly, been forgotten or are known only to a small circle of
specialists. The Academy's assistance helped all of them to continue
their creative work, thereby enriching cultural life in exile. We
received numerous applications via the tireless Richard Bermann,
who, with Prince Löwenstein's support, took a particular interest in
those of Hans Flesch and Walter Mehring. On 31 December 1937
Bermann wrote from Locarno to Villard, in New York:

Top of my list of nominations is Herr Dr Hans Flesch von Brunningen, currently in London ... In my judgement Flesch is the most talented of the impoverished authors in exile. His novel, *Alkibiades*, which was written in exile and has also been published in English [as *Alcibiades, Beloved of Gods and Men*] under the pseudonym of V. Brun (by G. P. Putnam, London), is a great masterpiece. He has also written an equally outstanding drama, which there is no chance of staging. He is very close to starvation. Enabling him to continue his work would be entirely consistent with the Academy's aims.[1]

In his memorandum 'A German Sanctuary' Bermann had already praised the stage play that Johannes Flesch Edler von Brunningen (as he was originally called) had completed in Vienna. Without actually naming the play or its author, Bermann had described it as symptomatic of the predicament of young authors in exile that no theatre had so far staged or even asked to see this 'masterpiece'. Flesch was indeed the name at the top of that first list of scholarship awards in January 1938, whilst Mehring headed the list approved on 28 February 1938.

The Academy's second award went to Alfred Wolkenstein, who was twelve years older than Flesch, having been born in Halle in 1883. He had made his debut with a volume of poetry, *Die gottlosen Jahre*, in 1914. In the 1920s he had written several stage plays: first, in Berlin in 1921, *Sturm auf den Tod*, then *Umkehr, Der Herr der Insel, Bäume in den Himmel, Celestina* and *Die Nacht vor dem Beil*. In 1936, as an exile in Czechoslovakia, he published a collection of 30 stories entitled *Die gefährlichen Engel*. He was another whom it proved impossible to rescue from France when war broke out. He spent years on the run, only to be arrested. Released by a German officer, he was admitted to the Rothschild Hospital in Paris and committed suicide shortly before the end of the war, on 22 January 1945.

Exile was also tragic, albeit in another way, for Paul Zech, an author who had enjoyed great success in Germany before Hitler emerged. In the Academy's questionnaire, which he sent to us with his application for a grant on 6 June 1937 at the instigation of Max Herrmann-Neisse, he listed fourteen works he had written between 1912 and 1932 (in fact there were several others): expressionist poetry, novels, stories, a war diary, a novel (*Peregrins Heimkehr*),

two plays – one of which, *Das trunkene Schiff*, I had read as a schoolboy back in 1926 in Berlin – and his renderings of poems by Rimbaud and Villon. He had written nine further works in exile, but
had failed to find a publisher for any of them.

Before becoming an editor, poet and dramatist, Paul Zech – who
had studied German literature and obtained a doctorate – had been
inspired by his sense of social responsibility to labour as a miner,
stoker and metalworker. Later he found a job at Berlin's city library.
In 1933 he was arrested, but he eventually managed to reach Buenos
Aires via Prague, Paris, Genoa and Naples. His brother lived in
Argentina and took care of his basic needs. Since his books were
banned and the Nazis had seized his property, he was unable to pay
for his wife to join him. She was forced, as he told us in a letter of 18
February 1938, to eke out a living working twelve-hour shifts at a
factory for 16 marks a week. In 1941 she committed suicide.

His scholarship was renewed more often than anyone else's,
and it quite literally saved his life. It gave him the strength and
the courage to continue his work despite the hardship. On 12
September 1938 he wrote to Prince Löwenstein:

> Without this help there would be no work. I suppose that one
> day the history of all these émigrés will be written. And your
> work on our behalf will undoubtedly occupy a place of hon-
> our within it. Please do not dismiss this as mere politeness: I
> am completely serious and in fact I am doing no more than
> stating a fact.[2]

It was unfortunate that, despite all our efforts, we were unable to
have any of Paul Zech's works published in the United States. Nor
was his heart's desire – a reunion with Germany – to be fulfilled. On
7 September 1946 he finally succumbed to the privations he had
suffered. The Löwensteins and I received the news shortly before
our return to Germany. At least Zech did have the satisfaction of
seeing four of his books published in Buenos Aires. The others followed posthumously: *Indianische Legenden* in 1947 under the title of
Die schwarze Orchidee, *Paul Verlaine und sein Werk* in 1949, *Kinder von
Paraná* in 1952, *Das rote Messer: Begegnungen mit Tieren und seltsamen
Menschen* in 1953, *Die Vögel des Herrn Langfoot* in 1954 (also published in English as *The Birds in Langfoot's Belfry* in 1994), and *Die
grüne Flöte von Rion Beni* in 1955. Many of these works had been

financed by the Academy, some with supplementary assistance (which we had been able to arrange for him) from Wilhelm Dieterle. Another book by him was published as late as 1980: *Deutschland, dein Tänzer ist der Tod*, to be followed in 1985 by his manuscript, *Michael M. irrt durch Buenos Aires*, which he entered in the Academy's literary competition under the pseudonym of 'Rhenanus'.

Gustav Regler, who was then in Paris after being seriously wounded in the Spanish Civil War, received a grant in 1938 for his work on *The Great Crusade*, which was published a year later in New York. He had been deprived of his German citizenship on 3 November 1934, along with Hubertus Löwenstein, Klaus Mann, Alfred Kantorowicz, Erwin Piscator and Bodo Uhse. He was a native of the Saarland and had taken part in the struggle there against Hitler in 1934–5. He had also worked on Willi Münzenberg's *Braunbuch über den Reichstagsbrand und den Hitlerterror* (*The Brown Book of the Hitler Terror and the Burning of the Reichstag*) and won the Heinrich Mann Prize in 1935. He enjoyed success as an author even in exile. Querido, in Amsterdam, published his novel *Der verlorene Sohn* as early as 1933 (*The Prodigal Son*, 1934). In 1934 *Im Kreuzfeuer. Ein Saarroman* came out in Leningrad and Moscow (where *International Literature* published an excerpt in English translation as 'Cross Fire. A German Short Story of the Saar Basin') and *Die Saat. Roman aus den deutschen Bauernkriegen* in Amsterdam in 1936.

In 1940 Regler succeeded in fleeing to Mexico. He left the Communist Party and settled down to write *The Hour 13* (1942), *Wolfgang Paalen* (1944), *The Bottomless Pit* (1944) and *Jungle Hut* (1945). He went on to produce many more books after the war.

One particularly high-profile case was that of Horst Galley. Galley was a Protestant born in Danzig, who, after studying theology and art history, had left Germany because his fiancée was Jewish. In 1937 he was ordered to leave Austria because he had 'no secure income', thereby evidently posing a 'threat to public order' in the semi-Fascist corporative state, as the supreme court, the *Bundesgerichthof*, confirmed in its verdict. Against that background, the Academy's grant for his novel about the Thirty Years' War, *Das tausendjährige Reich*, represented his salvation. At the same time Richard Bermann managed, through a concerted campaign in the press, to have the expulsion deferred. Together we managed to bring Galley, his partner and their newborn child first to Switzerland and later to the United States.

Oskar Maria Graf, the 'revolutionary in Lederhosen', was also on the first list of scholarship awards. When the Nazis neglected to include his books in the book burning, he caused an international sensation by firing off a sarcastic letter of protest demanding: 'Burn me!'[3] He published many books while in exile, including his novel about farming life, *Der harte Handel* (1935), and *Anton Sittinger* (1937). His biographical novel, *Das Leben meiner Mutter*, which he entered in the literary competition, was published in English in New York in 1940 as *The Life of My Mother* and in Germany by Desch, of Munich, in 1946.

The only woman on the first list was the socialist and pacifist, Anna Siemsen-Vollenweider. Having been a local education officer in Berlin, she went on to manage the secondary school and teacher training reforms in Thüringen. In 1923 she became an honorary professor at the University of Jena, and she was a member of the Reichstag from 1928 until 1930. In 1933 she moved to Switzerland, where she worked in the education office of the Swiss Social Democratic Party. Her scholarship in 1937 was for two books, *Spanisches Bilderbuch* and *Die Schweiz und das tschechoslowakische Schicksal*. The first was published in the same year, 1937, and the second in 1938 by Réunion Universitaire Pacifiste. After the war, in 1946, the senate of Hamburg appointed her director of the *Institut für Lehrerbildung* (Institute for Teacher Training). At the same time, she began teaching at Hamburg's *Universität für Literatur und Pädagogik* (University for Literature and Education). Her political work included her involvement in the German council of the *Europabewegung* and in the Socialist Movement for the United States of Europe, the German arm of which was later renamed the *Anna Siemsen Kreis* in her honour.

Alexander Moritz Frey, born in 1881 and the author of novels (such as *Die Pflasterkästen*, published in Berlin in 1929 and in English as *The Cross Bearers* in New York, 1930, and London, 1931), novellas, fairytales and literary criticism, was recommended for an award by Thomas Mann. In World War I, Frey had served as a medic in the same regiment as Adolf Hitler, and was fond of recounting that the future dictator had offered him a job as arts editor of the Nazi newspaper, the *Völkischer Beobachter*. In 1933, Frey emigrated first to

Salzburg and then to Switzerland. The book he worked on with the help of the Academy's grant was published in Amsterdam in 1940, entitled *Der Mensch*.

The rest of the first round of scholarships went to René Schickele, a friend of Thomas Mann from the Alsace and also recommended by him; Max Zimmering in Prague, who had been an active member of the *Revolutionäre Gewerkschaftsopposition* (Revolutionary Trade Union Opposition) and the *Bund Proletarisch-Revolutionärer Schriftsteller* (Association of Proletarian Revolutionary Writers) in Germany and was awarded the National Prize in East Germany after the war; the poet and essayist, David Luschnat, who survived the war as an illegal resident of France; and Julius Curt Cohn in Cape Town, South Africa.

As noted above, Walter Mehring headed the Academy's second list of scholarships of 28 February 1938. Bermann had written to Löwenstein on 27 November 1937 about Mehring's predicament: 'At the moment Mehring is going hungry ... Genuine malnourishment, yes indeed. Do you understand how furious the slow progress of the "Guild" is making me?'[4] Mehring, the famed Expressionist, Dadaist and performer at Max Reinhardt's well-known cabaret theatre in Berlin, *Schall und Rauch*, was a *bête noir* to the Nazis because of the way he had held them up to ridicule with his biting wit. He eluded them on 27 February 1933, the day of the Reichstag fire, by fleeing to Paris. The book of chansons, ballads and legends he published there was entitled *Und Euch zum Trotz* (And Despite You). In 1934 he moved to Vienna, where he published *Müller, Chronik einer deutschen Sippe*. This was followed a year later by his collection of 33 satirical biographies of Nazi bigwigs, entitled *Naziführer sehen dich an* (Nazi Leaders are Watching You) – an allusion to the notoriously anti-Semitic *Juden sehen dich an* (Jews are Watching You). In 1937 he published *Die Nacht des Tyrannen* and, in 1944 in New York, *No Road Back*.

Mehring had been sufficiently cautious to adopt a pseudonym for his book about the Nazi leaders, but this did not prevent the German ambassador in Vienna – none other than the notorious Herr von Papen, who, as German chancellor in 1932, had smoothed Hitler's path to power – from demanding that the Austrian government prosecute Mehring for denigration of the 'Führer'. In view of that threat, the Academy included Mehring among those it tried to help by wiring money to them when Austria was occupied in 1938. When we arrived in Paris on 30 March from New York, Mehring called on us the same evening and told us about his successful escape via Switzerland to France. The scholarship was awarded to enable Mehring to finish a novel he was working on at the time.

When war broke out we were able to help Mehring once again. He had been interned and sent to one camp after another. Finally we learned that he was in the camp of Le Vernet. The Guild sent him a small sum of money with a covering letter, which had of course to go through the censorship process. That alerted the camp author-ities to the American interest in the addressee and to the influential figures involved in the American Guild. In the meantime Löwen-stein had also made a plea on Walter Mehring's behalf to the French ambassador in Washington, Comte René de Saint Quentin, describing him as a 'personal friend'.

Our efforts were not in vain: Mehring was released. He made his way to Marseilles, where the Emergency Rescue Committee, led by one of the Guild's directors, Frank Kingdon, saved him from fresh detention. He eventually reached Miami, Florida, on 1 March 1941, having travelled via Casablanca and Martinique, helped by Varian Fry, whom we had also approached on Mehring's behalf.

The other names on the Academy's second list of scholarship awards of 28 February 1938 were those of Joseph Roth, Annette Kolb, Wilhelm Speyer, Klaus Berger, Uriel Birnbaum, Magnus Hen-ning, Hans Reisiger, Gerhard Hermann, Franz Blei and Alfred Pol-gar. The awards allowed them all to continue their work and led to a bountiful literary harvest. As Löwenstein informed the Guild's directors in November 1938, the reports from recipients of the first 25 scholarships and printing subsidies showed that 28 literary pro-jects had been helped along by the contributions. They included 20 novels, two stage plays, two volumes of poetry and four scholarly works. More significant still, however, was the confirmation that with relatively modest means it was possible to have an effect that went far beyond the material significance of the sponsorship. The awards had, he pointed out, lent German intellectuals new hope, strength and courage to continue speaking for the other Ger-many in exile. Löwenstein quoted from the report written by Heinz Politzer, one of the most gifted poets of the younger generation:

I had asked, some weeks after the occupation of my country, Austria, for a scholarship from the Guild, and I received within a short time a positive answer. While the material help the scholarship provided was to me of almost inestimable value, I feel that the moral support it meant ought to be mentioned first. At a time when I had come to doubt whether my life had any meaning left at all and whether I might ever be able to continue my work, it has shown to me that there were still, somewhere far away, believers in the true German spirit, that we were not lost and abandoned, and that for the sake of these friends of the true German spirit it was necessary to hold on and keep going. What the scholarship did for me was to, not merely spiritually, save my life. The material support enabled me to complete my second volume of poetry, *Das blau geblasene Glas*, and to start even a third one, the title of which has not yet been decided upon . . .

It was due to the assistance accorded by this scholarship awarded to me that I was fortunate enough to overcome the critical phase of my emigration. What I am facing now are just problems of practical life.[5]

As it became ever harder for even eminent exiles to secure a livelihood, more exceptions had to be made to the principle that Academy members could make recommendations for scholarship awards but not apply for one themselves. There were Academy members even in the first two lists of awards, such as Oskar Maria Graf, René Schickele, Walter Mehring, Walter Speyer, Alfred Polgar, Joseph Roth, Franz Blei, A. M. Frey and Annette Kolb. Many others would follow, among them Ernst Bloch, Bert Brecht, Hermann Broch, Alfred Döblin, Leonhard Frank, John Heartfield, Alfred Kantorowicz, Kurt Hiller, Hermann Kesten, Egon Erwin Kisch, Ernst Krenek, Otto Lehmann-Russbueldt, Siegfried Marck, Robert Musil, Alfred Neumann, Rudolf Olden, Gustav Regler, Anna Seghers, Fritz von Unruh, Franz Werfel, Hermynia ZurMühlen and Arnold Zweig. The sheer hardship experienced in exile by many men and women who had enjoyed respect and success in Germany is illustrated by the letter Leonhard Frank wrote to Prince Hubertus zu Löwenstein on 24 June 1939:

I possess nothing. Literally nothing! The money I had brought with me from Germany has been used up in my six years in exile. In the last three and a half years I have earned 550 French Fr. I have done my utmost to earn something through film work. Nothing! I have written two new stage plays. Nothing too, it seems! . . . I do not even possess the knack of gaining support from private individuals. That is a knack one either has or has not. What options are left to me? In September I will turn 57.

Today there are many people in my situation. I know that. Only the dead are prospering. But probably everyone still breathing considers himself to be a particularly deserving case. Should I fill another dozen pages to present a clearer picture of my situation? Better not! Is there anyone in America who might be saying to himself: Leonhard Frank must of course receive help?

Maybe there really is such a person. But how do I find him –?

I am aware of how shameless this letter is. The only way I can perhaps excuse myself is by expressing how indifferent to everything the utter hopelessness of my situation has left me.[6]

There were awards to an increasingly diverse range of recipients as the number of applications from all parts of the world rapidly rose. We kept a list of the literary and scientific projects to be supported, with precedence determined on the basis of the appraisals by the senators and other members of the Academy. The American Guild's Board of Directors was responsible for deciding on the second criterion, the urgency of the individual applications. It wasted no time in approving awards and authorizing the payments as soon as the necessary funding had become available. By the time the donations gradually dried up with the outbreak of war, the total number of recipients had swollen to 163. At the time each award was made (many of the exiles had to move to new host countries several times), 52 of them lived in France, 25 in the United States, nineteen in Czechoslovakia, sixteen in Switzerland, fifteen in England, nine in Austria, five in Holland, three each in Belgium, Italy and Palestine, two in Luxembourg and one each in Denmark, Sweden, Norway, Rumania, Tunisia, Liberia, South Africa, Argentina, Columbia, Australia and China. As Rudolf Olden said in his article for the *Pariser Tageszeitung* of 7 June 1938, only in the future would the true scope of what the Academy in Exile and the American Guild had accomplished become apparent: 'One day, when readers in German libraries find books marked "Written –" or "Printed with the help of the American Guild for German Cultural Freedom" ', he predicted, such readers would look back at Hitler and gain an insight into 'an age armed to the teeth and empty inside, an age of impoverishment, of weakness, of eroding, parching despotism'. Olden summed up: 'Back then the torch was, somehow, kept alight so that it could be passed on to future generations. That was the achievement of the fabulous "Guild".' And, of course, of the German Academy of the Arts and Sciences in Exile.

CHAPTER THIRTEEN

The 'Literary Contest'

This prize is the first response to Hitler's pronouncements of 30 January 1937, in which he was presumptuous enough to decree that recipients of Nazi awards should henceforth be considered as the representatives of German intellectual life. In the Senate of its German Academy in New York, the American Guild for German Cultural Freedom has united an overwhelming majority of the men and women whom the world in general, and intellectually free Germany in particular, regard and respect as the true representatives of German culture. The Guild itself offers conspicuous proof of the fact that there is no room for the spirit of German intellect within the Nazi domain.

Press statement by Prince Hubertus zu Löwenstein,
London, 23 April 1937[1]

One of the ways in which the Academy decided to promote and foster German literature in exile was by offering competitive, international literary awards. Like the scholarships, the prizes were intended as acknowledgements of special achievements which would encourage and assist literary creativity. Such competitions were also an effective means of awaking interest in the exiles' works among the public and the media. They demonstrated convincingly that Germany's true identity had nothing to do with pernicious Nazi ideology and that – despite Hitler's best efforts – German culture lived on. It might be suppressed, persecuted and forced underground within Germany itself, but in exile it was present for all the world to see.

On 20 April 1937, the Guild's vice-president and chairman of the Executive Committee, Alvin Johnson, signed an initial contract for the contest with the American publishing house Little, Brown &

Company in New York. The publisher agreed to make an advance payment of 2,500 dollars to the winning author for the right to publish the successful work in the United States and Canada. Later that same day, Thomas Mann announced this agreement at the annual gathering of the Academy and Guild in the Ritz Carlton, New York. His audience included representatives of the international press as well as eminent cultural, scientific, political and social figures.

Even during the months of preparation before the contest, we seized every opportunity to keep the public informed. One such opportunity was the international forum represented by the XVth P.E.N. Congress in Paris, where, in a speech of 24 June 1937, Prince Löwenstein was able to announce that a second publishing house, Querido in Amsterdam, had also decided to collaborate in the competition.

That there was substantial international interest was evident even at this preliminary stage. Other publishers from various countries expressed their desire to participate: William Collins of England on 22 October, Albin Michel of France on 13 December and, a few days later on 17 December, A. W. Sijthoff of the Netherlands. When the Academy's inaugural literary contest was officially launched on 26 February 1938, it boasted a total purse of 4,520 dollars and the winning author could also look forward to having his entry published both in America and across Europe.[2]

Three further publishing houses climbed aboard in May and June of 1938: Albert Bonnier in Stockholm, the Gyldendal Norsk Forlag in Oslo and the Danish Gyldendalske Nordisk Forlag in Copenhagen. Shortly before the deadline for submitting manuscripts, 1 October 1938, a ninth company also signed up: Towarzystwo Wydawnicze Rój of Warsaw. This brought the purse up to 5,365 dollars. The number of works submitted also rose quickly. Fifty manuscripts arrived after the initial announcement of the contest, and by the deadline we had received 177.

It seemed likely that the jury would need longer than had been foreseen to consider all these entries, particularly since the five Academy senators it comprised lived in four different countries: Rudolf Olden in England, Lion Feuchtwanger in France, Alfred Neumann in Italy, Bruno Frank and Thomas Mann in the USA. It was therefore decided that a preliminary selection would have to be made. Thirty entries were immediately excluded because they failed to meet the formal conditions. As enthusiastic and keen to help as ever, Richard Bermann, who had been elected to the Guild's Board of Directors on 11 October 1938 in New York and had immediately become chairman of the contest's organizing committee, volunteered to read the remaining 147 texts. We had already begun by sending a substantial number of manuscripts to Thomas Mann, the chairman of the jury, to assess. On the basis of his and Bermann's suggestions, 31 entries were selected to be sent in rotation to all the jurors.

Richard Bermann had noted with satisfaction that it was 'astonishing how many good manuscripts'[3] there were among those he read in order to make the preliminary selection – despite the impoverished and even desperate circumstances of many of the exiled writers. The high overall quality of the entries was indeed an encouraging sign that the flame of creativity had not been doused by the difficulties of life in exile, even among the new generation of writers. The more prominent figures had elected not to enter the contest in order to give the youngsters a fair chance. Later, when the veil of pseudonymity was lifted, we discovered that the only members of the Academy to enter had been Bert Brecht, A. M. Frey, Oskar Maria Graf, Georg Hermann-Borchardt and Paul Zech. Another indication of the depth of talent among the competitors was that none of these Academy members was among the three far less renowned writers whose entries made the final shortlist. Nine of the twelve other authors who received special commendations from one or more of the judges were also non-members.

The process of coming to a final decision was long and difficult. It dragged on for almost twelve months. The contract with the American publisher stipulated that the judges would agree not to award the prize to any manuscript unless they found a first-class book, which they would unanimously agree to declare as such.[4] Unfortunately, the five judges from four countries were ultimately unable to make a unanimous selection. Thomas Mann, Bruno Frank and Alfred Neumann chose Arnold Bender's *Es ist später denn ihr wisst*; Rudolf Olden voted for *Das Abenteuer des Bewusstseins*, a first novel by Gertraute Goetze-Fischer; and Lion Feuchtwanger preferred the 'prose-ballad',[5] as he called Jo Mihaly-Steckel's *Der Hüter des Bruders.* Olden ultimately agreed to support Bender's entry, but Feuchtwanger stuck to his guns without regard to the consequences.

When Little, Brown & Company received Bender's manuscript they had a respected expert assess its suitability for the American market. A special clause in the contract stipulated:

> If Little, Brown & Company should find that the prize book selected by the judges has no possibility of a fair-sized reading public in America, then the Committee on Awards of the American Guild shall be the final arbiter, and the judges and Little, Brown & Company agree to accept its decision as to the award and publication.[6]

This clause had been added to the contract while Löwenstein and I were in Europe. Löwenstein had immediately objected in a telegram from London, but Alvin Johnson, in his capacity as the Guild's vice-president and chairman of the Executive Committee, had already accepted it in order not to jeopardize the agreement upon which the competition depended. He omitted, unfortunately, to inform the judges of this passage in the contract.

Little, Brown & Company solicited appraisals from a second, a third and finally a fourth expert, and when all of them came to the same negative conclusion as the first, the company asked the Guild for a decision. Now came the bitterest pill of all for us to swallow: Henry Seidel Canby, one of our own directors and one of America's leading literary savants, agreed with the publisher's experts. His reasoning, as he told me, was that if a work adjudged by the jury to be the best work written in exile had turned out a flop, it would have done more harm than good to publish it.

Arnold Bender's novel *Es ist später denn ihr wisst* never was published in America – unlike other entries in the contest such as Oskar Maria Graf's *Jugendjahre meiner Mutter*, which Howell, Soskin & Company of New York published in 1940 as *The Life of my Mother*. Before the war was over, however, Bender's book was published in England – by William Collins in 1943 as *The Farm by the Lake* – and even before this, in 1941–2, the German text was serialized under the title *Der Winter in Schweden* by *Die Zeitung* in London. Albin Michel, as the company informed us on 6 April 1940,[7] had immediately commissioned a translation of the manuscript with the intention of publishing it as a prize-winning work in France. Little, Brown & Company's decision was based entirely on its assessment of the American market and had no relevance to Europe: the prize-winning novel had every prospect of being published by all eight of the European publishing houses involved in the contest.

Then, however, international political events intervened, with the end of the 'phoney war' which had followed the declarations of war of 3 September 1939. The Polish publisher dropped out as soon as Hitler invaded the country in September 1939. On 9 April 1940 the invasion of Denmark and Norway began, and that of Belgium and the Netherlands on 10 May. Paris was occupied on 14 June. Collins, in London, and Bonnier, in Stockholm, were therefore the only European publishers left. By now, however, Swedish anxiety about the country's own neutrality and security was so great that publication of a work by a German exile was out of the question.

The literary contest ended unsatisfactorily in several ways: the failure of the judges to reach a unanimous decision; the American publisher's view, supported by the American Guild's own Committee on Awards, that the jury's majority choice was not suitable for the American market; and the fact that wartime events eliminated all the publishers except the British one. Inevitably, the author, the judges and the Academy as a whole were bitterly disappointed. Bruno Frank resigned from the organization and Thomas Mann, who had invested so much time and energy as the chairman of the jury, also considered doing so. A detailed memorandum from Hermann Broch[8] and some lengthy discussions subsequently persuaded him that, in the interests of the common cause, he should not do so. It was hardly surprising that there were some expressions of annoyance and resentment from members of the exile community. There were recriminations in some of the exile journals, culminating in a grotesque article by Leopold Schwarzschild in April 1940 in the *Neues Tage-Buch*, insinuating that the contest had been 'buried', because 'a few weeks after the Stalin-Hitler pact' it was no longer of any use to the 'Communists'. Most absurd of all was Schwarzschild's claim that none other than Löwenstein was to blame and that the prince harboured secret Stalinist sympathies.

Of course, no one was more bitterly disappointed than Arnold Bender, who sought legal advice. Eventually the parties involved reached a compromise based on an *ex gratia* payment from Little,

Brown & Company, augmented by contributions from the Guild's directors. Even 1,000 dollars, however, offered scant consolation to the writer.

The progress of the war meant that hardly anyone outside the exile community took any notice of these latter stages of the literary contest. Suddenly people had other worries. This applied even to Americans, who were almost more horrified by the catastrophe unleashed in Europe in 1939 than they were by the Japanese attack on the US Pacific Fleet at Pearl Harbor on 7 December 1941 and Hitler's declaration of war on America on 11 December. The hoped-for grand finale to the competition, with publication of the winning work in several countries, would therefore have been over-shadowed by political events even if the judges' decision had been more satisfactory.

Nevertheless, there was still interest in the publication of works which had been entered in the contest. Although some such titles only reached the bookshops years or even decades later, their quality testified to the fact that Germany's cultural life and creative energy continued to thrive in exile. Such works included Johannes R. Becher's *Abschied* (Moscow, 1940; translated as *Farewell*, Berlin, 1970), Oskar Maria Graf's *The Life of my Mother* (New York, 1940), Jo Mihaly-Steckel's *Der Hüter des Bruders* (Zürich, 1942), Hannah Arendt's *Rahel Varnhagen* (Munich, 1959; translated as *Rahel Varnhagen, the life of a Jewess*, London, 1958 and Baltimore, 1997), Günther Anders's *Die molussische Katakombe* (Munich, 1992) and Bert Brecht's *Die Geschäfte des Herrn Julius Caesar* (published in 1957[9]). The latter work was in fact disqualified from the contest because Brecht had broken the rules by revealing his identity. The manuscript he had submitted was, moreover, only half finished.

The fact that so many women entered the contest was another of its more gratifying aspects, particularly since women frequently suffered the greatest hardship in exile, often having to provide for their husbands. One in five of the manuscripts was from a woman writer, and one in three of those specially commended by the judges. Of the three works on the shortlist for the overall prize, two were written by women: Gertraute Goetze-Fischer – Olden's choice – and Jo Mihaly-Steckel, whose work Feuchtwanger was determined to support even at the expense of a unanimous decision.

Jo Mihaly, born in 1902, was a dancer. She had been a member of the Haas-Heye Ballet in Berlin before joining the *Volksbühne* and becoming a solo dancer using her own choreographies in 1928. The Nazis were keen to enlist her for their own cause and tried to persuade her to stay, but she emigrated to Switzerland in 1933. A year later she founded and directed the 'Neuer Chor' choral society in Zürich. She had published her first book, *Die Ballade vom Elend*, in 1927, and had gone on to write two books for children. She also made a name for herself as a journalist in both Germany and Switzerland. She was no less energetic as a political activist, for example co-founding and leading the *Kulturgemeinschaft der Emigranten in der Deutschland-Bewegung* (Cultural Community of Exiles in the Germany Movement). Her pamphlets and fliers were distributed illegally in Germany. In 1945 the poems she had written in England were published under the title *Wir verstummen nicht: Gedichte in der Fremde* (We Do Not Fall Silent: Poems From Abroad), to be followed by many of her novellas, novels and animal stories.

Gertraute Goetze-Fischer's *Abenteuer des Bewusstseins* represented an even greater achievement, as it was her first book. Aged 42 at the time, she had worked in the Prussian civil service before choosing to emigrate to New York in 1935, although all her relatives remained in Germany. She had published nothing at this point. On 16 July 1937 she wrote to Prince Löwenstein:

> I am entering a novel I wrote immediately after leaving Germany in the winter of 1935 and spring of 1936, here in the United States … In it I describe the Third Reich's assault on the private lives of independent women.[10]

I do not know what fate held in store for this talented and courageous woman. She does not appear to have published any further works.

Arnold Bender, born in 1904, the winner of the contest, had published poems, essays and short stories in the *Dortmunder Generalanzeiger* newspaper from 1928 onward, but his first book, *In einer grossen Stadt*, was not published until shortly before his emigration. In 1934 he reached England via Denmark and Sweden. There he continued to write, contributing to London's German-language newspaper *Die Zeitung* and other publications, whilst making his living principally as a language teacher. *Die Zeitung* published his novels in instalments, including the one which won him the literary contest.

Looking back today, the sheer variety of creative writing produced under the difficult conditions of life in exile still seems astonishing. More such works are still being discovered and published posthumously; 1998, for example, saw publication of Rudolf Frank's manuscript, *Fair Play*, which the author – who was, like so many others, in receipt of an Academy scholarship – had entered in the literary contest under the pseudonym Francis Ruddy.[11] He wrote it in 1938 after emigrating for a second time, from Vienna via Italy to Zürich. *Fair Play* is a distinctly autobiographical *Zeitroman*, engaging with the spirit and events of the time. It tells the story of the author's experiences in Austria during the Dollfuss-Schuschnigg era. Frank left Germany in 1936. When asked why he waited so long before doing so, he replied: 'My God, the whole Hitler thing just seemed so extraordinarily ridiculous to us that we did not want to bolt from it.'[12]

Frank's biographer, Walter Heist, wrote of that multi-talented individual: 'How to describe him? Theatre director, journalist, novelist, writer (or co-writer) of stage and radio plays, editor, translator: he was all of them!'[13] Frank had performed in Max Reinhardt's *Deutsches Theater* in Berlin even before the First World War. Later he discovered Elisabeth Bergner; as an artistic director he made Brecht famous by giving *Trommeln in der Nacht* (*Drums in the Night*) its premiere at the Munich *Kammerspiele* in 1922 and organized a stage debut for Karl Valentin, who later achieved such popularity as a comedian and actor. His famous pacifist 'war novel for the younger generation' of 1932, *Der Schädel des Negerhäuptlings Makaua*, was one of the works the Nazis threw on the fire at the book burning of 10 May 1933. In 1992 it was republished under the title *Der Junge, der seinen Geburtstag vergass*.[14]

In retrospect it is evident that the international literary contest between 1937 and the beginning of the war did make a valuable contribution to anti-Nazi German culture and thus helped the exile community fulfil its political agenda. It was in this light, as the international interest and participation in it showed, that the competition was viewed: as a manifestation of another Germany outside the Nazi regime's sphere of influence. And this had important implications for the future.

CHAPTER FOURTEEN

After the Outbreak of War

Germany has been kicked, bloodied and mocked because of its current 'national' governors . . . Do you fail to see that this nationalist, Fascist Germany is a betrayal and the worst enemy of the true Germany? Such policies are a crime not just against the spirit of humanity but also against the very nation that spawned them. Not only do they rob it of much of its energy, they deny it the respect of the best friends it has in the world.

Romain Rolland, May 1933

When the Nazis let slip the dogs of war to devastate even their own country, the days of the German Academy's patronage of culture in exile, supported by the American Guild and the British Arden Society, were clearly numbered. Suddenly the eyes and energies of people throughout the world were focused on the war itself. Such funds as we could raise would henceforth be sufficient, at best, for emergency assistance to those in need. Since the war put an end to all links with the countries invaded by Hitler, and since the recipients of scholarships in Great Britain and the United States (America was still untouched by the war) were not, however difficult their circumstances, in immediate danger, our most urgent task was now to help those who had been able to escape to France but who were now – above all after the capitulation – at the mercy of the Gestapo.

Löwenstein and I were still in France when Hitler and Stalin sliced up Poland between them in the infamous Ribbentrop-Molotov Pact of 23 August 1939. A few days later came the invasions – Hitler's on 1 September, Stalin's on the 17th of the same month – by which they took possession of their agreed shares of the prize. On 10 August, the eve of the twentieth anniversary of the declaration of the Weimar Constitution, Prince Löwenstein, as general secretary of the Academy, had hosted a commemorative celebration in Paris. It was attended by members and scholarship recipients, but also by a broad range of other guests. Among them were many exiled politicians, including the former government ministers Hugo Simon and Rudolf Hilferding (whom the Vichy regime would hand over to the Gestapo two years later), and former elected members of the Reichstag such as Friedrich Wilhelm Wagner, subsequently a member of the parliamentary council and also, for many years, of the Bundestag. Also present were Max Cohen-Reuss, Peter Maslowski and Willi Münzenberg, editor of the journal *Die Zukunft*, which also appeared in German-English and German-French editions and led to the founding of the Union Franco-Allemande in France (with a membership that included prominent politicians such as Paul Boncour and Edouard Herriot); the leader of the Social Democratic Party, Hans Vogel, along with Erich Ollenhauer; Hermann Budzislawski, who edited *Weltbühne*, first in Prague and then in Paris; and the former Austrian secretary of state for defence, Julius Deutsch, who had fought on the front in the Spanish Civil War as a general.

Soon afterwards we travelled to Le Brusc, a village in the South of France near Sanary-sur-Mer – the town which Ludwig Marcuse dubbed the 'capital of German literature in exile' because so many émigré poets and authors were to be found there. Indeed, in 1987 a commemorative plaque was unveiled in Sanary, dedicated to the 'German and Austrian writers, and their relatives and friends, who gathered in Sanary-sur-Mer while fleeing the tyranny of National Socialism'. Most of the 36 émigrés honoured on the plaque were members of the Academy in Exile, and some were in receipt of scholarships.

One of the 36 members was Marcuse himself, who had lived in the region since 1933. Lion Feuchtwanger and his wife, Marta, had been there since 1934, welcoming a steady stream of visitors to the Villa Valmer. Franz Werfel and Alma Mahler-Werfel had moved into an old mill, Le Moulin Gris, shortly before our arrival. Hans Siemsen visited us several times while we were in Le Brusc. Wilhelm Herzog, whose collected poems, *Gedichte aus dreissig Jahren*, had just been published, was also back in Sanary, in the Villa

Roge, as was the doctor and writer Friedrich Wolf, whose son
Marcus Wolf was to make his name as the head of East Germany's
secret service. Various other exiles lived in the surrounding villages.

On 1 September 1939 we boarded a – blacked-out – train back to
Paris. Feuchtwanger, who had once exulted: 'The sooner the war,
the sooner our return',[1] remained behind. Only three weeks later he,
along with so many others, was interned in the camp of Les Milles.
Their first incarceration was brief, but then, in May 1940, they were
detained again. Marta Feuchtwanger was taken to the women's
camp of Gurs. Twenty years later, when I was in Los Angeles for the
West German foreign service, I often visited her – she was by then a
widow – at her seaside home in Pacific Palisades, the Villa Aurora,
built in the Spanish colonial style. There she told me, still in her
unaffected Munich vernacular, the dramatic story of Feuchtwanger's escape. After much effort she had managed to persuade
the American vice-consul, Miles Standish, to smuggle women's
clothes into the camp, which Feuchtwanger donned to disguise
himself as an old lady. He succeeded in slipping out of the camp
and took a taxi to Marseilles. Marta also managed to get out of Gurs.
Together they crossed the Pyrenees on foot, just as Heinrich, Nelly
and Golo Mann and Alma and Franz Werfel had recently done, and
crossed Spain to reach Portugal. Walter Benjamin had begun the
same journey, only to end it by committing suicide in Port Bou.
Immediately after his arrival in America, Lion angrily dictated a
book about his experiences in 'unholy France'. It was published
there under the title *The Devil in France*; Marta Feuchtwanger
contributed her own account of the escape for the German edition.

In the chaos which gripped Paris in the early stages of the war it
took us a long time to obtain our exit visas. I was still a German
citizen, and would therefore have been interned at the Camp de
Colombes with all the other 'enemy aliens', irrespective of the fact
that I was in exile, had I not been fortunate enough to receive a 're-
entry permit' when I left America with the Löwensteins. Yet even
the princess and her husband, who had been stripped of his
German citizenship and now held a Czech passport, were unable to
leave aboard the *MS Washington* on 9 September as planned, as they
were denied an exit visa. The reason for this could hardly have been
more absurd: the military department responsible did not yet have
the appropriate rubber stamp.

I spent day after day wandering the labyrinth of officialdom, being sent from one department to another, from the police commissioner's office to the prefecture; from there to the interior ministry and then to the military authorities, with long, pointless waits in between. I was turned away only to be repeatedly summoned again, and was even detained by a police patrol and obliged to spend the night in custody. On top of all this, I also had to try to obtain berths aboard another ship. Despite my protests I was sent to Colombes three times, before the acting camp commander, Battalion Commander Vayer, an elderly and amiable reserve officer who was evidently impressed by the re-entry permit with its big, red American seal and the testimonial from the US embassy, finally issued me a *laissez-passer*. He justified this by stating that on 13 September I had 'mistakenly reported to the Colombes transit camp for foreigners' and declaring me inaccurately, or perhaps generously, as an 'American citizen'.

Equipped with this priceless document, I managed to join the Löwensteins and reach Bordeaux, where the *MS Roosevelt* was due to sail on 20 September. The last hurdle before boarding was the passport check: my German passport was still the only one I had. If the border official had turned me back I would probably have had to resort to the same escape route taken by Heinrich Mann and the Feuchtwangers. To my relief, I was allowed through, perhaps because I was in such notable company: along with the Löwensteins, Toscanini was on the way to America, accompanied by Eleonore von Mendelssohn.

We arrived in New York on 28 September. By then the Guild's funds were exhausted, so our first priority was either to give the organization a shot in the arm or, if we could not reanimate it, to dissolve it and clear the way for a more effective alternative. Löwenstein had to take up his academic post, this time at Pullman in Washington State, on the day of our arrival. In view of the need for urgent steps to be taken, however, he allowed me to stay in New York to make clear to the directors just how precarious the situation was. To the same end, he wrote to them proposing the Guild's dissolution. This shocked them into action, and after a short period of reflection it was decided that the organization's work should continue.

Löwenstein then urged first the treasurer, Villard, and then (at the meeting of 17 January 1940) the whole Board to pursue new sources of revenue. He added force to his appeal by making a donation of his own. Two fundraising letters were sent out, one in Villard's name and the other signed jointly by the Guild's president Governor Wilbur L. Cross, the respected journalist Dorothy Thompson, and Thomas Mann in his capacity as president of the Academy.

This course of action proved successful once again. Soon it was possible to issue all the outstanding scholarship payments and to send contributions to many other needy individuals, particularly those still in France. Apart from financial support, émigrés also needed assistance in obtaining residence and work permits, finding employment and gaining introductions. They often required recommendations or testimonials, and several were also grateful for advice and help with personal problems. Many, of course, wanted to obtain visas, and there was an ever greater need for the affidavits from American citizens upon which applications for entry into the United States depended. All too often, these applications were matters of life and death. Since exiles, unlike other foreign nationals, did not enjoy the backing of their native country – and often not even of individuals or organizations of any import to the authorities in the host country – the Academy and the Guild were frequently the only support they could count on. The two organizations did their utmost for them.

On 15 January 1940, Löwenstein approached the French ambassador in Washington, Comte René de Saint Quentin, in the hope of securing the release of internees in France. The American Guild, with a state governor as its president and a US senator as honorary chairman, was an organization with the status needed to secure results. The ambassador asked for a list of names. We immediately gave him details of the most urgent cases, to be followed later by others. The embassy notified us of each release when it took place, upon which we did our best to help the person in question to leave France as quickly as possible. Vichy France remained a dangerous place: when the French government capitulated on 22 June 1940 it was required under Article 19, Paragraph 2 of the armistice agreement to hand all Germans over to the Gestapo on demand.

Some émigrés joined the French resistance, among them Rudolf Leonhard, who managed to escape from the extradition centre at Castres in autumn 1943. He was far from being the only foreigner in the fight against France's oppressors. In the Carmagnoles group in Lyon, for example, fewer than a fifth of the partisans were French; there were nearly as many Germans, Austrians, Hungarians and Rumanians; one in three was Polish, and the others were Spaniards, Italians and Belgians. A German émigré, Norbert Kugler, led the group from 1943.[2]

Entry to the United States was limited by annual quotas, depending on country of origin. Due to restrictions imposed by the American authorities until 1943, these quotas were not even fully exploited. Löwenstein therefore urged the Guild's Board to petition the government in Washington for a special dispensation to apply to exiled writers. When the directors decided against the idea for legal reasons at a meeting on 4 June 1940, he took the initiative himself.

He had by now freed himself of other commitments, and at the start of June a political controversy also involving Thomas Mann prompted him to resign as general secretary of the Academy and from the Guild's Board of Directors. I took over a share of his administrative duties. None of this deterred him from vigorously pursuing his rescue campaign, to which end he continued to work closely with the Guild. When he received two appeals for help from Rudolf Leonhard and Berthold Jacob, both of whom were detained at the Le Vernet camp, urging him to have the American Red Cross save émigrés from extradition to the Gestapo, Löwenstein forwarded them to, among others, First Lady Eleanor Roosevelt, who took an active interest in the fate of refugees at the time.

Löwenstein warned that even Portugal might not be a safe transit country for much longer and insisted on the need to act fast. The subsequent fate of Berthold Jacob proved just how accurate Löwenstein's assessment of the situation was: although Jacob was released, all the representations Löwenstein organized on his behalf could not prevent him from being repeatedly re-interned. The Guild approached the Emergency Rescue Committee in New York and also contacted the Committee's local representative in Marseilles, Varian Fry, directly. He approached the French authorities, while Villard provided the necessary affidavit and made a personal appeal to the American consul in Marseilles – but in vain. We never discovered what grounds the consul had for refusing to rescue Jacob. Perhaps, absurdly, he suspected Jacob of being a Communist or an agent of the French *Deuxième Bureaux*. Fry finally managed to smuggle Jacob to Lisbon under another name and with false papers, only for him to be arrested in a city street by Gestapo agents on 25 September 1941 and sent to Germany. He died on 26 February 1944, shortly after being transferred from prison to the Jewish hospital in Berlin.

Löwenstein also approached the Justice Department in Washington, to which the Immigration and Naturalization Office belonged. In view of the urgency of the cases in question, there appeared to be two possible options: visitors' visas or transit visas. These were not limited by quotas like the immigration visas. The only requirement for a transit visa was an entry permit to another country. On the same day Löwenstein therefore urged the British embassy to persuade its government to help those in danger by approving visas, if not to Britain itself, at least to British possessions on the American continent or to Australia. The British response was equivocal, but Mexico's ambassador, Don Castillo Najera, proved to be much more accommodating. In fact he received Löwenstein with open arms, and the prince presented him with a list of the Academy's scholarship recipients and of those who had approached us for assistance. Encouraged by Don Castillo's attitude, he also went so far as to ask for 500 blank visas, a request which the ambassador agreed to put to his government. He was as good as his word. Not only those on the list, but also many other refugees were permitted to travel to Mexico, often with transit visas through the United States. A good number of them were able to convert their transit or visitor status into permanent residence once they had reached the United States.

At the Justice Department, Löwenstein was assured that it would be possible to obtain ships for the crossing. In addition, however, he approached the Washington office of the Red Cross on the same subject and particularly with regard to Rudolf Leonhard's plea for protection and help in escaping. At the Academy's office in New York we concentrated mainly on obtaining affidavits for visa applications. Concerns about a rise in unemployment meant that immigration policy was applied strictly, and two affidavits were required for a simple visitor's visa and even for the Special Emergency Visitors Visa which the administration finally introduced. In one affidavit the signatory had to vouch for the visitor's political and moral integrity; the other involved personally underwriting all financial obligations he or she might incur. On top of these, one or more testimonials were required about the person in question, with proof that he or she was in acute danger.

Löwenstein also contacted George L. Warren, executive secretary of the President's Advisory Committee on Political Refugees. Warren's committee was responsible for the collation, sorting and preliminary examination of rescue applications. Löwenstein agreed to send him a list of urgent cases – members of the Academy and scholarship recipients – who were still stuck in France. We drew up the list in the New York office and immediately dispatched the 84 names with all relevant details to Warren. The line of communication thus established proved to be an immensely valuable one; from then on we could telephone on a personal basis whenever necessary.

Oswald Garrison Villard, as the Guild's treasurer, drafted a dramatic appeal for affidavits, which we sent to 346 public figures on 8 August 1940:

> The American Guild has aided hundreds of refugees, German, Austrian and Czechoslovakian writers, scholars and artists in exile ... Many of these unfortunates, all of whom have much to give to the world through their constructive writings, all of whom are profoundly anti-Nazi, many of them being voluntary exiles, are now in France in the gravest danger of falling into the hands of the Nazis, to undergo the torture of concentration camps, or to face the firing squads. It is the last hour for them.
> If they cannot be saved now, they are lost![3]

This appeal produced 44 affidavits and was followed by another, to 255 addressees and signed by Frank Kingdon, on 7 October.

Since we still had too few affidavits for our needs, I suggested to the Board that each member of it provide eight or ten such documents. When the directors decided that legal advice should first be sought, I appealed to their consciences, insisting that only the Guild could help the trapped émigrés:

> They are hiding in [unoccupied] France, under assumed names, and any day they may be caught. They implore the Guild to act immediately; nothing else can save them from certain death. It is simply [heart-rending]. I wish so much that

I could give affidavits, it would make me happy to do so; but I
am not an American citizen. It has become so literally true
what was written in some appeal letters of the Guild: 'If we fail
them, they are lost.'[4]

There were many other relief organizations for immigrants and
refugees in America, most of them based in New York. The various
religious agencies included the American Joint Jewish Distribution
Committee (which had been in existence since 1914), the Hebrew
Sheltering and Immigrant Aid Society of America (HIAS), the
Committee for Catholic Refugees from Germany, the American
Committee for Christian German Refugees (from 1934) and the Uni-
tarian Service Committee (from 1940). Academics were served by
the Emergency Committee in Aid of Displaced German Scholars,
co-founded by Felix Warburg in 1933, which worked in close
collaboration with the Rockefeller Foundation, the Oberlaender
Trust and the Quakers' American Friends Service Committee.
Immigrants who were already in America founded the Selfhelp of
German Émigrés in 1936, renaming it the Selfhelp of Émigrés from
Central Europe in 1940, and the European Film Fund was set up in
1938 in Hollywood. The Film Fund, with which we frequently
coordinated our relief programmes, was run by Ernst Lubitsch,
Paul Kohner and Charlotte Dieterle. There were also the International Relief Association, the American Friends of German
Freedom, the German Labor Delegation, the German-American
Emergency Conference, the German-American Congress for Democracy, and later also the Council for a Democratic Germany and
many other organizations. Guild members or sponsors were active
in a number of them, and Academy members were also represented
here and there. In several instances these organizations assisted us
and sometimes they even took over particular cases for us.

It was, however, the Emergency Rescue Committee (ERC) upon
which we most depended. It was founded in 1940 by Frank Kingdon, then the Guild's executive vice-president, with the sole aim of
helping writers, artists, composers, scientists, journalists and politicians to escape abroad from danger. Three of the seven well-known
figures who lent weight to the ERC on its national committee were
directors of the Guild too: Alvin Johnson, George Shuster and Dorothy Thompson. The Emergency Rescue Committee also did its best

to coordinate rescue plans with the many organizations involved before forwarding them to the president's advisers, with whom it had a close working relationship. In October 1940 Kingdon decided to dedicate all his energy to the Emergency Rescue Committee and resigned from his executive position at the Guild.

Despite the existence of the ERC, we did still sometimes have to take direct action ourselves, as in the cases of the Berlin curator, Bernhard von Bothmer; the publisher and author, Siegfried Thalheimer; and Helmut Hirsch, another of the Academy's beneficiaries. We had always insisted that the Academy and Guild must never be influenced by the religious, ethnic or political background of proven opponents of Hitler who needed our help – least of all when lives were at stake. Frank Kingdon, however, declared that his first loyalty was to his own country and that he was not minded to risk America being infiltrated by 'poisonous influences' – by which he meant the Communist tendencies certain individuals were suspected of harbouring. Although in practice things were rather different (not least because the ERC's courageous representative in France, Varian Fry, paid no heed whatsoever to such considerations), it now became clear how valuable it was to have Mexico available as a transit option.

When I was able to show Kingdon that Thalheimer, whom I knew well, had been confused with the opposition Communist politician August Thalheimer, he immediately withdrew his objections and submitted the application two days later. Thalheimer received his visa on 16 November 1940, and Bothmer a month later. In the case of Helmut Hirsch, however, Löwenstein had to circumvent the ERC and make a personal approach to George Warren of President Roosevelt's advisory committee. He managed to organize the transatlantic crossing with the help of the HIAS, and on 21 June 1941 we were able to welcome Hirsch and his wife to New York. Today he is an emeritus professor and still active in the fields of both literature and politics: the only living witness among the Academy's former beneficiaries.

The Emergency Rescue Committee, which was relatively well funded thanks to generous contributions from Ingrid Warburg and other patrons, was able to dispatch Varian Fry to take charge of the rescue operations on the spot, in Marseilles, by 4 August 1940. He was an inspired choice. Fry was a Harvard graduate and a lover of

German literature and European art who had experienced the per-
verted spirit and brutality of Hitler's regime at first hand on a visit
to Germany in 1935. As soon as he got to Marseilles he sought out
Franz Werfel, of whom he was a particular admirer, and Werfel's
wife, Alma Mahler-Werfel. Not long afterwards he assisted them,
along with Heinrich Mann, the latter's wife, Nelly, and Golo Mann
to flee over the Pyrenees.

As Fry admits in his book, *Surrender on Demand*, he had 'no
experience in refugee work, and none in underground work',[5] but
soon he was an expert on all the routes, including the most round-
about ones, on all the illegal methods, secret ploys and ruses needed
in order to rescue persecuted individuals in Vichy France from
under the noses of the collaborators and despite the constant, lurk-
ing menace of the Gestapo. Such rescues required false names,
forged passports and documents, and secret paths across country.
Sometimes the police and officials had to be outwitted, on other
occasions they were actually involved illicitly in the operation. Fry's
own account of all this is a fascinating and moving one. In order to
disguise his illegal activities, he created – in true secret agent style –
an innocent-seeming charity for the support of refugees in need, the
Centre Américain de Secours. The Centre's letterhead featured an
impressive list of luminaries as its *Comité de Patronage*, including
Jean Giraudoux, Aristide Maillol, André Gide, Wladimir
d'Ormesson, Henri Matisse and Georges Duhamel.

Hans Sahl, one of our beneficiaries whom we had entrusted to
Varian Fry, described in his novel *Die Wenigen und die Vielen* (*The
Few and the Many*) how much the first encounter with Fry meant to
those who were marooned and in constant fear of their lives. Asked
about his rescue, the protagonist, Kobbe, recounts how he had been
sitting in a café in Marseilles at his wits' end:

> Just then a friend came up to my table, a very witty chap, and
> said to me quietly that a man had put up at the Hotel Splen-
> dide, an American, with a stack of dollars and a list of people
> to be rescued. 'Your name is on it. Telephone him this minute!
> He's waiting for you.' I said I wasn't in the mood for jokes, but
> in fact I did telephone the hotel and ask for the mysterious
> gentleman. He came on the line immediately. 'What was your
> name again? Oh, yes, Kobbe, come over here right away, I'm

waiting for you.' Ten minutes later, when I arrived at the hotel, there were two German officers in the lobby. I walked past them to the elevator, went up, and when I opened the door and entered, a friendly young man in shirtsleeves came up to me, put his arm around me, stuffed a few banknotes in my pocket, led me to the window and whispered, like a not very good actor trying to play the part of a conspirator: 'If you need more, come back for it. In the meantime I'll cable your name to Washington. We'll get you out. There are ways, you'll see, there are ways . . .' He poured me a glass of whisky . . . You have to imagine what it was like: the borders were closed, you were completely trapped, you could be rearrested at any moment, life was as good as over – and then suddenly there is this young American in shirtsleeves stuffing your pockets full of money, putting his arm around you and murmuring with a hammy conspiratorial expression on his face, 'Oh there are ways to get you out', while your tears, damn it all, are running down your cheeks . . . and next the chap . . . actually takes his silk handkerchief from his jacket, which is draped over the chair, and says: 'Here, take it. It's not completely clean. You must forgive me.' And so you see, ever since then I've loved America, because it does these things so casually and yet with circumspection and commonsense and because after all, whenever you seem to be at the end of the road, some man in shirtsleeves appears before you and says: 'Oh, there are ways, you know . . .'[6]

Before Hans Sahl himself, bearing a Danish passport, reached America on April 1941, he became one of the many recruits who helped Fry with his work in Marseilles.

The grateful testimonials to Varian Fry, the 'guardian angel of Marseilles' as Carl Misch dubbed him,[7] are legion. According to figures Kingdon published in an ERC pamphlet, Fry rescued 602 people from France in his first year there, and helped 3,500 more in various other ways. Almost 2,000 of them are named in an alphabetical list drawn up by the Centre; those who also had Academy connections included Alfred Döblin, Lion Feuchtwanger, Leonhard Frank, Hans Habe, Berthold Jacob, Annette Kolb, Siegfried Kracauer, Golo Mann, Heinrich Mann, Hans Natonek, Alfred

Neumann, Karl Otto Paetel, Alfred Polgar, Hans Sahl, Anna Seghers, Hans Siemsen, Wilhelm Speyer, Fritz von Unruh, Walter Victor and Franz Werfel.

On one occasion when Löwenstein warmly expressed his grati-tude to Fry, the latter replied that he also wanted to thank Löwen-stein for his help in making his work possible. 'I know,' wrote Fry, 'that you have been one of the most helpful of all our friends and I want to thank you in the name of all the refugees for what you have done for them.'[8]

On 29 August 1941, the Vichy government, which was steadily caving in to pressure from the occupiers, had Fry arrested. Fry had already taken the precaution of asking for help from the American embassy and Washington, but in vain. Even Eleanor Roosevelt, doubtless constrained by her position as first lady, wrote to Varian Fry's wife to say that she could do nothing for him: 'I think he will have to come home because he has done things which the govern-ment does not feel it can stand behind.'[9] Many of Fry's activities in France were indeed contrary to his government's policy – but they had saved many lives.

Fry was expelled from France at the start of September 1941. The organization he left behind, however, ran so smoothly that it was able to continue its work for half a year without him. Fry himself was also determined to carry on, as he told Löwenstein in a letter from Lisbon whilst still *en route*.[10] Fry was a true friend of humanity and, as Will Schaber recorded in an obituary, remained committed to the cause of refugees until his premature death in 1967, at the age of 59.[11]

Even in 1940 the American Guild continued to act as a patron insofar as its resources allowed. That year it helped 56 writers and scholars, some with scholarships, but most with one-off, emergency contributions. As the war continued, however, income from donations inevitably dropped still further. When the donations produced by a final appeal to 2,000 addressees, signed by Governor Wilbur L. Cross as the Guild's president, failed to cover the expenses incurred in making it, it became clear that work could not go on.

On 25 October 1940, the Board of Directors decided that the American Guild's activities should be halted temporarily. On 8 November 1940, the end was postponed until the conclusion of the literary competition, before being made final by a unanimous vote on 10 January 1941. The archive shared by the Academy and the Guild was entrusted to me, and my offer to attend to the remaining correspondence and other outstanding matters, in exchange for reimbursement of my postage and telephone expenses, was accepted by another unanimous vote. And then the American Guild for German Cultural Freedom formally concluded its beneficent work with a final entry in the minutes: 'There being no further business, the meeting adjourned *sine die*.'

For the Academy in Exile, the evaporation of the financial support it had received from the Guild came simply as confirmation that now, in time of war, it would have to find other ways to continue the mission it had successfully undertaken in the years of peace: that of addressing the world as the representative of the other Germany through intellectual and cultural means and media.

The goal which the members and patrons of the Academy felt themselves bound to pursue was that of maintaining awareness that this other Germany of justice, freedom and human dignity persisted even amid the emotional turbulence of war, and of keeping alive the general will to preserve that Germany despite the obscenities of Hitler's regime. Now that the war had started, they pursued their campaign in the interests of preserving a basis for future peace. The fact that they had managed to take their message to a considerable section of the international public by intellectual and cultural means before the outbreak of war was hugely important – not least in political terms. It laid the foundations for what was, in the long run, a successful continuation of the struggle for peace based on understanding between nations – although from now on that struggle would depend more on political means and resources.

CHAPTER FIFTEEN

The Way Forward: The Continuing Influence of the Academy in Exile

> The millions of Germans . . . who never submitted to Hitler . . . have a
> right to be heard, and they did not dedicate themselves to the struggle
> simply to see their Reich destroyed and the present system of repression
> replaced with another one.
>
> Prince Hubertus zu Löwenstein in Der Aufbau (New York),
16 April 1943

> And so it was the émigrés who, throughout the world, saved both the
> German name and the awareness that there was always and for ever
> another, better, Germany.
>
> Gunter Groll, De profundis, 1946

When the American Guild discontinued its work on 10 January 1941, the German Academy in Exile lost its whole financial basis. This meant it would have to abandon its sponsorship and aid programmes, but it did not spell the end of its influence, which was far-reaching and by no means dependent on its existence as an institution. This influence had been built up through a worldwide network of writers, artists, architects and scientists in exile on all four continents. The presence and activities of these individuals were a convincing indication to the rest of the world that when, from 1933 onwards, Hitler's barbarous administration drove so many from their native land, the result was indeed, as Claus-Dieter Krohn termed it, the 'exclusion of a whole culture'.[1] Helge Pross described it even more vividly as the 'intellectual and spiritual decapitation'[2] of Germany. It was also abundantly clear that German culture, bloodily suppressed as it was inside the country, was now validly represented only in exile. Moreover, the Academy's success in creating worldwide solidarity among the émigrés made it easier for them to denounce the horror of National Socialism from exile and develop political concepts for post-Hitler Germany.

This was a task that became even more important after the outbreak of war. As we have seen, intellectual and cultural émigrés established firm and indispensable foundations for the politics of exile. Members of the Academy were also key participants in this political endeavour – not just in their own right, through what they stood for and did, but also through the organizations they founded or helped to found and which quickly began to turn their attention to the approaching peace and the construction of a future Germany. The individuals concerned were not just the 100 senators and members and the 163 scholarship recipients, but also a much broader selection of the Academy's co-workers, candidates, friends and patrons. Among them were political as well as cultural émigrés.

Thomas Mann, for example, became patron of the German-American Congress for Democracy, founded in June 1940, to which the former member of the Reichstag Gerhard Seger, who was now editor of the *Neue Volkszeitung* in New York, and Max Brauer, who had been mayor of Altona (in Hamburg) and a member of the former Prussian state council, also belonged. Brauer, a co-founder of the Guild destined to become mayor of Hamburg, was also one of the leading figures in the German Labor Delegation (GLD), established in 1939. The GLD really amounted to the representative in America of the Social Democratic Party, the leadership of which was based in London following Hitler's invasion of Czechoslovakia. Gerhard Seger and Friedrich Stampfer, who was the SPD's *éminence grise* both in Germany and then in exile and had edited *Vorwärts* as well as being a member of the Reichstag from 1920 until 1933, were both members of the GLD, as were Albert Grzesinski (the former Prussian interior minister and *Polizeipräsident* of Berlin), Rudolf Katz and other prominent Social Democrats. In its political blueprint for the treatment of Germany after the war, 'What Is to be Done with Germany', the GLD came out vehemently against enslaving and partitioning Germany. It advocated allowing Germans themselves to reconstruct democracy in their country and insisted on an internationally binding right of self-determination, so that territorial concessions could only be made with the consent of the population affected. At that time it was inconceivable that contraventions of international law could be backed by the Western Allies and followed by mass expulsions.

Grzesinski was also chairman of the German-American Council for the Liberation of Germany and, from 1941, of the Association of Free Germans. Other organizations which emerged to work on plans for Germany's future included the German-American Emergency Conference in New York (founded in 1942) and the German American Anti-Axis League in Chicago, both founded by the left-wing socialist Kurt Rosenfeld, and the American Friends of German Freedom, whose members included Academy and Guild representatives such as Thomas Mann, Paul Tillich, Frank Kingdon and Paul Kellogg.

Of outstanding importance was the Council for a Democratic Germany. It was a kind of exiles' council, co-founded and led by figures in or close to the Academy such as Heinrich Mann, Bert Brecht, Siegfried Marck, Lion Feuchtwanger, Veit Valentin, Wolfgang Stresemann, Fritz Kortner, Elisabeth Bergner, Alfred Kantorowicz, Erwin Piscator, Maximilian Beck, Karl Paetel, Hans von Hentig, Otto Zoff, Berthold Viertel and Herbert Weichmann. And just as the Academy was supported by an organization consisting of respected, influential Americans – the American Guild for German Cultural Freedom – so the Council had the American Association for a Democratic Germany, many of whose leading members also belonged to the Guild: Alvin Johnson, Henry Seidel Canby, Dorothy Thompson, Horace M. Kallen, Robert McIver, Lewis Gannett, Raymond Walsh, Rabbi Stephen Wise, Paul Kellogg and others.

Many of the émigrés in such organizations were vehement opponents of Britain's permanent under-secretary for foreign affairs, Robert Vansittart (chief diplomatic advisor to the British foreign secretary from 1938), and of America's secretary of the treasury, Henry Morgenthau Jr. In 1944 Lord Vansittart (as he now was), who had paid diplomatic court to Hermann Goering before the war, declared that all Germans would have to go down on their knees and beg forgiveness. Stampfer objected in the *Neue Volkszeitung*:

All? All? – Even the Germans in Dachau and Buchenwald? – Even those who were shot, beheaded, hanged? – Those who were driven out, deprived of their citizenship? – All those Goering hunted down like animals? – None of his fellow hunters? – None of the gentlemen from the Foreign Office? We, to our knees? After you, Lord Vansittart, after you![3]

One example from my own experience illustrates the profound impression some of these men and women made on those around them and the general public. In 1943, while I was his academic assistant, Prince Löwenstein gave lectures at Bowdoin College in Brunswick, Maine. The war was at its height. At the graduation ceremony, the dean, Paul Nixon, paid tribute to the visiting professor who had spoken of the 'true Germany', and said that those present wanted to thank him not in words, but by singing a hymn. He regretted that they were unable to sing it in German, but was sure that the prince would understand the message anyway. And then, as everyone rose – many of the thousand or so students were already in American army, navy or air force uniform – the organ began to play the German national anthem.[4]

Not only was a large part of the public welcoming and receptive, but, in America at least, the media were generally also very fair. In their pursuit of the common goal of peace and international understanding, émigrés were able to avail themselves of all the means by which public opinion may be influenced in a democracy: lectures, essays, readings, radio talks; the whole apparatus of a free press. Throughout the war, even when emotions were at their height, public debate in America was characterized to a quite astounding extent by independence of judgement and freedom of opinion, even with regard to the American government itself. Members of the Academy had no need to censor their public pronouncements, even if their opinions ran absolutely counter to official policy.

Nevertheless, speaking out did require a degree of courage, for the forces advocating the annihilation of Germany – such as the 'Society for the Prevention of World War III', led by detective novelist Rex Stout – were becoming increasingly vociferous. Support for them grew, of course, as more was revealed about the atrocities committed by the Hitler regime, about its inhumanity and the millions of murders of which it was guilty. This spawned, for example, the book by Tete H. Tetens (and with a foreword by Emil Ludwig!) entitled *Know Your Enemy*, which used quotations to try to prove

that Germans – including everyone from Wilhelm II to some representatives of the émigré community – were possessed of an
irredeemably evil collective character.

The American press, however, had little time for such aberra-
tions, tending to find them embarrassingly reminiscent of the tir-
ades of racial hatred from the likes of Joseph Goebbels and Julius
Streicher.[5] When members of the Academy or Guild wished to
protest that Hitler's dictatorship should not be equated with the
German people as a whole and to criticize the government – sometimes quite sharply – they were always able to find publications or
some other kind of forum prepared to carry their views. In 1943, for
example, Löwenstein wrote:

> The millions of Germans . . . who never submitted to Hitler . . .
> want a free Europe . . . They have a right to be heard, and they
> did not dedicate themselves to the struggle simply to see their
> Reich destroyed and the present system of repression replaced
> with another one.[6]

And at an official service held in New York in March 1945[7] to com-
memorate the twentieth anniversary of the death of Reich President
Friedrich Ebert, he declared that the degrading plans to annihilate
Germany after the war, to enslave its people and destroy its industry, were aimed not at Hitler and National Socialism (which would
have disappeared by then), but rather at the democratic forces to
whom it would fall to reconstruct the second republic from the
ruins and devastation left behind. Later that same year, in August,
he criticized the resolutions of the Potsdam Conference in damning
terms:

> Never were smugness, shamelessness, surrender of principles,
> stupidity and guilt so closely knitted into one . . . And then
> they talk about 'a just peace!' This is a willful deceit committed
> against the American people who would not stand for it, if all
> the facts were known.[8]

Dorothy Thompson, one of the American Guild's directors and a
journalist of international repute, was equally scathing about the
Potsdam Protocol in her 'On the Record' column in the *New York
Herald Tribune*, calling it 'the lowest debasement of American history . . . an appeal, not to reason but to revenge, and an invitation to

loot, plunder, starve, dispossess millions, smash Europe, produce chaos, divide the Allies . . .'. Thompson, who had once been expelled from Germany at Hitler's personal behest, fulminated: 'If there were a scrap of imagination, an iota of intellect, a modicum of historical perspective, a shred of democratic principle, or even a whiff of morality operating at Potsdam, it was never indicated.'[9]

The process of planning and constructing post-war Europe would have been a much smoother one if the Allied governments had been able to bring themselves to work with the German opposition movement. Right from the start, émigrés attempted to convince England, France, the United States and other powers of the threat posed by Hitler. They did their best to persuade these foreign governments to make common cause with exiles and the resistance movement in order to avert the catastrophe of war and ensure a future of peace and reconciliation. Had a government in exile been recognized – as those of the Netherlands and other states overrun by Hitler were – those goals would have been a step nearer.

There were plenty of moves towards creating such a government, with Hermann Rauschning, for example, the former president of the senate in Danzig, taking soundings in Paris and London even before the war. And from within Germany itself, representatives of the resistance repeatedly suggested to Allied governments that there should be some sort of anti-Hitler agreement: Count Gerhard von Schwerin did so as early as the summer of 1939, and was echoed by Carl-Friedrich Goerdeler and Pastor Dietrich Bonhöffer. In 1942 the same message was communicated by Adam Trott zu Solz, and later that year by the Englishman, Bishop Bell of Chichester.[10] The American press occasionally expressed expectations that a German government in exile would soon be recognized, as in the article published by the monthly magazine *Scoop* in November 1941, quoted above, speculating about its composition and duties. Löwenstein himself had developed concrete plans for a government in exile shortly before the United States was drawn into the war. These were published in *American Mercury*, also in November 1941. The aim was to create a psychological basis for a successful *coup d'état* by convincing the leaders of the German army and the population at large that there was a real chance of peace and of a rapprochement with Hitler's adversaries.

The governments, however, were not prepared to support such

initiatives for reasons of, as they saw it, *realpolitik*. Before the war, Prime Minister Neville Chamberlain's policy of appeasement was aimed not at toppling Hitler but rather at winning him as a partner to counter the growing might of the Soviet Union.[11] During the war, President Roosevelt brushed all else aside in pursuit of 'unconditional surrender'. He was determined to have a free hand when it came to deciding Germany's future and was not prepared to let consideration for the German opposition prevent him from making the country pay for what Hitler and his regime had done.

The idea of forming and recognizing a German government in exile came to the fore again when the *Nationalkomitee Freies Deutschland* (National Committee for a Free Germany, also known as the 'Free Germany Committee') was founded in Moscow in June 1943. Speculation immediately arose about whether this was the first step towards a government in exile under the Soviet aegis. At first glance there was nothing unreasonable in the manifesto issued by the Communist exiles, led by Walter Ulbricht, Wilhelm Pieck, Erich Weinert, Friedrich Wolf, Johannes R. Becher and an 'association of German officers' consisting of men such as General von Seydlitz, Lieutenant Count Einsiedel and Field Marshal Paulus, who had survived Hitler's disaster at Stalingrad:

> Hitler has been preparing for this war for years, without inquiring what the will of the people might be. Hitler has isolated Germany politically. He has unscrupulously provoked the three greatest powers in the world and united them for a ruthless struggle against Hitler's supremacy. He has made Europe the enemy of the German people and sullied that people's honour. He is responsible for the hatred surrounding Germany today. No external enemy has ever dragged us to such calamitous depths as Hitler . . . If, however, the German people takes its courage in its hands before it is too late and proves by its deeds that it wishes to be a free people, and that it is intent on ridding Germany of Hitler, it will win the right to determine its own destiny.[12]

There were also demands for the complete 'elimination of all laws based on nationalist and racial hatred', 'compensation for all victims' and the establishment of 'a rigorous court for war criminals, the ringleaders, the individuals behind them and their assistants'.[13]

We realized immediately that, however seriously many officers might take the manifesto, the Soviets and the Ulbricht-Pieck group viewed it as mere propaganda. It was not directed merely at the *Wehrmacht* and the German population: through the implied threat of a separate peace accord, Stalin hoped to exert pressure on the Western powers. In fact those powers had already excluded the possibility of a separate peace by demanding an unconditional surrender not just from the *Wehrmacht* but also from the German state. Now, however, Stalin wanted a second front – the American and British invasion of the continent – in order to lighten his own military burden. He also wanted recognition of all the territorial concessions which he had wrung from Hitler when they carved up Europe in the Ribbentrop-Molotov Pact.

Stalin had calculated correctly. Only a few months later, at the Tehran Conference of 28 November–1 December 1943, Roosevelt and Churchill agreed to all his demands, as well as to 'compensating' Poland for land annexed by the Russians with German territories in Silesia, Pomerania and East Prussia. Yet the Western Allies could quite justifiably have resisted Stalin's pressure and countered it by themselves recognizing and sponsoring a German government in exile. Löwenstein urged them to do just that when he wrote in the *New York Herald Tribune*:

> One may regret that the initiative was not taken by the Western powers a long time ago. According to a statement by the President [Roosevelt] of July 23, 'a lot of suggestions have been received in the last few years, but absolutely nothing has been done about it.' This I can readily confirm, for during the last ten years my republican friends and myself have urged, most unsuccessfully, the formation and recognition of a German national council in exile in the democratic world.[14]

He argued that now, however, the West would have to reconsider its attitude and offer encouragement and support to such a council, similar to that enjoyed by the Committee formed in Moscow.

The American Friends of German Cultural Freedom made an appeal to the government in Washington along the same lines. Meanwhile, an Organizing Committee was formed, becoming known informally as the 'Tillich Committee' after its chairman, Paul Tillich. Bert Brecht, Hans Staudinger, Carl Zuckmayer and

Hermann Budzislawski were all involved, as was Löwenstein; I also attended meetings occasionally.

It was this Organizing Committee that created the Council for a Democratic Germany, which included many Academy members and amounted to a Western council in exile. Constituted at the beginning of 1944, it involved all sections of the exile community in planning the reconstruction of Germany when peace returned to Europe.

On 3 May 1944 the Council issued a declaration, signed by 65 well-known exiles, about the form the new Germany should take. This enjoyed the emphatic support of the American Association for a Democratic Germany, which issued its own 'Statement Endorsing the Declaration of the Council for a Democratic Germany', signed by 57 prominent Americans including many of the American Guild's sponsors. The Council's declaration noted:

> It is inevitable that the German people will have to bear the consequences of the war into which *Hitler* has driven them. It is, however, self-evident that a lasting solution of the European question is only possible if there is a creative solution of the German question.
>
> The prerequisite for any such solution is the defeat of Nazism, the destruction of those who brought Nazism into power and the obliteration of its spirit in Germany and throughout the world . . .
>
> . . . It is taken for granted that Germany must return all conquered territory and that she must make good the damages she has caused to the limit of her ability. But it must not be forgotten the first victims of National Socialism were large numbers of Germans who dared to oppose *Hitler*, and who did not want this war . . . Policies leading to an enslavement of the German people and their pauperization must therefore be regarded as unwise and unjust . . .
>
> It would be disastrous for the future of Europe if Germany were to be dismembered and split up economically and politically . . .
>
> . . . German democracy, permanently secured, will prove to be Germany's main contribution to the peace of Europe and the world.[15]

The Organizing Committee had already formed several sub-committees, variously dedicated to drafting guidelines; to research (this was later divided into specialist areas of law and administration, economy, finances, education and science, art and press); to consulting with representatives of other European nations about how to solve post-war problems; to dealing with public relations in America; and to supervising prisoners of war. Several others were formed later. Together they soon created a comprehensive blueprint for post-war Germany.

This council in exile was intended to stand for the other Germany as a whole, with all the various political and ideological sections of society represented more or less in proportion to their general prevalence. The members included conservatives, Catholics, Protestants, Jews, democrats, liberals, socialists and even Communists. In order for the body to remain comprehensively representative, all its resolutions had to be passed unanimously. The Council for a Democratic Germany was thus closer to being a government in exile than any other émigré organization outside the Soviet Union. Even after the foundation of the *Nationalkomitee Freies Deutschland* in Moscow, however, the government in Washington could not bring itself to recognize the Council. Thomas Mann, who approached the US secretary of state regarding the matter, had already received a negative response from Assistant Secretary Adolf A. Berle on 25 November of the previous year. And when the Federal Council for a Just and Durable Peace, which was allied to the Council for a Democratic Germany, presented the same question to President Roosevelt in person, his reaction was reportedly 'devastating'.[16]

Nevertheless, the Council – like the Academy in Exile before it – did make an impressive and important impact on public opinion, as subsequent developments would show. Even before it was actually founded, there were several reports about it in the media. When the Council then stepped into the public arena by issuing the Declaration on 3 May 1944, there were detailed and positive commentaries the same day in major national newspapers and magazines such as the *New York Times*, the *Herald Tribune*, the *Nation* and *PM*. They demonstrated not only that it was generally taken for granted that German émigrés should be allowed to express their views about the approaching peace and the future of their country, but also that there was genuine interest in their opinions.

In the United States this impact on opinion was not restricted to particular groups or sections of society: it was a nationwide phenomenon. The American public's response to the Morgenthau Plan offered startling evidence of just how fair its attitude towards Germany – the real Germany – had remained even during the war, and of how effectively it was able to make itself heard even in opposition to its own government. Although Secretary of State Cordell Hull once estimated that Secretary of the Treasury Henry Morgenthau Jr's plan to divide Germany, flood the Ruhr mines and dismantle most industry would make it impossible for 40 per cent of the population to survive,[17] President Roosevelt had given it his personal seal of approval. He went on to have it endorsed by the Allies at the Quebec Conference of September 1944.

Then something quite extraordinary occurred. It was overwhelming and unforgettable even to those of us who had been living in America and had become familiar with the attitudes of its people. Thanks to an indiscretion, an American journalist learned the details of the top-secret Quebec resolution, which he promptly published. This triggered such a wave of outraged opposition to the 'project for mass starvation' that within a few days President Roosevelt – not wanting to prejudice his chances of re-election – found himself forced to deny that there was any such plan.[18] Before long there were assurances that the story was simply disinformation sown by Joseph Goebbels, whose horror stories about the victorious Allies' plans were part of his effort to maintain his hold over the German people to the bitter end.

The immediate and resolute popular protest against the Morgenthau Plan certainly reflects great credit on the American public and its unwavering sense of humanity. The opposition extended to the highest levels of government. One of the plan's most prominent critics was Secretary of War Henry L. Stimson, as the memoirs of General Lucius D. Clay make clear.[19] General Dwight D. Eisenhower, with whom Morgenthau discussed the plan in August 1944, shortly before the Quebec conference, called it 'silly and criminal',[20] and Secretary of State Hull openly opposed it after a second conference in Quebec. British Prime Minister Winston Churchill also initially resisted the American scheme, saying it would mean 'England's being chained to a dead body'.[21] When, however, Morgenthau helped him arrange an urgently needed loan of six and a half billion dollars, Churchill voted with the Americans at Quebec.[22]

At the time of the American public's protest it was not even generally known that, as John T. Flynn concluded in 1951, the so-called Morgenthau Plan was 'actually the Stalin plan'.[23] Morgenthau's closest associate was the deputy secretary of the treasury, Harry Dexter White, who was one of a small group of highly placed agents in the government working for the Soviet Union. In spring 1944 they received information from Moscow about the Kremlin's plans for Germany, basically corresponding to the Morgenthau Plan,[24] and were instructed to steer the US government towards a similar plan of its own. White was responsible for using Morgenthau to obtain Roosevelt's backing for the scheme. In 1948, when proof of this came to light and charges were laid against him, he committed suicide.

In retrospect, Stalin's goal seems abundantly clear. He hoped to set himself up as a friend to the Germans and win them over: his motto of 23 February 1942 was: 'Hitlers come and go, but the German people and the German state live on.' Hence also the founding of the *Nationalkomitee*. At the same time, however, Germany had to be left impotent, for he wanted not an equal partner, but rather a satellite at his beck and call. Yet it was the Americans who were to take the blame for destroying the country, for all the hunger and poverty, thus predisposing Germans towards Moscow's advances.

It is inconceivable that the protests which greeted news of the Morgenthau Plan would have been so spontaneous and so resolute if émigrés – particularly members of the Academy in Exile and the Council – had not been persistently reminding Americans that Hitler did not embody Germany. In their campaign, they were always able to point to opposition and inner exiles within Germany. Shortly before the Quebec conference, the conspiracy and attempted *coup d'état* of 20 July 1944, in which Colonel Count Claus Schenk von Stauffenberg tried to assassinate Hitler, provided graphic evidence that there was indeed domestic resistance to the Nazis.

The success of the émigrés in communicating their message to such a large section of the international public was certainly a consequence of the sheer numbers in which they had fled Germany, but it was the Academy members and other cultural exiles who lent the message its convincing profundity. This was not just because of the respect in which they were held, but also because of the growing recognition of their contribution to the development of culture, art and science in their host countries. Much has been written on this subject.

Claus-Dieter Krohn has observed that the way Germany's cultural elite was driven out struck intellectuals in the countries which received them as surprising, indeed amazing:

> In several studies of this phenomenon a parallel is drawn to the exodus of the Greek leading class after the Osmanian [i.e. Ottoman] conquest of the Byzantine Empire in the fifteenth century ... If the westward flight of the Greeks could be regarded as the starting point of the Renaissance and of Humanism, the expulsion of German intellectuals after 1933 seemed like the transfer of an entire culture, primarily to the United States.[25]

From 1933 to 1941 America was host to more than 100,000 German-speaking exiles, of whom 8,000 were academics and between 1,500 and 2,000 artists, writers, journalists or freelance intellectuals. The Nazis dismissed, transferred, or forcibly retired half of Germany's sociologists after 1933. Those who fled to America gave a major boost to sociology in their new home. The New York School for Social Research, led by Alvin Johnson, one of the American Guild's directors, was indebted to them for its swift progress in becoming the leading institution in its subject and acquiring the rank of a university – the 'University in Exile', as it was generally known. Nearly all the official bodies in America concerned with planning for post-war Europe turned to the New School for advice and information. Its Institute of World Affairs, founded in 1943, drew up a blueprint for peace in Europe. Members of the faculty, such as Arnold Brecht, who had in the meantime taken charge of a Government Structures Branch in the occupation, and Hans Simons, once a director of the *Hochschule für Politik* (University of Political Science) in Berlin who was now on General Clay's staff, advised the administration on the reconstruction of Germany. Amongst the matters they dealt with were a catalogue of fundamental rights and the problems of federalism, and they even gave initial consideration to the issue of a new currency.[26]

Two other subjects which were still in their infancy in the United States, art history and musicology, also profited greatly from the influx of German and Austrian academics, to the extent that America acquired a leading position in some fields.[27] In English universities, it was the émigrés who established art history as a respectable academic subject.[28]

Exiled representatives of the Bauhaus – particularly Walter Gropius, Mies van der Rohe, Erich Mendelsohn and Marcel Breuer – helped change the appearance of American cities such as New York, Chicago and St Louis. With their bold concrete, glass and steel constructions, and their radical reorganization of the syllabus particularly in Harvard and Chicago, they left their mark on a whole generation of architecture students and on American architecture in general.

Allan Bloom, by no means a friend of Germany, concludes: 'American university life was ... revolutionized by German thought.' Furthermore: 'Our intellectual skyline has been altered by German thinkers even more radically than has our physical skyline by German architects.'[29]

In Germany itself, the returning émigrés also contributed substantially to the spiritual and intellectual renewal of the country in both the political and the cultural spheres. Their influence, according to Claus-Dieter Krohn in the book on this subject that he edited with Patrick von zur Mühlen, 'was not restricted to the rebuilding of democracy in the early years . . . in fact it extended to the general modernization of German society and culture.'[30] One out of three intellectuals returned to Germany from exile.[31]

As Stimson showed,[32] and as Morgenthau's memoirs confirm,[33] policies in Washington continued more or less along the lines Morgenthau had advocated, despite the nationwide protests against the Morgenthau Plan which led to Roosevelt's denial. The occupying authorities were given strict instructions in the secret directive JCS 1067/4 of 26 April 1945: 'Germany will not be occupied for the purpose of liberation but as a defeated enemy nation.'[34] It was made equally clear to the military governor that no measures should be taken to normalize, encourage or even maintain economic activity. The period following Germany's surrender was a hard one indeed.

The turnaround came more quickly than might have been expected in view of the usual pace of international political processes. On 6 September 1946, the new American secretary of state, James Byrnes, gave his famous policy speech in Stuttgart, heralding a completely new approach towards the occupation:

> The American people who fought for freedom have no desire to enslave the German people . . .
>
> The United States cannot relieve Germany from the hardships inflicted upon her by the war her leaders started. But the United States has no desire to increase those hardships . . .
>
> The American people want to return the government of Germany to the German people. The American people want to help the German people to win their way back to an honorable place among the free and peace-loving nations of the world.[35]

This approach – diametrically opposed to the simplistic policies of vengeance – was in the spirit of the Academy and of the Council for a Democratic Germany's peace plans. It was an early signal that most of the schemes championed by the likes of Vansittart and Morgenthau would quickly turn out to be ill-conceived. None of those which were implemented after Roosevelt's death (or which it was too late to cancel) contributed anything towards a stable post-war political order. The only possible exception was the policy of de-nazification, which in fact coincided with one of the émigrés' principal demands.

Even so, soon after the end of the war it was also clear that the exiles' plans for a European and global community of reconciled peoples – which, even today, commentators sometimes dismiss as illusionary or even presumptuous – were actually, in many respects, astonishingly far-sighted. They were certainly prescient in looking forward to rapprochement and collaboration between eastern and western Europeans, as we are now seeing in the wake of the reunification of Germany, the collapse of the Soviet system and the growing cohesion of Europe.

Secretary of State Byrnes confirmed that the spirit of the exile community, speaking for the 'other' Germany, did indeed influence his attitude towards Germany. The president of Columbia University in New York, Nicholas Murray Butler, had given him a copy of Löwenstein's *The Germans in History* (published by the university's own Press in 1945) with the recommendation:

Prince Löwenstein's book just published on *The Germans in History* is in my judgement the best book that has ever been written by anyone in any language on the German people and their characteristics. It will be widely read not only in this country but elsewhere and will greatly aid our public opinion in dealing with the problems and the reorganization of the German State on a democratic and peaceful basis.[36]

Shortly before our return to Germany we learned from Butler – a friend of Byrnes – that the secretary of state had mentioned in a letter that the book did indeed influence the tenor of his speech in Stuttgart.

In July 1947, JCS 1067 was rescinded and replaced with the a new directive, JCS 1779. Then, on 17 December 1947, the American Congress approved a comprehensive programme for economic aid to Europe in the form of the Marshall Plan. After being admitted to the Organization for European Economic Co-operation (OECC) on 31 October 1949, the Federal Republic of Germany (West Germany) was also able to enjoy the benefits of the plan. On 19 October 1953 the country joined the West European Union and on 23 October of the following year it entered NATO. On 5 May 1955 the Allied Control Council was dissolved, thereby conferring full sovereignty, and on 25 March 1957 West Germany signed the Treaty of Rome to become one of the six founder members of the European Economic Community, predecessor of the European Union. Germany had, in the words of Secretary of State Byrnes in 1946, won her way 'back to an honorable place among the free and peace-loving nations of the world'.

In 1944 Prince Löwenstein had written:

After its liberation from the swastika, the other Germany, purified and steeled by so much suffering and pain ... and conscious of its Christian inheritance, will reassume its responsibility: the responsibility of being a country which seeks honour not through power and conquest, but in the service of the common ideal of the Western peoples. Many – famous and nameless – martyrs have bled for that ideal. Torture and death could not break their courage and their readiness to sacrifice themselves – for all the power on earth is not equal to their faith and their historic mission, to the creative forces of a living past and the pledge of a future realm of justice, peace and liberty.[37]

The success of the émigré community in maintaining awareness of this other Germany, even beyond the war and despite all the atrocities committed by the regime, represents its greatest, most admirable achievement. The German Academy of Arts and Sciences was one of the most effective mediators in that success,[38] and therein lies its historic significance. Moreover, its significance persists to this day. For it was this other Germany – represented by the exile community, the domestic resistance and those who went into inner exile – which was the inspiration for the founding of the Federal Republic of Germany. Irrespective of how many exiles had by then returned to their native land, it was the spirit of that other Germany which permeated our state and our society and which survives as a fundamental facet of our spiritual, intellectual and political existence.

CHAPTER SIXTEEN

Afterword: Resistance by Cultural and Intellectual Means

This book represents the first comprehensive account of the German Academy of Arts and Sciences, founded by Prince Hubertus zu Löwenstein-Wertheim-Freudenberg, and of its aid organizations, the American Guild for German Cultural Freedom and the Arden Society for Artists and Writers Exiled in England.

The fact that no such volume has appeared until now is all the more remarkable since, with Thomas Mann and Sigmund Freud as its presidents, the Academy in Exile united most of the members of Germany's intellectual élite – writers, artists and scientists – who refused to accept the Nazi regime from the start. By campaigning publicly and internationally on behalf of the other Germany – a civilized nation to which, despite the barbaric atrocities of Hitler and his henchmen, the future must belong – they helped prepare the intellectual ground for Germany's rapid readmission to the Western community of shared values after the war. Then in 1989–90, aided by the economic, technological and military power of the Atlantic alliance and the will for change among the forces of reform in the Soviet bloc, Germany was able to overcome its own division and lend momentum to the process of European unification following the collapse of the East–West conflict. In the wake of Gustav Stresemann's foreign policy, the members of the Academy in Exile had had a vision of a democratic Germany at the heart of an ever more unified Europe; that vision was now reality.

Yet in Germany – which foreigners still often refer to as the 'land of poets and thinkers' – the resistance of those intellectuals who went into exile from 1933 onward has nowadays been largely forgotten. This is not the consequence merely of our much-criticized reluctance to come to terms with a thousand years of history or of our selective memory, but also of a particular approach to culture in which there is often a stark contrast between reverent words and actual deeds.

The forgetfulness is even more astonishing when one considers that the Academy's archive survives intact and has been generally available as a part of the *Exilarchiv* at the Deutsche Bibliothek in Frankfurt am Main for more than 30 years. Moreover, in 1993 these collections went on show in Frankfurt, and subsequently in Leipzig, Bonn, Berlin and Erfurt, in an impressive exhibition called 'Deutsche Intellektuelle im Exil: Ihre Akademie und die American Guild for German Cultural Freedom' ('German Intellectuals in Exile: Their Academy and the American Guild for German Cultural Freedom'), accompanied by an outstanding catalogue.

The Academy in Exile had its headquarters in New York, and offices in Vienna, London and Paris. Its 100 senators and members and the 163 recipients of its scholarships, scattered among 27 countries, considerably enriched the arts and sciences in their respective host nations. After the war they contributed towards a modern, cosmopolitan culture in Germany, even if no German federal government, regardless of its political hue, ever made the gesture of inviting them to return.

The present volume is an eyewitness account and is based on personal experience, although it does, of course, also draw on the results of historical research, if only to ensure that events dating from over half a century ago have been remembered accurately and as vividly as possible.

It is to be hoped that this book will help broaden and deepen people's awareness that the Third Reich was not just a period of culprits and victims, but also of countless men and women who opposed the regime with their bodies and souls, often at the cost of their lives. They were to be found within Germany – in the resistance movement and in inner exile – and in exile abroad, where their resistance was by intellectual and cultural means. Together they were immensely effective, not least in a political sense. It should be noted that Germans of the Jewish faith were among the major contributors.

The book's author and its German publisher would like to thank all the many individuals and institutions who offered their moral and practical support to the project, and most particularly the long-serving director of the *Exilarchiv* at the Deutsche Bibliothek, Werner Berthold; his successor, Brita Eckert; and Frank Wende, all of whom were unflaggingly ready to help. The exhibition catalogue they put together with the archival assistance of Mechthild Hahner and Marie-Luise Hahn-Passera, and which was edited by Klaus-Dieter Lehmann, proved to be a most valuable resource in many instances.

We thank Prince Rupert of Loewenstein, Botho von Schwarzkopf and Wally Brack, along with Ursula Seuss-Hess (as director of the *Verband für Freiheit und Menschenwürde* and the *Union Deutscher Widerstandskämpfer- und Verfolgtenverbände*) and Georg Prinz, for their generous assistance, and, not least, Anita Krätzer for editing the manuscript so enthusiastically and knowledgeably. Concerning the English edition, the author is most grateful indeed to Professor Kenneth Newton for his invaluable advice and assistance, to Claudia Eisenring for her encouragement and most generous support, and in particular to Martin Bott, not only for his sensitive, precise rendition of the text but also for enriching it through so many references to the English translations, in all their various editions, of the German publications quoted in the book.

Volkmar Zühlsdorff, author
Ernst Martin, publisher

Notes

1 The Background

1 See W. Berthold (1981), *Die 42 Attentate auf Adolf Hitler*. Munich: Blanvalet, and also: A. Leber, W. Brandt and K. D. Bracher (1966), *Das Gewissen steht auf. 64 Lebensbilder aus dem deutschen Widerstand 1933–1954*. Berlin, Frankfurt am Main: Verlag Annedore Leber (English: (1957), *Conscience in Revolt; Sixty-four Stories of Resistance in Germany, 1933–45*. London: Vallentine, Mitchell); F. von Schlabrendorff (1984), *Offiziere gegen Hitler. Deutscher Widerstand 1933–1945*. Berlin: Ullstein (English: (1966), *The Secret War Against Hitler*. London: Hodder & Stoughton); D. Graf von Schwerin (1991), *Dann sind's die besten Köpfe, die man henkt. Die junge Generation im deutschen Widerstand*. Munich: Piper; A. Stahlberg (1987), *Die verdammte Pflicht. Erinnerungen 1932 bis 1945*. Frankfurt am Main: Ullstein (English: (1990), *Bounden Duty: the Memoirs of a German Officer, 1932–45*. London: Brassey's); P. Steinbach and J. Tuchel (1994), *Lexikon des Widerstandes 1933–1945*. Munich: C. H. Beck (English: (1997), *Encyclopedia of German Resistance to the Nazi Movement*. New York: Continuum).

2 Prinz M. von Baden (1927), *Erinnerungen und Dokumente*. Stuttgart: Deutsche Verlagsanstalt, p. 634.

3 Quoted in Prince H. zu Löwenstein (1984), *Deutsche Geschichte. Der Weg des Reiches in zwei Jahrtausenden* (8th edn). Munich, Berlin: Herbig, p. 528.

4 K. D. Bracher (1979), *Europa in der Krise. Innengeschichte und Weltpolitik seit 1917*. Frankfurt, Berlin, Vienna: Ullstein, p. 169.

5 Cf. Prince H. zu Löwenstein (1945), *The Germans in History*. New York: Columbia University Press, p. 440.

6 *Kunst der Zeit* Nos. 1–3, Berlin, 1928, 12. Quoted in B. Schrader and J. Schebera (1987), *Kunst-Metropole Berlin 1918–1933. Dokumente und Selbstzeugnisse*. Berlin, Weimar: Aufbau-Verlag, p. 36.

7 Quoted in P. Gay (1968), *Weimar Culture. The Outsider as Insider*. New York: Harper & Row, p. 108.

8 P. Klee (1920), 'Schöpferische Konfession', *Tribüne der Kunst und Zeit*, No. 13, 28–40.

9 Manifesto of April 1919, in H. M. Wingler (ed) (1962), *Das Bauhaus 1919–1933: Weimar, Dessau, Berlin*. Bramsche: Rasch, pp. 38–41 (English: (1969), *The Bauhaus: Weimar, Dessau, Berlin, Chicago*. Cambridge, Mass: MIT Press).

10 A. Whittick (1940), *Erich Mendelsohn*. London, New York: Faber & Faber, p. 64.

11 T. Heuss (1963), *Erinnerungen 1905–1933*. Tübingen: Wunderlich, p. 354.

12 W. Worringer: 'Fragen und Gegenfragen' quoted in J. Hermand and F. Trommler (1978), *Die Kultur der Weimarer Republik*. Munich: Nymphenburger Verlagsbuch-handlung, p. 130.

13 R. A. Bermann (i.e. A. Höllriegel) (1998), *Die Fahrt auf dem Katarakt. Eine Autobiographie ohne einen Helden*, ed. H.-H. Müller. Vienna: Picus, p. 84.

14 P. Gay (1970), *Weimar Culture: The Outsider as Insider*. New York: Harper & Row, p. xiv.

2 Prince Hubertus zu Löwenstein

1 Cf. also (in English) Prince H. zu Löwenstein (1968), *Towards the Further Shore*. London: Victor Gollancz, p. 425.

2 *Ibid.*, p. 80; cf. also Prince H. zu Löwenstein (1972), *Botschafter ohne Auftrag. Lebensbericht*. Düsseldorf: Droste, p. 57.

3 Prince H. zu Löwenstein (1931), *Umrisse der Idee des faschistischen Staates und ihrer Verwirklichung (unter Vergleichung mit den wichtigsten Gebieten des deutschen Staatsrechts)*, diss., Hamburg. Kirchhain: Zahn & Baendel, p. 61.

4 Prince H. zu Löwenstein (1937), *A Catholic in Republican Spain*. London: Victor Gollancz, p. 109.

5 Löwenstein (1937), *ibid.*, p. 148. (German: (1938), *Als Katholik im Republikanischen Spanien*. Zürich: Stauffacher).

6 Quoted in W. Berthold, B. Eckert and F. Wende (eds) (1993), *Deutsche Intellektuelle im Exil. Ihre Akademie und die 'American Guild for German Cultural Freedom'; Eine Ausstellung des Deutschen Exilarchivs 1933–1945 der Deutschen Bibliothek, Frankfurt am Main*. Munich, London, New York, Paris: K. G. Saur (Sonderveröffentlichungen/Die Deutsche Bibliothek, No. 18, ed. K.-D. Lehmann), pp. 110–11.

7 Löwenstein (1972), pp. 9 ff.; cf. also (in English) Löwenstein (1968), pp. 17–18 and 22–3.

8 Prince Löwenstein wrote several autobiographical works about his dramatic childhood and subsequent career: (1938) *Conquest of the Past*. Boston: Houghton Mifflin; and (1942) *On Borrowed Peace*. New York: Doubleday, Doran & Co. (both also published by Faber & Faber in London, 1938 and 1943 respectively) describe his childhood and his time in exile; his German career is covered by *Towards the Further Shore* (*op.cit.*); *Botschafter ohne Auftrag* (*op.cit.*); and (1983) *Abenteurer der Freiheit*. Frankfurt am Main, Berlin, Vienna: Ullstein.

9 H. Duderstadt (1933), *Vom Reichsbanner zum Hakenkreuz. Wie es kommen musste. Ein Bekenntnis*. Stuttgart, Berlin, Leipzig: Union Deutsche Verlags-Gesellschaft, pp. 31–2.

10 E. Anderson (1973), *Hammer or Anvil. The Story of the German Working-Class Movement*. New York: Oriole Editions, p. 145.

11 In E. Schumacher: Die Parteikonferenz vom 19. Juni 1933.

12 Prince H. zu Löwenstein (1934b), *The Tragedy of a Nation. Germany 1918–1934*. London: Faber & Faber, pp. 183 ff. Also (in manuscript form): Deutsche Bibliothek, Exilarchiv, Nachlass Prinz Löwenstein: Arthur Neidhart's letter to Löwenstein of 25 January 1965; Reuben S. Nathan, 'Zwei gegen den Maelstrom', West Redding, USA, 28 March 1983; Prince H. zu Löwenstein: 'Der 20. Juli 1932: Schicksalstag des Jahrhunderts'.

13 Löwenstein (1934b). Also published in America by Macmillan, New York; and in German and Dutch editions by Steenuil of Amsterdam as *Die Tragödie eines Volkes* and *De Tragedie van een Volk* respectively. All these editions appeared in the same year, 1934.

14 Prince H. Löwenstein (1934a), *After Hitler's Fall. Germany's Coming Reich*. London: Faber & Faber and (1935) New York: Macmillan.

15 Vienna, 10 September 1934. Bundesarchiv Koblenz, Nachlass Prinz Löwenstein.

16 Löwenstein (1934a), p. 62.

17 R. A. Bermann, *Deutsche Freistatt. Eine Denkschrift, dem Prinzen Hubertus Friedrich zu Löwenstein überreicht von Arnold Höllriegel* (A German Sanctuary. A Memorandum presented to Prince Hubertus Friedrich zu Löwenstein by Arnold Höllriegel), p. 24. Bundesarchiv Koblenz, Nachlass Richard Bermann. See Appendix 1 to the present volume.
18 Löwenstein (1942), pp. 46–7.
19 *Ibid.*
20 'Prinz Löwenstein stellt sich vor', *Sonntagsblatt der New Yorker Staatszeitung und Herold*, 3 February 1935.
21 *Los Angeles Times*, 6 February 1935.
22 Berthold, Eckert, Wende (eds) (1993), p. 57.
23 Cf. Löwenstein (1983), p. 147.
24 German consulate general in San Francisco to the German embassy in Washington, 27 February 1935, Auswärtiges Amt (Foreign Ministry), Bonn; also in Löwenstein (1983), p. 149.
25 Prince H. zu Löwenstein (1935), 'Eine Reise nach Amerika', *Der Wiener Tag*, 24 March.
26 E. and K. Mann (1939), *Escape to Life*. Boston: Houghton Mifflin, p. 309. Published in German as (1991), *Escape to Life. Deutsche Kultur im Exil*. Munich: Edition Spangenberg; paperback edition (1996), Reinbek bei Hamburg: Rowohlt.

3 Richard Arnold Bermann

1 *Berliner Tageblatt*, 7 November 1929, insert 1.
2 Cf. Löwenstein (1968), p. 136.
3 M. Ondaatje (1992), *The English Patient*. London: Bloomsbury.
4 In January 1934 Bermann gave a lecture to the Royal Geographical Society on 'Historic Problems of the Libyan Desert'; cf. (1933), 'Tagebuch von der Saharafahrt' [Sahara Expedition Diary]: Deutsche Bibliothek, Exilarchiv, Nachlass Richard Bermann, pp. 45–6.
5 L. E. Almásy (1939), *Unbekannte Sahara. Mit Flugzeug und Auto in der Libyschen Wüste*. Leipzig: Brockhaus. New edition: (1997) *Schwimmer in der Wüste. Auf der Suche nach der Oase Zarzura*. Innsbruck: Haymon. (No English translation appears to have been published to date.)
6 H.-H. Müller and B. Eckert (eds) (1995), *Richard A. Bermann alias Arnold Höllriegel. Österreicher – Demokrat – Weltbürger. Eine Ausstellung des Deutschen Exilarchivs 1933–1945. Die Deutsche Bibliothek, Frankfurt am Main*. Munich, New Providence, London, Paris: K. G. Saur (Sonderveröffentlichungen/Die Deutsche Bibliothek, No. 22, ed. K.-D. Lehmann).
7 R. A. Bermann (i.e. A. Höllriegel) (1998), *Die Fahrt auf dem Katarakt. Eine Autobiographie ohne einen Helden*, ed. H.-H. Müller. Vienna: Picus.
8 R. A. Bermann (1933), p. 3.
9 Quoted in Löwenstein (1942), pp. 29–30.
10 *Ibid.*, p. 30.
11 Hermann Broch: 'Nachruf', 1939, quoted in Müller and Eckert (eds) (1995), p. 2.
12 Quoted in Berthold, Eckert and Wende (eds) (1993), p. 37.
13 Quoted *ibid.*, p. 38.
14 Quoted *ibid.*
15 Quoted *ibid.*
16 R. A. Bermann, *Deutsche Freistatt. Eine Denkschrift* – see Appendix 1 to the present volume. In his books in English, Löwenstein termed the 'sanctuary' (*Freistatt*) a 'homestead' – cf. for example Löwenstein (1968), p. 157.

17 Cf. Berthold, Eckert and Wende (eds) (1993), p. 119, and Müller and Eckert (eds) (1995), p. 334.
18 Deutsche Bibliothek, Exilarchiv.
19 Bundesarchiv Koblenz.
20 Bundesarchiv Koblenz, Nachlass Hubertus Prinz zu Löwenstein. Extracts quoted in Berthold, Eckert and Wende (eds) (1993), pp. 113–14.
21 Quoted in Berthold, Eckert and Wende (eds) (1993), p. 119.
22 Cf. Müller and Eckert (eds) (1995), p. 393.
23 Quoted *ibid.*, p. 392.
24 Alfred Polgar, *Die Zukunft*, 10 November 1939, 5.

4 The American Guild for German Cultural Freedom

1 Löwenstein (1968), p. 87.
2 See H. Villard (1904), *Memoirs of Henry Villard. Journalist and Financier*, 2 vols. Boston, New York: Houghton Mifflin.
3 O. G. Villard (1933), *The German Phoenix. The Story of the Republic*. New York: Harrison Smith & Robert Haas, foreword.
4 See Appendix 1.
5 'Certificate of Incorporation of American Guild for German Cultural Freedom', 4 April 1935. Bundesarchiv Koblenz.
6 *Ibid.*
7 Vienna, 6 August 1935.
8 Since the purpose, aims and duties of the Guild were already laid down in the official Certificate of Incorporation, the 'By-Laws' approved by the board set out its internal regulations, organs and offices and the corresponding responsibilities. Cf. Berthold, Eckert and Wende (eds) (1993), pp. 71–2.
9 Quoted in P. Kurth (1990), *American Cassandra. The Life of Dorothy Thompson*. Boston, Toronto, London: Little, Brown, p. 364.
10 *Ibid.*, p. 365.
11 *Ibid.*, p. 372.
12 *Jewish Exponent*, Philadelphia, Pennsylvania, 18 December 1936.
13 Löwenstein (1972), p. 130; cf. also (in English) Löwenstein (1968), pp. 171–3.

5 The German Academy of Arts and Science in Exile

1 Cf. Prince Hubertus zu Löwenstein's letter to Fritz Demuth, quoted in Berthold, Eckert and Wende (eds) (1993), p. 72.
2 C. J. Leuchtenberg (i.e. Peter de Mendelssohn) (1935), *Wolkenstein*. Vienna, Leipzig: R. A. Höger.
3 P. Wedekind Regnier (1978), 'Beheimatet in dieser Welt', in J. H. Freund (ed), *Unterwegs. Peter de Mendelssohn zum 70. Geburtstag*. Frankfurt am Main: S. Fischer, p. 11.
4 See Appendix 2.
5 Bundesarchiv Koblenz, Nachlass Hubertus Prinz zu Löwenstein.
6 On 30 July 1936, for example, Mendelssohn wrote to Alfred Neumann in Fiesole, near Florence, telling him that the Academy would like to found institutions such as the following:

> 1. An organization for exchanges of non-Nazi students between Europe and America. There are presently twelve annual scholarships available for this organization, enabling non-Nazi German students living in exile to visit

American universities. A special committee has been formed which is responsible for allotting these scholarships. Its chairman is the former editor of *The Nation*, Oswald Garrison Villard.

2.   The creation of a comprehensive, non-Nazi library and associated archive. In this the Guild will collaborate with institutions of the same sort which already exist in Europe, and in particular with the newly founded 'Institute for Central European Affairs', led by Dr G. P. Gooch in London.

3.   The creation of a book club modelled on the American book guilds, with the aim of helping German books achieve the general impact they have failed to make for so long, as well as increasing their sales very substantially.

4.   The creation of an organization which will enable those German writers, artists and scientists who are as yet unknown or little known in America to draw themselves to the attention of the American public through lecture tours, thus winning new, potent opportunities . . .

5.   Finally, the creation of a journal or bulletin to appear under the Academy's auspices and publicise the progress of non-Nazi German cultural activity in the United States and elsewhere. It will serve as a mouthpiece for the members of the Academy, their friends, supporters and patrons. This bulletin will be published in English in New York and in German and French in Paris.

(Deutsche Bibliothek, Exilarchiv).

7   Deutsche Bibliothek, Exilarchiv.
8   G. Mann (1978), 'Festvortrag', in J. H. Freund (ed), *Unterwegs. Peter de Mendelssohn zum 70. Geburtstag*. Frankfurt am Main: S. Fischer, p. 54.
9   Letter by Löwenstein from the Isle aux Moines, 8 July 1938, reprinted in Berthold, Eckert and Wende (eds) (1993), p. 223.
10 A. Söllner (1996), *Deutsche Politikwissenschaftler in der Emigration. Studien zu ihrer Akkulturation und Wirkungsgeschichte*. Opladen: Westdeutscher Verlag, p. 250.

6 Thomas Mann

1   T. Mann (1978), *Tagebücher 1935–1936*, ed. P. de Mendelssohn. Frankfurt am Main: S. Fischer, p. 330 (English: for an abridged translation of Mann's diaries in the period dealt with in this chapter, but not including this entry, see (1982), *Thomas Mann Diaries 1918–1939* (selection and foreword by H. Kesten, trans. R. and C. Winston). New York: Harry N. Abrams).
2   Cf. *Börsenblatt des deutschen Buchhandels*, 14 October 1933.
3   T. Mann (1935), *Leiden und Grösse der Meister*. Berlin: S. Fischer.
4   T. Mann (1977), *Tagebücher 1933–1934*, ed. P. de Mendelssohn. Frankfurt am Main: S. Fischer, p. 356.
5   Cf. G. Bermann-Fischer (1967), *Bedroht – Bewahrt, Weg eines Verlegers*. Frankfurt am Main: S. Fischer, p. 87.
6   *Neue Zürcher Zeitung*, 4 February 1936. Reprinted in T. Mann (1961–5), *Briefe*, ed. E. Mann (3 vols). Frankfurt am Main: S. Fischer; Vol. 1 (1961), *1889–1936*, pp. 409–13. (An English translation of the letter appears in the first volume of (1970), *Letters of Thomas Mann, 1889–1955* (selected and trans. R. and C. Winston, 2 vols). London: Secker & Warburg, pp. 244–9.) Mann quotes August von Platen's poem beginning 'Es sehnt sich ewig dieser Geist ins Weite' in (1982), *Werke in zwei Bänden*, ed. K. Wölfel and J. Link. Munich: Winkler; Vol. 2 (*Lyrik*), pp. 399–400.
7   Deutsche Bibliothek, Exilarchiv.
8   Quoted from the *New York Times*, 12 December 1936. Mann's article is reprinted in German under the title 'Die deutsche Akademie in New York' in T. Mann (1986), *An die*

gesittete Welt. Frankfurt am Main: S. Fischer (Vol. 20 of (1980–86), *Gesammelte Werke in Einzelbänden: Frankfurter Ausgabe*, ed. P. de Mendelssohn), pp. 154–60.

9 Quoted in English in T. Mann (1961), p. 362.

10 Cf. K. Harpprecht (1995), *Thomas Mann. Eine Biographie*. Reinbek bei Hamburg: Rowohlt, p. 915.

11 Quoted in P. E. Hübinger (1974), *Thomas Mann, die Universität Bonn und die Zeitgeschichte. Drei Kapitel deutscher Vergangenheit aus dem Leben des Dichters. 1905–1955.* Munich, Vienna: Oldenbourg Verlag, p. 182.

12 Auswärtiges Amt (Foreign Ministry), Bonn. Reprinted in Berthold, Eckert and Wende (eds) (1993), pp. 90–1.

13 T. Mann (1980), *Tagebücher 1937–1939*, ed. P. de Mendelssohn. Frankfurt am Main: S. Fischer, p. 3 (and in English in (1982) *Thomas Mann Diaries 1918–1939*, *op.cit.*, p. 269).

14 Letter to Wilbur L. Cross quoted in Berthold, Eckert and Wende (eds) (1993), p. 96.

15 Quoted *ibid.*

16 Quoted *ibid.*, p. 98.

17 Quoted from the English text preserved in the Deutsche Bibliothek, Exilarchiv. The German version of the same text, entitled 'Zur Gründung der American Guild for German Cultural Freedom und der Deutschen Akademie', appears in T. Mann (1986), pp. 177–81.

18 Quoted in Berthold, Eckert and Wende (eds) (1993), p. 100.

19 Heywood Brown in the *New York World Telegram*, 22 April 1937.

20 T. Mann (1986), p. 188. (An English translation of the essay, 'Mass und Wert', appears in T. Mann (1942), *Order of the Day. Political Essays and Speeches of Two Decades*. New York: Knopf.)

21 Quoted in Berthold, Eckert and Wende (eds) (1993), p. 108.

22 E. and K. Mann (1939), *Escape to Life*. Boston: Houghton Mifflin, p. 314. German edition subtitled *Deutsche Kultur im Exil* (1996). Reinbek bei Hamburg: Rowohlt, pp. 336–7.

23 Prince H. zu Löwenstein in *Die Neue Weltbühne*, 6 May 1937. Quoted in Berthold, Eckert and Wende (eds) (1993), p. 109.

7 Sigmund Freud

1 Cf. Löwenstein (1942), p. 217.

2 Quoted *ibid.*

3 *Ibid.*, p. 219.

4 6 June 1938. Quoted in E. Freud, L. Freud and I. Grubrich-Simitis (eds) (1976), *Sigmund Freud. Sein Leben in Bildern und Texten*. Frankfurt am Main: Suhrkamp, p. 295 (English: (1978), *Sigmund Freud: His Life in Pictures and Words*. London: A. Deutsch).

5 Cf. Löwenstein (1942), p. 218.

6 Bermann (1998), p. 328.

7 Quoted in Müller and Eckert (eds) (1995), p. 386.

8 Sigmund Freud in a letter of 8 June 1938. Quoted *ibid.*, p. 385.

9 Quoted in Berthold, Eckert and Wende (eds) (1993), p. 220.

10 Quoted *ibid.*, p. 221.

11 Ile aux Moines, France, 9 July 1938. Quoted *ibid.*, pp. 224–5.

12 Quoted *ibid.*, p. 225.

13 'Die Stellung Freuds in der modernen Geistesgeschichte', in T. Mann (1982), *Leiden und Grösse der Meister*. Frankfurt am Main: S. Fischer (Vol. 8 of (1980–86) *Gesammelte Werke* in Einzelbänden: Frankfurter Ausgabe, ed. P. de Mendelssohn), p. 902.

14 T. Mann (1988), *Briefwechsel mit Autoren*, ed. H. Wysling. Frankfurt am Main: S. Fischer, p. 183.

15 Quoted in S. Freud (1960), *Briefe 1873–1939*, ed. E. L. Freud. Frankfurt am Main: S. Fischer, p. 419 (English: (1970), *Letters of Sigmund Freud, 1873–1939*, ed. E. L. Freud, trans. T. and J. Stern. London: Hogarth Press).

16 Quoted in S. Freud/A. Zweig (1968), *Briefwechsel*, ed. E. L. Freud. Frankfurt am Main: S. Fischer, p. 117 (English: (1970), *The Letters of Sigmund Freud and Arnold Zweig*, ed. E. L. Freud. London: Hogarth Press for the Institute of Psycho-Analysis).

17 K. Mann (1989–91), *Tagebücher*, ed. J. Heimannsberg, P. Laemmle and W. F. Schoeller. Munich: Edition Spangenberg; vol. 3 (1990), *1936–37*, p. 60.

18 See Appendix 3.

19 Quoted in Berthold, Eckert and Wende (eds) (1993), pp. 225–6.

20 Quoted *ibid.*, pp. 228–9.

21 Quoted *ibid.*

22 Letter from Prince Hubertus zu Löwenstein to Sigmund Freud, 26 July 1938, quoted in Berthold, Eckert and Wende (eds) (1993), p. 229.

23 *Ibid.*

24 Letter from Sigmund Freud to Prince Hubertus zu Löwenstein, 7 August 1938. Quoted *ibid.*, p. 230.

25 Letter from Prince Hubertus zu Löwenstein to Sigmund Freud, 23 February 1939. Quoted *ibid.*, p. 261.

8 Rudolf Olden

1 See the chapter about Prince Hubertus zu Löwenstein in the present volume.

2 B. Olden (1977), *Das Paradies des Teufels. Biographisches und Autobiographisches. Schriften und Briefe aus dem Exil*, ed. R. Greuner. Berlin: Rütten und Loening, p. 16.

3 R. Olden (1938), 'Nachruf auf einen Freund', *Das Neue Tagebuch*, Paris, 5 February, 141.

4 R. Olden (1933), *Hitler der Eroberer. Die Entlarvung einer Legende. Von einem deutschen Politiker*. Berlin, Prague: Malik. Later published in an English translation as *Hitler the Pawn* (see below).

5 R. Olden (1934), *Das Schwarzbuch. Tatsachen und Dokumente: Die Lage der Juden in Deutschland*. Paris: Comité des Délégations Juives.

6 Reprinted in *Die neue Weltbühne*, Prague, No. 24, 15 June 1933, 743–4.

7 Cf. *P.E.N. News*, London, No. 59, November 1933, 4.

8 W. Berthold and B. Eckert (1980), *Der deutsche P.E.N. Club im Exil 1933–1948. Eine Ausstellung der Deutschen Bibliothek* (Sonderveröffentlichungen/Deutsche Bibliothek, No.10, ed. G. Pflug). Frankfurt am Main: Buchhändler-Vereinigung, p. 46.

9 Cf. *ibid.*, p. 51.

10 Reprinted *ibid.*, p. 82.

11 Letter from Rudolf Olden to Thomas Mann, London, 8 May 1934, reprinted *ibid.*, p. 83.

12 Letter from Heinrich Mann to Rudolf Olden, Nice, 1 March 1935, reprinted *ibid.*, p. 128.

13 *P.E.N. News*, London, No. 65, September 1934.

14 Cf. Berthold and Eckert (eds) (1980), p. 113; *P.E.N. News*, London, No. 72, June 1935, 5; 'Der P.E.N. Club in Barcelona', *Die Sammlung*, Amsterdam, July 1935, 662.

15 'Deutsche Schriftsteller im Exil', *Ost und West I*, No. 4, 1947, 47 ff.

16 According to the membership list of 18 November 1938. Cf. Berthold and Eckert (eds) (1980), p. 254. Other names were added later.

17 Cf. Berthold, Eckert and Wende (eds) (1993), p. 108.

18 Letter from Rudolf Olden to Richard Bermann, Oxford, 1 December 1938, Deutsche Bibliothek, Exilarchiv.

19 Cf. Rudolf Olden, 26 February 1939, Deutsche Bibliothek, Exilarchiv.

20 Quoted in Berthold and Eckert (eds) (1980), p. 325.
21 Cf. *P.E.N. News*, London, No. 106, October 1939, 5–7.
22 Rudolf Olden quoted in Berthold and Eckert (eds) (1980), p. 343.
23 Quoted *ibid.*, p. 206.
24 7 September 1939, quoted *ibid.*, p. 327.
25 Quoted in Peter Olden's obituary of his brother Rudolf and the latter's wife, Deutsche Bibliothek, Exilarchiv. Here taken from Prince H. zu Löwenstein (1943), *On Borrowed Peace*. London: Faber & Faber, pp. 280–1.
26 London, 15 August 1940, quoted in Berthold and Eckert (eds) (1980), pp. 346–8.
27 Cf. Gilbert Murray's foreword to R. Olden (1946), *The History of Liberty in Germany*. London: Gollancz, p. 6, and the correspondence between Rudolf and Peter Olden: C. Brinson and M. Malet (eds) (1987), *Rudolf Olden – Peter Olden: Briefe aus den Jahren 1935–1936*. Berlin: Verlag Europäische Ideen (No. 64), p. 13.

9 The Arden Society

1 A. Koestler (1954), *The Invisible Writing*. London: Collins with Hamish Hamilton, p. 425.
2 J. Willett (1984), 'The Emigration and the Arts', in G. Hirschfeld (ed), *Exile in Great Britain – Refugees from Hitler's Germany*. Leamington Spa: Berg and New Jersey: Humanities Press (for the German Historical Institute, London), pp. 209–10.
3 H. Krug (1986), 'Exil und Rückkehr. Hilde Spiel im Gespräch', in Neue Gesellschaft für Bildende Kunst, Berlin, (ed.) *Kunst im Exil in Grossbritannien 1933–1945*. Berlin: Frölich & Kaufmann, p. 289.
4 London, December 1933.
5 Deutsche Bibliothek, Exilarchiv.
6 Löwenstein (1942), p. 174.
7 See Appendix 4.
8 Deutsche Bibliothek, Exilarchiv.
9 *Ibid.*
10 *Ibid.*
11 Leaflet: *The Arden Society – For Artists and Writers Exiled in England*. Texts and lists of the sponsors and directors. Deutsche Bibliothek, Exilarchiv.
12 London, No. 1965, 22 February 1939, p. 338.
13 Letter from Rudolf Olden to Prince Hubertus zu Löwenstein, Oxford, 13 April 1939. Quoted in Berthold, Eckert and Wende (eds) (1993), pp. 262–3.
14 Cf. Bundesarchiv Koblenz, Nachlass Hubertus Prince zu Löwenstein.
15 Memorandum from Volkmar Zühlsdorff to Oswald Garrison Villard, treasurer of the American Guild, 15 January 1940, and letter from Villard to the treasurer of the Arden Society, 23 January 1940, Deutsche Bibliothek, Exilarchiv, Personalakte Ludwig Winder.

10 Jesse Thoor

1 Translator's note: In endeavouring to convey the sense and the rhythm of the sonnets quoted in this chapter as accurately as possible, I have had to sacrifice the rhyme-schemes. The original German is included to mitigate somewhat my disservice to the poet.
2 Brno (German: Brünn), August 1938: Deutsche Bibliothek, Exilarchiv.
3 J. Thoor (1956), *Die Sonette und Lieder*, ed. A. Marnau. Heidelberg-Darmstadt: Lambert Schneider (Veröffentlichungen der Deutschen Akademie für Sprache und Dichtung, Darmstadt, No. 7), p. 61.

4 Reprinted in Berthold, Eckert and Wende (eds) (1993), pp. 288–9.
5 Fiesole, 25 August 1938, quoted *ibid.*, p. 286.
6 Brno, September 1938, reprinted *ibid.*, p. 289.
7 Nice, 22 October 1938, quoted in G. Thom (1986), *Rufer ohne Fahne. Der Dichter Jesse Thoor*. Vienna: Österreichischer Bundesverlag, p. 118.
8 Sanary-sur-Mer, 21 October 1938, reprinted in Berthold, Eckert and Wende (eds) (1993), p. 286.
9 Brno, November 1938, reprinted *ibid.*, p. 290.
10 G. Thom (1986), p. 43.
11 Brno, 4 December 1938, reprinted in Berthold, Eckert and Wende (eds) (1993), pp. 290–1.
12 J. Thoor (1958), *Dreizehn Sonette*, ed. and with an afterword by Wilhelm Sternfeld. Stierstadt im Taunus: Eremitenpresse, 'Nachwort', p. 5.
13 G. Thom (1986), p. 40.
14 *Mass und Wert*, November 1939.
15 Alfred Marnau in his afterword to J. Thoor (1956), p. 142.
16 J. Thoor (1956), p. 75.
17 London, February 1940: Deutsche Bibliothek, Exilarchiv.
18 G. Thom (1986), p. 56.
19 Deutsche Bibliothek, Exilarchiv.
20 J. Thoor (1956), p. 72.

11 The Academy in Exile's Public Relations Work and its Influence

1 For example in the *Chicago Herald and Examiner*, 13 February 1935, quoted in Löwenstein (1983), pp. 148–9.
2 'William Tell', *B'nai B'rith Messenger*, Los Angeles, California, 2 June 1939.
3 Cf. *New York Times*, 10 April 1937.
4 *Citizen*, New York, 22 April 1937.
5 *Evening Sun*, New York, 12 April 1937.
6 *The State*, Columbia, South Carolina, 19 April 1937.
7 Cf. *Evening Sun*, New York, 12 April 1937.
8 Cf. Thomas Mann, *New York Herald Tribune*, 16 April 1937.
9 E. Toller, 'The Responsibility of the Writer', Deutsche Bibliothek, Exilarchiv. An abridged German translation appeared under the title 'Die Verantwortung des Schriftstellers' in *La otra Alemania. Das andere Deutschland*, Buenos Aires, December 1942, 10–12.
10 *Ibid.*
11 Thomas Mann: speech on the occasion of the American Guild dinner of 11 May 1938, here quoted from the English typescript preserved at the Deutsche Bibliothek, Exilarchiv. A German translation appears in Berthold, Eckert and Wende (eds) (1993), pp. 136–8.
12 *Ibid.*
13 *Ibid.*
14 New York Times, 12 February 1939.
15 *Chronicle*, 18 February 1939.
16 *New York Times*, 19 February 1939.
17 Quoted in Berthold, Eckert and Wende (eds) (1993), p. 267.
18 In the Academy archive there are over 300 cuttings on the subject, including some from Europe.

19 Cf. *New York Times*, 28 June 1939.
20 *Ibid.*
21 Cf. *ibid.*
22 Harold. L. Ickes, 'Culture Requires Freedom', Deutsche Bibliothek, Exilarchiv. Excerpts quoted in Berthold, Eckert, Wende (eds) (1993), p. 267.

12 Academy Scholarships

1 Quoted in Berthold, Eckert and Wende (eds) (1993), p. 119.
2 Quoted *ibid.*, p. 529.
3 *Wiener Arbeiterzeitung*, 11 May 1933.
4 Quoted in Berthold, Eckert and Wende (eds) (1993), p. 119.
5 'Report on the results of scholarships awarded by the American Guild', 1 November 1938, pp. 3–4, Deutsche Bibliothek, Exilarchiv.
6 Reprinted in Berthold, Eckert and Wende (eds) (1993), p. 336.

13 The 'Literary Contest'

1 Translated from the German, the original text in English having been lost.
2 The rules and regulations for the competition issued by the Guild and Academy were as follows (translated from the German information sheet, which is reprinted in Berthold, Eckert and Wende (eds) (1993), pp. 374–5):

Prizes: Total sum of $4,520

a) Little, Brown & Co. will pay the author of the best manuscript (novel or other) the following sums for the American and Canadian book rights: when the contract for the winning book is signed, an advance of $2,500.00 on the proportional royalties based on the US (retail) selling price – 10% for the first 5,000 copies, 12% from 5,000 to 10,000 copies and thenceforth 15%, including the usual Canadian royalties. Little, Brown & Co. receives 20% of the total revenue from publication of the book in instalments in the United States and Canada (pre-printing and post-printing).

b) William Collins, Ltd., London, will pay an advance of 200 English pounds on the usual royalties for the rights to publish the book in the British Empire except Canada.

c) Querido Verlag, Amsterdam, will pay an advance of $400 on the usual royalties for the rights to publish the book in the German language.

d) Albin Michel, Paris, will pay an advance of 10,000 francs towards royalties of 10% of the (retail) selling price for the rights to publish the book in the French language.

e) Sijthoff Verlag, Leiden, will pay an advance of 500 guilders on a royalty of 10% of the (retail) selling price for the rights to publish the book in the Dutch language.

Conditions

1. Only typewritten manuscripts of works which have never been published in book form, magazines or newspapers are eligible.

2. The manuscripts must be written in German.

3. Whatever the entrant's nationality might be, he must have been driven out of his original homeland for political reasons.

4. The manuscript must bear only the writer's chosen pseudonym, not his real name.

5.   The choice of theme is left to the author. The entry can be a novel or another kind of work. In the latter case, however, it must be a work of biography, autobiography, history, travel or adventure – in other words, a book for the general public, not an academic work! Albin Michel (the French publisher) and Sijthoff (the Dutch publisher) are, however, only interested in a novel.

6.   An entrant can submit more than one manuscript, but each must be submitted separately. Each must also be accompanied by a special declaration of consent.

7.   It is expected that all manuscripts, whether or not they are awarded prizes, will be offered to Little Brown & Co. and the other participating publishers; it will then be for the author and the publisher to agree terms.

8.   The author of the prize-winning book and those authors whose submissions have been accepted must declare their readiness to offer the publishers an option on their next two books; the conditions will then be subject to negotiation.

9.   The publishers plan to publish several other submissions apart from the prize-winning work, but they must reserve the right to reject all except the prize-winning manuscript if the judges award the prize. If the prize-winning manuscript is not a novel, Albin Michel and Sijthoff reserve the right to reject it . . .

13.   None of the judges will know the names of the entrants before the verdict.

14.   No judge may enter the competition . . . The judges reserve the right to reject all the entries . . . The deadline for submissions is 1 October 1938.

3 R. A. Bermann: letter to Stefan Zweig, New York, 2 December 1938. Quoted in Müller and Eckert (eds) (1995), p. 393.
4 Cf. contract between Little, Brown & Company and the American Guild, 7 October 1937, Deutsche Bibliothek, Exilarchiv.
5 Berthold, Eckert and Wende (eds) (1993), p. 394.
6 Contract between Little, Brown & Company and the American Guild, 7 October 1937, *op.cit.*.
7 Albin Michel to Volkmar Zühlsdorff, Paris, 8 April 1940. Deutsche Bibliothek, Exilarchiv.
8 'Memorandum zum Prize Contest der Guild', 11 December 1939. Deutsche Bibliothek, Exilarchiv.
9 In English: B. Brecht (1958), 'The Private Life of Mister Julius Caesar: An Extract', trans. Dorothea Alexander, *Nimbus / New English Review*, 4: 2, 2–13.
10 Deutsche Bibliothek, Exilarchiv.
11 R. Frank (1998), *Fair Play, oder Es kommt nicht zum Krieg. Roman einer Emigration in Wien*. Berlin: Aufbau-Verlag.
12 *Ibid.*, p. 345.
13 Quoted in *ibid.*, p. 323.
14 (1992) Ravensburg: Otto Maier Verlag (English: (1986), *No Hero for the Kaiser*. New York: Lothrop, Lee & Shepard).

14 After the Outbreak of War

1 Quoted in M. Flügge (1996), *Wider Willen im Paradies. Deutsche Schriftsteller im Exil in Sanary-sur-Mer*. Berlin: Aufbau Taschenbuch-Verlag, p. 88.
2 Cf. K.-M. Mallmann (1997), 'Frankreichs fremde Patrioten. Deutsche in der Résistance', in C.-D. Krohn, E. Rotermund, L. Winckler and W. Koepke (eds), *Exil und*

Widerstand. Munich: edition text + kritik (Gesellschaft für Exilforschung/Society for Exile Studies, Exilforschung Vol. 15), pp. 33 ff.

3 Deutsche Bibliothek, Exilarchiv; quoted in Berthold, Eckert and Wende (eds) (1993), p. 434.

4 *Ibid.*, p. 435.

5 V. Fry (1997), *Surrender on Demand*. Boulder, Colorado: Johnson Books, p. xii. First published: (1945), New York: Random House.

6 H. Sahl (1959), *Die Wenigen und die Vielen. Roman einer Zeit*. Frankfurt am Main: S. Fischer, pp. 256–7 (English: (1962), *The Few and the Many* (trans. R. and C. Winston). New York: Harcourt, Brace & World).

7 C. Misch (1941), 'Der gute Engel von Marseille', *Aufbau*, New York, 5 September.

8 Marseilles, 25 July 1941: Bundesarchiv Koblenz, Nachlass Prinz Löwenstein.

9 Washington, 13 May 1941. Quoted in Fry (1997), p. 251.

10 18 September 1941. Bundesarchiv Koblenz, Nachlass Prinz Löwenstein.

11 Cf. W. Schaber (1967), 'Ein unbesungener Held starb. Varian Fry half Tausenden von Flüchtlingen', *Aufbau*, New York, 22 September.

15 The Way Forward

1 C.-D. Krohn and P. von zur Mühlen (eds) (1997), *Rückkehr und Aufbau nach 1945. Deutsche Remigranten im öffentlichen Leben Nachkriegsdeutschlands*. Marburg: Metropolis, p. 8.

2 Quoted in S. Papcke (1992), 'Entlastet von Gemeinschaftsmythen. Anmerkungen zur deutschen Soziologie im Exil', in E. Böhne and W. Motzkau-Valeton (eds), *Die Künste und Wissenschaften im Exil 1933–1945*. Gerlingen: Lambert Schneider, p. 403.

3 *Neue Volkszeitung*, New York, 14 October 1944.

4 Löwenstein (1972), p. 207 and (in English) (1968), p. 262.

5 Thus the magazine *Common Sense* described the Society for the Prevention of World War III's hate propaganda as 'perhaps unique in the history of responsible journalism'. Cf. U. Langkau-Alex and T. M. Rupprecht (eds) (1995), *Was soll aus Deutschland werden? Der Council for a Democratic Germany in New York 1944–1945*. Frankfurt am Main, New York: Campus Verlag (Internationales Institut für Sozialgeschichte, Amsterdam: Quellen und Studien zur Sozialgeschichte, Vol. 15), p. 45.

6 *Der Aufbau*, New York, 16 April 1943.

7 At the Rand School for Social Science, New York, 2 March 1945.

8 *The Tablet*, New York, 11 August 1945.

9 *New York Herald Tribune*, 17 July 1946. Quoted in P. Kurth (1990), *American Cassandra. The Life of Dorothy Thompson*. Boston, Toronto, London: Little, Brown, p. 377.

10 Bishop Bell of Chichester put the following questions to the Allies on behalf of the exiles: would the governments be prepared to negotiate peace with a trustworthy German government after Hitler's demise, and to guarantee this to an authorized representative from the German opposition? Or, better still, could they make an unambiguous declaration to that effect? (Cf. Bishop Bell of Chichester (1945), 'The Background of the Hitler Plot', *The Contemporary Review*, October 1945, 207, and W. H. Chamberlain (1950), *America's Second Crusade*. Chicago: Regnery, p. 228.) Such a guarantee was vital to undermine the Nazi regime's propaganda to the effect that defeat would lead to the destruction of Germany. After British Foreign Secretary Anthony Eden had consulted with the American government, however, he responded negatively on 17 July 1942.

11 The policy of appeasement led logically to the Munich Agreement of September 1938. Only when Hitler unscrupulously broke that agreement by invading Czechoslovakia and subsequently extended the hand of friendship towards 'arch-enemy'

Stalin by partitioning Poland with him in the Ribbentrop-Molotov Pact of August 1939 did London perform its volte-face. Yet even then the British government remained unwilling to recognize a government in exile. At the start of the war Chamberlain declared in a radio broadcast: 'In this war we are not fighting against you, the German people, for whom we have no bitter feeling, but against a tyrannous and forsworn régime which has betrayed not only its own people but the whole of Western civilisation and all that you and we hold dear.' (*White Book* No. 1, 1939, issued by the British Ministry of Information). Under Churchill, however, and under Roosevelt in America, this view was abandoned. Not only did Roosevelt approve the Morgenthau Plan, but at the conference with Churchill in Casablanca in January 1943, he also pushed through his demand for unconditional surrender. The British military expert General J. F. C. Fuller points out that this demand was a foolish one, as the division and disarmament of Germany automatically left Russia as the greatest military power on the continent. Cf. J. F. C. Fuller (1949), *The Second World War 1939–1945. A Strategical and Tactical History*. New York: Duell, Sloane and Pearce, p. 355.

12 Quoted in B. Scheurig (1960), *Freies Deutschland. Das Nationalkomitee und der Bund deutscher Offiziere in der Sowjetunion 1943–45*. Munich: Nymphenburger Verlagsbuchhandlung, pp. 46–7 (English: (1969), *Free Germany; the National Committee and the League of German Officers*. Middletown, Connecticut: Wesleyan University Press).

13 Quoted in *ibid.*, p. 48.

14 *New York Herald Tribune*, 22 August 1943.

15 'Declaration of the Council for a Democratic Germany', quoted in W. Link (ed) (1968), *Mit dem Gesicht nach Deutschland. Eine Dokumentation über die sozialdemokratische Emigration* (Aus dem Nachlass von Friedrich Stampfer ergänzt durch andere Überlieferungen. Herausgegeben im Auftrage der Kommission für Geschichte des Parlamentarismus und der politischen Parteien von Erich Matthias). Düsseldorf: Droste Verlag, pp. 649–52.

16 Langkau and Rupprecht (eds) (1995), pp. 271–2.

17 Cf. C. Hull (1948–9), *The Memoirs of Cordell Hull* (2 vols). New York: Macmillan, Vol. II, p. 1617. See also H. zu Löwenstein and V. von Zühlsdorff (1957), *Deutschlands Schicksal 1945–57*. Bonn: Athenäum, p. 18.

18 Löwenstein and Zühlsdorff (1957), pp. 15 ff.

19 At this time the first directives from Stimson's ministry concerning the treatment of Germany after its defeat foresaw the destruction of the Nazi apparatus of power, but not the decimation of the German population. There was no intention to wreck the economy or explode the social order, no insistence on the idea of collective guilt and no ban on fraternization (cf. 'Allied Expeditionary Force, Supreme Headquarters, Handbook for Military Government in Germany', issued on the basis of the directives of 17 April and 24 May 1944 by Lieutenant General Walter B. Smith on the orders of General Dwight D. Eisenhower. Duplicated manuscript, undated). General Lucius D. Clay reported that Stimson had spoken to him and Eisenhower during the Potsdam conference about the policy the occupying forces were to adopt: 'He would have no part of a policy based on vindictiveness and was certain that the American people would in the long run give their approval only to an occupation which was decent and humane and which was conducted under a rule of law. He could see no purpose in the deliberate destruction of the German economy, because he was convinced that its reconstruction was essential to create an atmosphere in which it might be possible to develop a true spirit of democracy. He knew that the innate kindliness and decency of the American people would lead them to disapprove the exercise of our supreme authority in Germany in other than the traditional American way.' L. D. Clay (1950), *Decision in Germany*, New York: Doubleday, p. 54.

20 D. D. Eisenhower (1948), *Crusade in Europe*. Garden City, New York: Doubleday, p. 287.
21 Hull (1948–9), II, p. 1615.
22 *Ibid.*, p. 1617.
23 J. T. Flynn (1951), *While You Slept. Our Tragedy in Asia and Who Made it*. New York: Devin-Adair, p. 51.
24 *Ibid.*, p. 50. On the background to this, see also: W. Chambers (1987), *Witness*. Washington DC: Regnery; S. Tanenhaus (1997), *Whittaker Chambers. A Biography*. New York: Random House; E. Bentley (1952), *Out of Bondage*. London: Hart-Davis.
25 C.-D. Krohn (1993), *Intellectuals in Exile. Refugee Scholars and the New School for Social Research* (trans. R. and R. Kimber). Amherst: University of Massachusetts Press, pp. 11–12. (Originally published in German (1987), *Wissenschaft im Exil. Deutsche Sozial- und Wirtschaftswissenschaftler in den USA und die New School for Social Research*. Frankfurt am Main, New York: Campus.) And in the book accompanying the Los Angeles County Museum of Art's 'Exiles and Emigrés' exhibition, which was also shown at the *Neue Nationalgalerie* in Berlin in 1997, Martin Jay writes: 'No student of the forced migration from Germany to the United States during the Nazi era can fail to be impressed by the extent of its impact on the cultural life of the country to which its members fled.' (1997), 'The German Migration: Is there a Figure in the Carpet?', in S. Barron and S. Eckmann (eds), *Exiles + Emigrés. The Flight of European Artists from Hitler*. Los Angeles County Museum of Art, p. 326.
26 Cf. 'Let us be prepared to win the peace. Nachkriegsplanungen emigrierter deutscher Sozialwissenschaftler an der New School for Social Research in New York', in T. Koebner, G. Sautermeister and S. Schneider (eds) (1987), *Deutschland nach Hitler. Zukunftspläne im Exil und aus der Besatzungszeit 1939–1949*. Opladen: Westdeutscher Verlag.
27 C.f. K. Michels (1997), 'Transfer and Transformation: The German Period in American Art History', in S. Barron and S. Eckmann (eds), *op.cit.*, p. 304.
28 H. Möller (1992), 'Die Remigration von Wissenschaftlern nach 1945', in E. Böhne and W. Motzkau-Valeton (eds), *Die Künste und Wissenschaften im Exil 1933–1945*. Gerlingen: Lambert Schneider, p. 604.
29 A. Bloom (1987), *The Closing of the American Mind*. New York: Simon and Schuster, pp. 148 and 152.
30 Krohn and Mühlen (eds) (1997), p. 8.
31 Möller (1992), p. 610.
32 H. L. Stimson and M. Bundy (1945), *On Active Service in Peace and War*. New York: Harper & Brothers, p. 582.
33 H. Morgenthau Jr. (1945), *Germany Is Our Problem*. New York: Harper & Brothers, Introduction, p. 11.
34 JSC 1067, Part 1, Paragraph 4b, in US Department of State (Released March 1950), *Germany 1947–1949. The Story in Documents*. Department of State Publication 3556 European and British Commonwealth Series 9 (Division of Publications, Office of Public Affairs), p. 23.
35 'Restatement of U.S. Policy on Germany. Address by Secretary James F. Byrnes', *ibid.*, p. 8.
36 Löwenstein (1968), p. 282.
37 Prince H. zu Löwenstein (1944), 'Das Eine Deutschland', *Deutsche Blätter*, Santiago de Chile, No. 5, p. 11.
38 It is astonishing that the Academy in Exile remained largely unheard of in Germany itself for decades. Even most scholarly publications refer to it only fleetingly or not at all. The first academic work to deal with it appeared in 1989, not in Germany, but rather in the form of a dissertation at the University of Paris: Pascale

Eberhard's *Les jeunes exilés allemands 1933–1949: Analyse des conditions de la création littéraire en exile. Thèse de troisième cycle sous la direction de Gilbert Badia.* Then, in 1991, Klaus Amann (a professor in Klagenfurt) published his essay 'Die American Guild for German Cultural Freedom und die Deutsche Akademie im Exil (1935–1940)', as a contribution to a work about Austrian literature in exile: J. Holzner, S. P. Scheichl, W. Wiemüller (eds) (1991), *Eine Schwierige Heimkehr. Österreichische Literatur im Exil 1938–1945.* Innsbruck: Institut für Germanistik (*Innsbrucker Beiträge zur Kulturwissenschaft*, Germanische Reihe, Vol. 40), pp. 181–204. The Academy was honoured for the first and only time to date in the outstanding book *Deutsche Intellektuelle im Exil* ((1993) Berthold, Eckert and Wende (eds)), much cited in the present volume. This catalogue publication accompanied the impressive exhibition by the Deutsche Bibliothek, Frankfurt am Main, and was the work of Werner Berthold and Brita Eckert with Frank Wende, librarians Mechthild Hahner and Marie-Luise Hahn-Passera, and the library's general director, Klaus-Dieter Lehmann. The general silence surrounding the topic is all the more surprising given that the archive relating to the Academy and the Guild, which Prince Löwenstein and I brought to Germany when we returned from America in 1946, has been freely available for consultation at the Deutsche Bibliothek in Frankfurt since 1970. It runs to 14,000 letters, manuscripts, evaluations, reports on work in progress, testimonials, affidavits, photographs and other documents as well as 1,000 personal files. They form the basis of the holdings in the library's Exile Collections (*Exilarchiv*) and form its most used section.

Appendices

Appendix 1: A German Sanctuary. A memorandum presented to Prince Hubertus Friedrich zu Löwenstein by Arnold Höllriegel (excerpt, translated from the German)

I: Preliminary Remarks

My dear Prince Löwenstein: what follows is my attempt to put into writing the trains of thought we have so often pursued in conversation, so that you – from whom I hope and expect the realization of the GERMAN SANCTUARY – can forward what I have written to other persons and recruit new helpers on behalf of an idea; for we both believe that much depends upon the fate of that idea in the realm of reality.

Within a very brief period, Hitler's rule has, if not destroyed, at least crippled and weakened intellectual culture in the German Reich. This overwhelming pressure also weighs on the German cultural area beyond the Reich. Herr Goebbels's propaganda dictatorship has acquired direct power over publishing, theatre and cinema in almost the whole of the German-speaking region, but even in those places where there is resistance to so barbaric an invasion the poisonous ideology of National Socialism exerts a devastating influence on German spiritual and intellectual life . . .

When the Propaganda Ministry in Berlin threatened a few months ago to prevent the London publishing firm of Lovat Dickson from ever publishing further translations of German authors if it did not toe Herr Goebbels's line, it received the nonchalant response that this would not matter, as all the *good* German authors already lived abroad in any case.

Any German author writing for the 'émigré presses' (be he an exile, or – if he is the citizen of another country – at least one deprived of his spiritual home) has, quite apart from the personal distress and the economic catastrophe which the triumph of Hitler's barbarism represents for him, lost his sounding-board, that aura which beams back from the reader to the writer and renews his energy . . .

The same fate befalls the German actor deprived of the stages and cinemas in the German Reich, the painter: every creative artist. In the midst of a wonderful blossoming which had earned the respect and wonder of all other nations, German literature, German theatre and German cinema have suddenly been condemned to wither and die. Nothing worthwhile can grow in a field upon which a man such as Goebbels spreads his poisonous manure . . .

It will probably never be possible to make good all the damage that has been done, but it was and still is possible to counter it through intelligent organization. There are, after all, many millions of German speakers living beyond the Reich's borders whom Goebbels cannot send to a concentration camp when a book the Nazis have not approved is discovered in their library; hundreds of German theatres are thirsting for new plays and lively dramatic art; thousands of cinemas yearn for good German sound-films. The citizens of many other nations apart from Germany have hitherto constituted the audience for German intellectual and artistic production. Is this audience to be estranged from German culture because the Reich has betrayed its historic duty to export that culture to the rest of the world?

This German and non-German audience for German art beyond the Reich's borders might, of course, remain available to exiled writers or actors. Many 'celebrities' who have been driven from their homeland have indeed managed to earn a living in other countries where German is understood. The 'émigré presses' publish the works of famous writers, which are outlawed in the Reich; foreign theatres are ready to welcome prominent actors, even if these stars are unable to perform in the Reich. It is only in the German language film industry outside Germany that Dr Goebbels has managed to assert his dictatorship almost totally . . . .

What is a talented young author to do if he cannot prove either that he has the right kind of grandmothers or that his convictions are in accordance with the Party line? At best he can offer his manuscript to a publisher in Austria or Switzerland. Publishers in German-speaking countries outside the Reich fall into two categories: those who want to sell their wares within the Reich and those who have renounced that market. The first are careful neither to print any line that might incite the wrath of Berlin's Propaganda Ministry, nor to publish any author on Berlin's blacklist. Those publishers who do not care about Berlin's dictates, the so-called émigré presses, were founded in such numbers after Hitler's seizure of power that it has been impossible for any one of them properly to fly the standard for literature in exile as a whole. Nearly all of them survive on the reflected prestige of elderly, famous authors ... What is needed is a SANCTUARY ...

And yet it would be only too easy to save genuine German culture outside Germany.

II: The Structure of the 'German Sanctuary'

People and resources will have to be found. Somewhere in Europe a provisional headquarters has to be set up, an office to deal with the preparatory work – initially publicity and finance. The choice of location is important. At the time of writing it still seems possible that the German people of the Saar might reject Hitler in a great expression of their will, whilst still pledging themselves to the greater German ideal. If ... an independent German political unit were to develop in the Saar territory, determined to wait in total freedom for the moment that all Germany becomes free and German as well as European again – in that case a free Saar would be the proper place to found the German Sanctuary for Germany's hard-pressed culture. If we lose the Saar to Hitler, it will be necessary to seek a place where Germans live in freedom ... Practical considerations will probably make it wise to found a BOOK CLUB modelled on the large organizations for readers in Germany and elsewhere. This will probably be the easiest way ... to draw people together who do not wish to derive their intellectual nourishment from Herr Goebbels's apothecary of poisons. Once the future 'Sanctuary Publishing Co.' has attracted a few thousand readers with a few good publications, it can use a . . . magazine to help unite those readers more closely . . . for the 'German Sanctuary' *Film Society*, its *Theatre Society* and finally its *Lecture Society*.

The 'German Sanctuary' will be just what its name suggests: a sanctuary for the German spirit and intellect. That means that it will be tolerant and cosmopolitan in the best German manner. It will also stand in stark internal contrast to German National Socialism . . . Everyone involved in the 'German Sanctuary' must feel love, not hatred, for Germany – the real, indispensable Germany . . . It is vital never to forget that here people will be working for the Germany of the future, for the return of German culture from exile to its great home . . .

There are also Germans outside Germany, and the German-Americans in particular ought to be informed in the most urgent terms of the lofty aims of the Sanctuary movement . . .

III: The Book Club

For the reasons given above, it would be a good idea to begin by founding a book club for the 'German Sanctuary' . . .

IV: Filmmaking

Apart from German literature, it is German filmmaking that is in greatest need of a sanctuary. Indeed, perhaps its need is even greater, for good German books continue to appear despite Hitler and Goebbels, whilst German sound-films are hardly being made at all any more . . . Here again the main and ultimate focus must be not so much on famous figures and those who have already achieved success, but rather on youngsters, on those as yet unheard of, on those to whom the future belongs. It is for the new and, one hopes, totally different kinds of film *they* will create that we really need to prepare the Sanctuary. If I knew that the film studio I am campaigning for were destined to end up as nothing more than a German Hollywood, I would cease to take any interest in the matter.

V: Theatre

I know of a dramatic masterpiece in the German language that was completed in the first year of the Third Reich, but not, of course, within the Third Reich. When I say a masterpiece, I mean the accomplished work of a great master. In years to come, this great work of literature will occupy an honoured place in the annals of German drama. So far, however, it has never been performed anywhere; nobody is interested in staging it. This is a shameful chapter in German history . . .

Once again, our principal interest is in the next generation, in the future. Our young dramatists and actors must be helped to survive. Those already well known, the stars, must offer their help. It is *their* German theatre, the theatre which fills their lives, that they need to stand up for. Even those who can earn more money in English theatres will be called up to join this irregular army. Anyone who does not report for duty simply does not belong within its ranks. He does not belong to the future of German theatre . . .

VI: The Lecture Society

It may seem strange that this memorandum has dealt with literature, theatre and film, but not yet with German science – as though it were not equally vital to free its spirit from the intolerable tyranny, to gather its émigrés in a Sanctuary, to help its smothered voice to speak loudly and clearly again.

VII: Concluding remarks

My dear Prince Löwenstein, I have tried to trace out a great map in a brief sketch; you must found the empire it illustrates! . . .

It is, however, important never to forget that there can only ever be *one* real sanctuary for the German spirit: a liberated, reconstructed German Reich. Our little Sanctuary must aim, so far as possible, to bring the greater one closer. To that end we will build a site hut, a model, a nursery. And that is why we must never allow temporary details to distract us from our future purpose, from our great cause: the fight for the political, social, spiritual and intellectual freedom of all Germans.

Appendix 2: Memorandum on the establishment of a German Academy in New York, submitted through the American Guild for German Cultural Freedom, June 1936 (excerpt, translated from the German)

A year ago in New York a group of men

- aware that intellectual freedom, as the first and highest pre-requisite for all human and cultural progress, is faced with a bitter and desperate struggle for survival in many parts of the world at present;
- mindful in particular that this defensive struggle is raging most violently of all within the German cultural region and that the cultural tradition of the German peoples is being systematically suppressed and destroyed by a ruthless tyranny, so that it is currently quite impossible for it to continue within the frontiers of the German Reich;
- and possessed by the urgent desire to create an additional and highly effective instrument to enable Germany's exiled intellectual community of authors, scholars and artists to continue their work and endeavours and – as free human beings, beyond the menace of the merciless political forces set on eradicating the true essence of the German intellectual spirit and cultural ambition – to keep alive the tradition of German intellect, to carry that tradition forward and to preserve every branch of it with the greatest conceivable scope for the benefit of the world;

formed a pilot committee which has created the organization dedicated to putting these aims into practice.

This association is incorporated in New York under the name of the AMERICAN GUILD FOR GERMAN CULTURAL FREEDOM and has had local groups in several other American states and various affiliated committees for some time now. Among its founders are many outstanding individuals who enjoy eminence and influence in the United States . . .

This American organization, which is flourishing most encouragingly, has the goal and intention of securing the liberty and survival, for the present and the future, of a German artistic and scientific culture that is not bound to any particular party. The American friends of German culture are aware of the extent of the practical problems and personal distress experienced by German writers, artists and scholars living outside the German Reich. They know how extraordinarily difficult it is, in view of the persistent deterioration of economic conditions and the shrinking market and readership on the European continent, even to maintain and develop that which already exists. In these circumstances they are particularly conscious of the extreme desperation among the younger generation, which has not yet been able to establish itself outside Germany and which would certainly despair in the absence of any present prospect of a breakthrough, if there were no help and encouragement from other sources. The American Guild for German Cultural Freedom therefore endeavours to raise funds in the United States to help the younger generation of working German intellectuals above all.

This assistance, however, should not and shall not take the form of personal benefits or charity. Rather, since Germany has closed its doors and its market to its own intellectual élite, the idea is to keep the German cultural tradition alive outside the frontiers of the Reich among those who think in or understand German. To this end the Guild aims to open up new markets to German writers and artists and to organize them, supporting German publishers abroad in their difficult venture and creating book clubs and other relevant organizations to serve German cultural and intellectual activity in exile (in addition to what has already been achieved) and help it progress as far and as inclusively as possible. This inclusiveness should embrace every writer and artist from the German cultural region, without regard to his religion, 'race' or particular nationality, and irrespective of his political affiliations within the front which opposes the political system currently prevailing in Germany . . .

The American friends of German culture are nevertheless very well aware that, however great their efforts, they can never be more than advisors and helpers. The banished artists, writers and scholars themselves must undertake the work which, they hope, will signify the salvation of German cultural endeavour for the present and the future, for a new Germany and for the whole world . . . The GERMAN ACADEMY shall act as the ultimate patron and protector of Germany's whole imperilled cultural tradition. It shall use the funds provided to it by the American Guild for German

Cultural Freedom in order to confer scholarships on needy and deserving artists and scientists, writers, musicians and scholars, thus enabling them to continue their work. In addition, it shall use these funds to put up prizes honouring truly outstanding achievements in all these fields, thereby encouraging and motivating both the prize-winners and others to work on unceasingly. The members of the Academy who award these literary and artistic prizes shall therefore have the pleasant duty of paying particular regard to the younger generation, which can thus be helped towards a greater reputation. The sense of intellectual and artistic responsibility among the members of the GERMAN ACADEMY will guarantee that these prizes enjoy the high level of publicity and recognition they require.

The GERMAN ACADEMY will, moreover, be able to assist greatly in propagating the best work by exiled German artists, writers, scholars and musicians by coming to arrangements with existing publishing houses in Europe and America for the publication of prize-winning works and those created with the help of the Academy and its scholarships; by, where necessary, subsidizing the publication and distribution of such works and translations of them; by making similar arrangements with music publishers and galleries; and by organizing the friends of German culture in German and English book clubs . . .

The work of the members of the GERMAN ACADEMY shall therefore be on an honorary basis . . .

The call for the founding of the GERMAN ACADEMY goes out to Germany's exiled intellectuals at a time when the powers currently prevailing in Germany are again resorting to far-reaching and reckless propaganda in their attempt to take over, subjugate and pervert to their own ends such free and independent German intellectual culture as still exists and thrives in the world. It is hardly necessary to go into details about the extent and depth of this propaganda across the globe, or the means by which it is disseminated. The people of the world are very well aware of all this, and none more so than Germany's banished intellectuals, for they encounter it, ever more pervasive, in the limited sphere of activity still open to them. The GERMAN ACADEMY can and must create a bulwark high and sturdy enough to repel the attacks of those forces hostile to culture and intellect. This bulwark of true intellectual and cultural authority will be the only structure capable of holding back the rising tide of anti-intellect and anti-culture. The American friends of German culture therefore appeal to their exiled German allies to join with them in building that bulwark, for both these parties know that if *they* do not build it, it will never be built at all. They hope, however, that such an authoritative organization can shield Germany's cultural heritage, allowing it to blossom and thrive, now and in the future, for the benefit both of Germany and of a world reluctant to lose it.

Appendix 3: Statutes of the German Academy of Arts and Sciences (translated from the German)

Preamble

Aware that intellectual and spiritual freedom is the most precious asset of any people and of the international community of peoples, and that no culture can survive when laws prescribe bondage and inequality;

knowing that in the intellectual and spiritual realm there can be no division by diversity of kind, language or confession and no form of service other than to truth, beauty and humanity;

and in the conviction that the spirit of a people can only exist in mutual dependency with other cultures whilst also maintaining its own creative forces at their freest and most vivid;

German scholars, writers and artists have come together in order to facilitate the survival of German culture, to preserve its values beyond the current persecution and to protect German language, art and learning from distortion and destruction. They have therefore decided to found the

GERMAN ACADEMY
OF ARTS AND SCIENCES IN EXILE

to which the following statutes shall apply:

I: The Structure and Membership of the Academy

Article 1: The German Academy of Arts and Sciences is a society of scholars, writers and artists, founded to maintain and foster a German culture which is not in spiritual or intellectual tutelage.

The Academy does not pursue any political aims.

Article 2: The Academy has two divisions, one for the artists and one for the scientists. They are of equal status.

No member of the Academy may belong to both divisions at the same time.

Article 3: The Academy consists of: 1. full members, 2. corresponding members and 3. honorary members. The honorary members do not belong to a division.

Article 4: Membership of the German Academy is conditional on a pledge of support for intellectual and spiritual freedom.

Article 5: Full membership is open to scholars, writers and artists of unblemished repute who are held in general respect on account of their outstanding achievements.

Article 6: Corresponding membership is also open to persons whose cultural background is not German.

Article 7: Individuals of any nationality can be elected honorary members if the Academy wishes to honour them for their contributions to intellectual freedom or for other reasons.

Article 8: An application for the election of a new member can be made by anyone possessing the rights of a full member. The application must make clear the nominee's suitability. The application shall be considered and approved or rejected either orally, at a private meeting, or in writing, under the aegis of the general secretary. In the latter case, the application should be made to the general secretary, who shall pass it on to the president and the full members in an appropriate form and gather the votes.

The general secretary must treat the individual votes as confidential.

Article 9: Members who belong to a division can only be elected on the recommendation of the relevant division. The recommendation is subject to the terms of Article 8.

Article 10: The full members and the corresponding members have the right and the duty to participate in the Academy's work.

The corresponding members can be entrusted particularly with academic tasks, such as producing assessments.

All members shall endeavour to further the work of the German Academy to the best of their abilities.

Article 11: If a member of the Academy requires written confirmation of his membership, the general secretary shall issue, sign and
seal such a document.

II: The Academy's Agents

Article 12: The president of each division is to be elected by the full
members of that division. The election is subject to the terms of
Articles 8 and 9.

The presidents of the two divisions are equal in status and take
turns to preside over the Academy as a whole for a year.

The general secretary is responsible for organizing contact and
collaboration between the two presidents.

Article 13: The vice-presidents are to be elected by the members of
each division on the recommendation of their presidents.

Article 14: The president and vice-presidents are subject to
re-election every two years.

If a presidency ends within the two years, the vice-president
takes over for the remainder of the term.

If the president in question was also the overall president of the
Academy, that office passes to the president of the other division.

Article 15: The Academy's administrative office is to be led by the
general secretary, who also determines its location and the
arrangements for it. He is elected by the full members on the recommendation of the presidents and has the rights of a full member.

The office prepares conferences and meetings, undertakes the
tasks delegated to it, drafts proposals, is responsible for correspondence and manages the archive. It maintains relations
between members and with other, allied organizations.

Article 16: The general secretary bears the Academy seal. He draws
up the Academy's certificates and official documents and signs
them wherever no other organ of the Academy is responsible for
doing so.

Matters which represent a commitment on behalf of the Academy
as a whole must be signed by the president, and those which repre-

sent a commitment on behalf of one of its divisions must be signed by the president of that division.

Certificates relating to a resolution of the full membership require the signatures of all full members.

Article 17: The Academy treasurer administers the funds available to the Academy. He is elected by the full members and is answerable to them for his management.

Financial dispositions must be countersigned by the Academy president.

III: The Academy's Conferences and Meetings

Article 18: The Academy president instructs the general secretary to convene Academy conferences. This should occur at least once per year.

Article 19: The meetings are either general or private. The private meetings are only open to corresponding and honorary members if they have received a written invitation, which the general secretary issues on the presidents' instructions.

All Academy members have the right to participate in the general meetings. Honorary and corresponding members have an advisory function at these events. One or both groups can, however, be granted full voting rights for any particular event if a resolution to that effect is passed by a simple majority.

Guests are also permitted to attend the general meetings if they have been invited in writing or if a member has introduced them to the president.

Article 20: The Academy president opens, chairs and concludes the meetings. He gives speakers the floor and imposes order. If necessary, he can nominate any full member to represent him.

The general secretary submits the agenda. The assembly can approve changes to it.

Article 21: At the annual general meeting, the general secretary presents a report on the work of the office and the progress made by the Academy since the last conference. He requests the assembly's endorsement and presents proposals which he considers necessary in respect of the continuing work of the Academy and its office.

The treasurer presents a report on his financial management and the Academy's financial situation and moves its approval.

Apart from these items, the structure of conferences and meetings depends on the relevant agenda.

Article 22: When the Academy is unable to hold annual general meetings, a written procedure takes their place. The regulations relating to the meetings shall apply as appropriate to the written procedure.

Article 23: The assembly can delegate specific matters to individuals or committees, such as readers, experts, prize juries, preparatory committees and so forth. In certain matters it can confer the right to make reports for the Academy upon any individual member, or upon a number of members in concert.

The committees are also open to corresponding and honorary members and non-members. At least one committee member, however, should be a full member of the Academy.

Article 24: Matters of an exclusively artistic or scientific nature may only be presented to the relevant division by the president of that division or the general secretary.

The regulations for the meetings of the Academy as a whole also apply, as appropriate, to meetings of each division.

IV: The Tasks of the Academy

Article 25: The German Academy of Arts and Sciences in Exile shall endeavour, as a representative of free German intellectual life, to protect and foster Germany's abused arts and sciences by the appropriate means.

Article 26: Insofar as the resources available to it allow, the Academy shall offer prizes for outstanding achievements in the fields of literature, art and science.

It can also grant subsidies for the creation or completion of a particular work if the Academy believes that the work in question will be of a kind likely to enhance the reputation of German intellectual endeavour and that it could not come into being without such assistance.

Article 27: In order to fulfil the tasks specified in Article 26, the Academy shall solicit assistance from allied organizations such as the American Guild for German Cultural Freedom in New York or entrust them to act as its representative.

The Academy may decide to support the activities of allied organizations which endeavour to foster German cultural life in exile. Such support shall be commensurate to the Academy's resources. The general secretary is responsible for establishing and maintaining such contacts.

Article 28: The Academy may submit assessments of works of German literature, art and science. The Academy may issue diplomas for outstanding achievements. The Academy shall not award prizes, scholarships or diplomas for works by its own full members.

Article 29: The Academy can extend its activities to all fields and enterprises which are compatible with its character and resources. It can create posts and organs which become necessary to fulfil such tasks.

Article 30: Changes to the Statutes require a resolution passed by a two-thirds majority of the full members, including the presidents and the general secretary.

Article 31: These statutes come into force today.

Appendix 4: Prince Hubertus zu Löwenstein's letter to Stanley Richardson regarding the aims and activities of a 'British Guild for German Cultural Freedom', summer 1938 (translated from the German, the original English having been lost)

My dear Stanley, I would like to thank you once again, in the name of the German Academy of Arts and Sciences, for so kindly offering to organize the British Guild for German Cultural Freedom in the United Kingdom of Great Britain and Northern Ireland. I am delighted that we were able to talk about its aims and about the successes which the American Guild has already achieved. Following on from those discussions, may I again set forth the idea behind such a British Guild and leave it to you to tidy up my still rather clumsy English.

The FIRST principle of the British Guild should be that it aspires to provide productive patronage rather than mere charity. This is of the utmost psychological importance to the intellectuals in all fields whom we wish to support and it also defines the whole thrust of our work.

The SECOND principle: the British Guild is fundamentally non-political. It pursues cultural goals whilst heeding the fundamental human rights of freedom of expression, artistic and scientific freedom, and religious and racial tolerance which are firmly established in British constitutional history and tradition. Totalitarian ideas are incompatible with intellectual freedom.

The THIRD principle: by serving German culture in exile, the British Guild serves the cause of peace and international understanding. It may fall to the Guild to sustain those forces which will one day be called upon to work on a peaceful solution to European and global problems.

Our main duties and responsibilities will include, for example, the following:

FIRST, the formation of a committee of respected representatives of religious, political, social and scholarly life in England, some of whom will be selected to hold office in the Guild. We will then have to organize a somewhat broader set of sponsors with local groups in all the cultural centres of Great Britain and the Empire. We shall have to print a statement of purpose for the Guild, in order to introduce it and its work to the public in general and the British public in particular. There will be lectures and all the other forms of public relations work to back up the statement.

SECOND, the considerable amount of material I have been able to accumulate as general secretary of the American Guild and the German Academy of Arts and Sciences in Exile, and which I continue to gather, will be available to the British Guild. This will enable it to launch its own initiatives, avoid unnecessary duplications, ensure that there is fruitful cooperation with the American organization (including exchanges concerning experiences and opportunities), and thus contribute to even closer contacts between the English and American cultures. Close and continual collaboration between the German intellectuals and their English friends will be another result.

THIRD, we shall create a practical basis for our activities along the following lines:

1. The patronage of needy German intellectuals through scholarships to allow them to continue their creative work. These should be allocated in proportion to the importance of their previous achievements and of the projects on which they are currently working. Such scholarships, worth from ten pounds upward per month depending on the living costs in each host country, should be awarded for six months at a time in each case, with the possibility of renewal if justified by the work in question and the hardship being experienced.

2. Since the German-speaking market for scholarly and literary works published in exile has contracted so greatly, many significant texts have no chance of being published at all if the exiled publisher has to bear the whole risk. The British Guild might therefore sometimes offer to underwrite or subsidize the printing costs. This applies in particular to works by the younger, lesser-known generation, and to those works of considerable cultural value but limited popular appeal.

3. Many important works are currently banned in Central Europe on account of 'racial' or political discrimination and cannot be published in English because the writer or his heirs cannot afford to have them translated. In such cases the British Guild ought to approach the publishers regarding the fees. The works of that last German Humanist, Friedrich Gundolf, would be a typical example.

His writings on Goethe, Shakespeare, Caesar, early historiography and other topics would enrich English cultural life, and having them translated would also save them from neglect or destruction.

4. The British Guild might also decide that it should help scientists and artists who have been driven from their native land and been granted asylum in Great Britain in their efforts to establish themselves there. It might also, by working closely with the authorities, assist cultural figures of outstanding importance who can no longer pursue their careers in their own country to find a new environment in which to work in Great Britain or the Empire. By doing so, the British Guild would also help counteract the pernicious influence of a certain type of propaganda to which dominions such as South Africa and Canada are particularly exposed.

5. Since feelings of hopelessness and futility are particularly prejudicial to creative work, the Guild could offer encouragement in the form of various competitions and prizes. These would also stimulate intellectual and cultural life in England, which would benefit from all kinds of German talent and expertise.

Themes for such competitions might include the problems associated with international understanding. One of the first could be about 'Principles of a European order – political, social and economic'. Or: 'On the basis of which concrete principles would the restoration of international trust be conceivable?' Or: 'Central Europe and the British Commonwealth' and so forth. The prizes for such competitions need not be exorbitant: amounts between 50 and 100 pounds would be acceptable.

6. The British Guild ought to arrange readings and lectures at British universities and colleges for German professors and scholars driven from their posts in Central Europe, as these men and women are at a disadvantage compared to their colleagues in other countries. The provisions most large organizations make for academic exchanges are irrelevant to emigrants, as no exchange is possible in such cases.

FOURTH, the British Guild should consider establishing an archive, which all those with a legitimate interest would be able to consult. The basic ideas behind such an archive should be the same as those detailed under III.5 . . .

My dear Stanley, you will doubtless realize that all this is merely an outline of the extensive task awaiting us if the forces of oppression and persecution are to be prevented from destroying a great culture that has contributed so much to human progress. We shall have to prepare for the development of a new Europe, in which England will work together in peace with the Continent. It is vital to keep alive those forces upon which the rebuilding of Germany will depend.

I am really very grateful that you want to help us, and I know that we could have found no better man for this immense undertaking.

Yours ever, H.L.

Appendix 5: Recipients of German Academy in Exile scholarships, 1938–40

Anders, Günther
Arzt, Arthur

Bach, David
 Joseph
Bauer, Norbert
Baum, Alfred
Baum, Oskar
Beck, Enrique
Behrendt, Ernst
Bender, Arnold
Berendsohn, Walter
 Arthur
Berger, Klaus
Biel, Egon Vitalis
Birnbaum, Uriel
Blei, Franz
Bloch, Ernst
Borchardt, Hermann
Born, Herbert
Bothmer, Bernhard
 von
Braun, Felix
Brecht, Bertolt
Broch, Hermann
Brügel, Fritz
Budzislawski,
 Hermann

Castonier, Elisabeth
Cohn, Julius Curt
Csokor, Franz
 Theodor

Döblin, Alfred
Dreyfus, Paul

Duschinsky,
 Richard

Eckstein, Isak
Ehrenstein, Albert
Ehrenzweig, Stefan
Eisler, Hanns
Epstein, Julius

Feldmann, Theodor
Flesch von
 Brunningen, Hans
Fraenkel, Ernst
Frank, Leonhard
Frank, Rudolf
Frei, Bruno
Frey, Alexander
 Moritz
Friedlaender, Otto
Friedlaender-
 Mynona, Salomo
Frisch, Efraim

Galley, Horst
Goldstein, Franz
Graf, Oskar Maria
Granach, Alexander
Grautoff, Christiane
Gundolf, Elisabeth

Häfker, Hermann
Halbert, Abraham
Hallgarten,
 Wolfgang
Hardekopf,
 Ferdinand

Heartfield, John
Heller, Otto
Henning, Magnus
Hermann, Gerhard
Herzog, Wilhelm
Heydorn, Richard
 W.
Hiller, Kurt
Hirsch, Helmut
Hochdorf, Max
Hönigswald,
 Richard
Hoffmann-
 Luschnat, Lotte

Jacob, Berthold
Jacob, Heinrich
 Eduard
Jacobi, Lotte
Jokl, Georg

Kahle, Hans
Kaiser, Georg
Kaiser-Blüth, Kurt
Kamnitzer, Ernst
Kantorowicz, Alfred
Kesten, Hermann
Keun, Irmgard
Kisch, Egon Erwin
Kobler, Franz
Kolb, Annette
Kracauer, Siegfried
Kramer, Theodor
Kreitner, Bruno
Krell, Max
Krenek, Ernst

Kuttner, Erich

Langer, Felix
Lehmann-
    Russbueldt, Otto
Leitner, Maria
Leonhard, Rudolf
Loewenberg, Alfred
Luschnat, David

Maass, Alexander
Mainzer, Otto
Marck, Siegfried
Marcuse, Ludwig
Mehring, Walter
Meisel, Hans
Menne, Bernhard
Mondo, Renato
Morgenstern, Soma
Müller (geb. Wolf),
    Ingrid
Musil, Robert

Nathan, Reuben
    Sigmund
Neisser, Artur
Neumann, Alfred

Olden, Balder
Olden, Rudolf

Paechter, Heinz
Paetel, Karl O.

Paulsen, Fritz
Polgar, Alfred
Politzer, Heinz

Regler, Gustav
Reichmann, Max
Reisiger, Hans
Renn, Ludwig
Reuss, Leo
Richter, Werner
Rieger, Erwin
Rikko, Grete
Roseck, Erich
Roth, Joseph
Ruest, Anselm

Saenger, Samuel
Sahl, Hans
Salomon, Bruno von
Salten, Felix
Schaber, Will
Scheuer, Ernst
Schickele, René
Schlüter, Herbert
Schnog, Karl
Seghers, Anna
Siemsen-
    Vollenweider,
    Anna
Speyer, Wilhelm
Steinen, Diether von
    den
Steiner, Friedrich

Steiner, Rudolf
Sterler, Hermine

Thoor, Jesse

Uhse, Bodo
Unruh, Fritz von
Urbach, Franz

Victor, Walther

Wadler, Arnold
Walter, Friedrich
Walter, Hilde
Weiss, Ernst
Weiss, Fritz
Weiss, Fritz A.
Winder, Ludwig
Wittkowski, Victor
Wittmann, Max
Wolfenstein,
    Alfred
Wolff, Ernst
Wüsten, Johannes
Wysbar, Eva

Zarek, Otto
Zech, Paul
Zimmering, Max
Zoff, Otto
ZurMühlen,
    Hermynia
Zweig, Arnold

Appendix 6: Participants in the German Academy's Literary Contest (so far as could be confirmed)

Abter, Adolphe
Amann, Paul
Anders, Günther
Apelbaum, Else
Arendt, Hanna
Arzt, Arthur

Bauer, Norbert
Baum, Alfred
Baum, Oskar
Becher, Johannes R.
Behr, Wilhelm
Bender, Arnold
Berall, Magdalena
Berges, Max Ludwig
Blaustein, I. Sela
Blei, Franz
Borchardt, Hermann
Brusto, Max
Bud, Elsa Maria
Bud-Lindholm,
  Carmen

Castonier, Elisabeth
Cohn, Julius Curt

Dauber, Doris
Daudistel, Albert

Ellbogen, Paul
Ello-Donnebaum,
  Anton
Engler, Hermann

Federn-Kohlhaas,
  Etta

Fraenkel, Heinrich
Frank, Rudolf
Freund, Grete
Frey, Alexander
  Moritz
Fried, Antonie
Friedländer, Albert
Friedlaender-
  Mynona, Salomo

Goetze-Fischer,
  Gertraute
Goldschmidt, Bruni
Gottschalk,
  Friedrich
Graf, Oskar Maria
Graumann, Heinz
Greid, Hermann
Gross, Fritz
Grossmann,
  Adolphe
Gundelfinger, Leo

Halbert, Abraham
Hermann-
  Borchardt, Georg
Heuser, Saffiyah
Heymann, Lida
  Gustava
Hinzelmann, Alfred
Hirsch, Helmut
Hirsch, Käthe
Hirsch, M.
Hochdorf, Max
Hoegner, Wilhelm
Hoffmann, Walter

Horwitz, Ernst

Ilberg, Werner
Infeld, Heinrich

Jakubowitz, Oskar
Joseph, Rudolph

Kaemmerer, E.
Kahn, Selma
Karpinski, Martin
Kieve, Rudolph
Koenigsgarten,
  Hugo F.
Krumschmidt,
  Eberhard
Kupfer, Manja

Lackner, Stephan
Langer, Felix
Lazar, Maria
Lehnert, G.A.
Levi, Julius Walter
Liebeck, Adolf
Lipschitz, Rudolf
Loewenstein, Alfred
Loewenthal, Anna
Loundine, Tamara
Ludmer, Joseph
Luschnat, David

Maeder, Hans
Mainzer, Otto
Masloff, Arcadi
Mayer, Goetz
Meisel, Hans

Merck, Valerie
Merz, Konrad
Mihaly-Steckel, Jo
Mohr, Walter
Mohr, Wilhelmine
Morgenstern,
  Soma
Moser, Werner

Natonek, Hans
Neumann, Robert

Otten, Karl

Petersen, Jan

Reinowski, Hans
  Johann
Rieser, Max
Rosenheim, Felix
Rubinstein, Hilde
Rühle-Gerstel, Alice
Ruez, Luis F.
Russ, Georg

Schiff, Hans
Schlüter, Herbert
Scholz, Hermann
Schubart, Edith M.
Schück, Karl
Schütz, Barbara
Schütz, Wilhelm
  Wolfgang
Schwarz, Joachim
Seidler-Schick, Ange
Sidon, Gertrud
Silber, Hans
Silbergleit, Arthur
Siliava, Sulamith
Sinko, Erwin
Sochaczewer, Hans
Somin, Willy Oscar
Sommerfeld-Brand,
  Renée
Spira, Mela
Starke-Lachmann,
  Margot
Steinen, Helmut von
  den

Struchhold, Edgar

Temple, R. de
Tergit, Gabriele
Traube, Maria
  Johanna
Treuherz, Peter
  Axel
Tyktin, Bella

Wadler, Arnold
Wald, Wolf
Walter, Friedrich
Weigel, Hans
Weiss, Ernst
Wertheim, Max
Wolff-Kolleritz,
  Ilse
Wolfradt, Willi
Wüsten, Johannes

Zech, Paul
Zehden, Franz
Zimmering, Max

Bibliography

Details of newspaper, magazine and archive material will be found in the relevant chapters and notes. Only books, academic articles and the major unpublished texts are listed below.

Adorno, T., 'Minima moralia. Fünfzig Aphorismen zum fünfzigsten Geburtstag Max Horkheimers' (typescript, 2 vols). Stadt- und Universitätsbibliothek Frankfurt am Main, Nachlass Max Horkheimer.

Almásy, L. E. (1939), *Unbekannte Sahara. Mit Flugzeug und Auto in der Libyschen Wüste*, ed. H. von der Esch. Leipzig: Brockhaus. New edition, (1997), *Schwimmer in der Wüste. Auf der Suche nach der Oase Zarzura*. Innsbruck: Haymon; includes chapters from the Hungarian edition of 1934 and a secret document about Almásy's 'Operation Salam' of 1942.

Amann, K. (1991), 'Die American Guild for German Cultural Freedom und die Deutsche Akademie im Exil (1935–1949)', in J. Holzner, S. P. Scheichl and W. Wiemüller (eds), *Eine Schwierige Heimkehr. Österreichische Literatur im Exil 1938–1945*. Innsbruck: Institut für Germanistik (*Innsbrucker Beiträge zur Kulturwissenschaft*, Germanische Reihe, Vol. 40), pp. 181–204.

Anderson, E. (1973), *Hammer or Anvil. The Story of the German Working-Class Movement*. New York: Oriole Editions. Re-issued (1945), London: Victor Gollancz.

Baden, Prinz M. von (1927), *Erinnerungen und Dokumente*. Stuttgart: Deutsche Verlagsanstalt.

Barron, S. and Eckmann, S. (eds) (1997), *Exiles + Emigrés. The Flight of European Artists from Hitler*. Los Angeles and New York: Los Angeles County Museum of Art and Harry N. Abrams. German: (1997), *Exil. Flucht und Emigration europäischer Künstler 1933–1945*. Munich: Prestel.

Bell, Bishop of Chichester (1945), 'The Background of the Hitler Plot', *The Contemporary Review*, October.

Bentley, E. (1952), *Out of Bondage*. London: Hart-Davis.

Bermann, R. A. (alias A. Höllriegel (1931)), *Die Derwischtrommel. Das Leben des erwarteten Mahdi*. Berlin: Volksverband der Bücherfreunde Wegweiser-Verlag. English: (1932), *The Mahdi of Allah. The Story of the*

Derwish Mohammed Ahmed, with an introduction by Winston Churchill. London, New York: Putnam.

— (1933), 'Tagebuch von der Saharafahrt'. Deutsche Bibliothek, Exilarchiv, Nachlass Richard Bermann.

— (1938), *Die Geschichte einer Expedition in die Libysche Wüste*. With 77 photographs by Hans Casparius and a map by Ladislaus Kádár. Zürich: Orell Füssli. Another edition was published in the same year by the Büchergilde Gutenberg im Exil in Zürich and Prague.

— (1998), *Die Fahrt auf dem Katarakt. Eine Autobiographie ohne einen Helden*, ed. H.-H. Müller. Vienna: Picus Verlag. Manuscript in Deutsche Bibliothek, Exilarchiv, Nachlass Richard Bermann.

Bermann-Fischer, G. (1967), *Bedroht – bewahrt. Weg eines Verlegers*. Frankfurt am Main: S. Fischer.

Berthold, W. (1997), *Die 42 Attentate auf Adolf Hitler*. Vienna: Ueberreuter Verlag. First published (1981) Munich: Blanvalet.

Berthold, W. and Eckert, B. (1980), *Der deutsche P.E.N. Club im Exil 1933– 1948. Eine Ausstellung der Deutschen Bibliothek* (Sonderveröffentlichungen / Deutsche Bibliothek, No. 10, ed. G. Pflug). Frankfurt am Main: Buchhändler-Vereinigung.

Berthold, W., Eckert, B. and Wende, F. (eds) (1993), *Deutsche Intellektuelle im Exil. Ihre Akademie und die 'American Guild for German Cultural Freedom'; Eine Ausstellung des Deutschen Exilarchivs 1933–1945 der Deutschen Bibliothek, Frankfurt am Main*. Munich, London, New York, Paris: K. G. Saur (Sonderveröffentlichungen / Die Deutsche Bibliothek, No. 18, ed. K.-D. Lehmann).

Bloom, A. (1987), *The Closing of the American Mind*. New York: Simon and Schuster.

Böhne, E. and Motzkau-Valeton, W. (eds) (1992), *Die Künste und Wissenschaften im Exil 1933–1945*. Gerlingen: Lambert Schneider.

Bracher, K. D. (1979), *Europa in der Krise. Innengeschichte und Weltpolitik seit 1917*. Frankfurt, Berlin and Vienna: Ullstein.

Braun, O. (1949), *Von Weimar zu Hitler*. Hamburg: Hammonia.

Brecht, B. (1957), *Die Geschäfte des Herrn Julius Caesar: Romanfragment*. Berlin: Weiss. English: (1958), 'The Private Life of Mister Julius Caesar: An Extract', trans. Dorothea Alexander, *Nimbus/New English Review* 4: 2, 2–13.

Brinson, C. and Malet, M. (eds) (1987), *Rudolf Olden – Peter Olden: Briefe aus den Jahren 1935–1936*. Berlin: Verlag Europäische Ideen (No. 64).

British Ministry of Information (1939), *White Book*, No. 1.

Broch, H. (1986), *Briefe über Deutschland 1945–1949. Die Korrespondenz mit Volkmar von Zühlsdorff*, ed. and with an introduction by P. M. Lützeler. Frankfurt am Main: Suhrkamp.

Bronson, D. (1974), *Joseph Roth. Eine Biographie*. Cologne: Kiepenheuer & Witsch.

Chamberlain, W. H. (1950), *America's Second Crusade*. Chicago: Regnery.

Chambers, W. (1987), *Witness*. Washington DC: Regnery.

Clay, L. D. (1950), *Decision in Germany*. Garden City, New York: Doubleday.

Duderstadt, H. (1933), *Vom Reichsbanner zum Hakenkreuz. Wie es kommen musste. Ein Bekenntnis*. Stuttgart, Berlin, Leipzig: Union Deutsche Verlags-Gesellschaft.

Duncan-Jones, A. S. (1938), *The Struggle for Religious Freedom in Germany*. London: Gollancz.

Eberhard, P. (1989), *Les jeunes exilés allemands (1933–1945). Analyse des conditions de la création littéraire en exile. Thèse de troisième cycle sous la direction de Gilbert Badia* (diss.). Paris: Université Paris XIII Vincennes à Saint Denis, Département d'Allemand.

Eisenhower, D. D. (1948), *Crusade in Europe*. Garden City, New York: Doubleday.

Emmerich, W. and Heil, S. (1985), *Lyrik des Exils*. Stuttgart: Reclam.

Flügge, M. (1996), *Wider Willen im Paradies. Deutsche Schriftsteller im Exil in Sanary-sur-Mer*. Berlin: Aufbau Taschenbuch-Verlag.

Flynn, J. T. (1951), *While You Slept. Our Tragedy in Asia and Who Made it*. New York: Devin Adair.

Frank, R. (1992), *Der Junge, der seinen Geburtstag vergass*. Ravensburg: Otto Maier Verlag. English: (1986), *No Hero for the Kaiser*. New York: Lothrop, Lee & Shepard.

— (1998), *Fair Play oder Es kommt nicht zum Krieg. Roman einer Emigration in Wien*. Berlin: Aufbau-Verlag.

Freud, E., Freud, L. and Grubrich-Simitis, I. (eds) (1976), *Sigmund Freud. Sein Leben in Bildern und Texten*. Frankfurt am Main: Suhrkamp. English: (1978), *Sigmund Freud: His Life in Pictures and Words*. London: A. Deutsch.

Freud, S. (1960), *Briefe 1873–1939*, ed. E. L. Freud. Frankfurt am Main: S. Fischer. English: (1970), *Letters of Sigmund Freud, 1873–1939*, ed. E. L. Freud, trans. T. and J. Stern. London: Hogarth Press.

Freud, S./Zweig, A. (1968), *Briefwechsel*, ed. E. L. Freud. Frankfurt am Main: S. Fischer. English: (1970) *The Letters of Sigmund Freud and Arnold Zweig*, ed. E. L. Freud. London: Hogarth Press for the Institute of Psycho-Analysis.

Freund, J. H. (ed) (1978), *Unterwegs. Peter de Mendelssohn zum 70. Geburtstag*. Frankfurt am Main: S. Fischer.

Fry, V. (1997), *Surrender on Demand*. Boulder, Colorado: Johnson Books. First published (1945), New York: Random House.

Fuller, J. F. C. (1949), *The Second World War 1939–1945. A Strategical and Tactical History*. New York: Duell, Sloane and Pearce.

Gay, P. (1968), *Weimar Culture. The Outsider as an Insider*. New York: Harper & Row.

Grimm, R. and Hermand, J. (1972), *Exil und Innere Emigration. Third Wisconsin Workshop*. Frankfurt am Main: Athenäum.

Haas, W. (1957), *Die Literarische Welt. Erinnerungen*. Munich: Paul List.

Hardt, H., Hilscher, E. and Lerg, W. B. (1979), *Presse im Exil. Beiträge zur*

Kommunikationsgeschichte des deutschen Exils 1933–1945. Munich, New York, London, Paris: Saur.

Harpprecht, K. (1995), *Thomas Mann. Eine Biographie*. Reinbek bei Hamburg: Rowohlt.

Hermand, J. and Trommler, F. (1978), *Die Kultur der Weimarer Republik*. Munich: Nymphenburger Verlagsbuchhandlung.

Heuss, T. (1963), *Erinnerungen, 1905–1933*. Tübingen: Wunderlich.

Hirschfeld, G. (1983), *Exil in Grossbritannien. Zur Emigration aus dem nationalsozialistischen Deutschland*. Stuttgart: Klett-Cotta. English: (1984), *Exile in Great Britain – Refugees from Hitler's Germany*. Leamington Spa: Berg and New Jersey: Humanities Press (for the German Historical Institute, London).

Höllriegel, A.: see Bermann, R. A.

Holzner J., Scheichl, S. P. and Wiemüller, W. (eds) (1991), *Eine schwierige Heimkehr. Österreichische Literatur im Exil 1938–1945*. Innsbruck: Institut für Germanistik (Innsbrucker Beiträge zur Kulturwissenschaft Germanische Reihe, Vol. 40).

Hübinger, P. E. (1974), *Thomas Mann, die Universität Bonn und die Zeitgeschichte. Drei Kapitel deutscher Vergangenheit aus dem Leben des Dichters, 1905–1955*. Munich and Vienna: Oldenbourg.

Hull, C. (1948/9), *The Memoirs of Cordell Hull*, 2 vols. New York: Macmillan.

Jay, M. (1997), 'The German Migration: Is there a Figure in the Carpet?', in S. Barron and S. Eckmann (eds), *Exiles + Emigrés. The flight of European Artists from Hitler*. Los Angeles and New York: Los Angeles County Museum of Art and Harry N. Abrams, pp. 326–37.

Kerr, A. (1984), *Ich kam nach England. Ein Tagebuch aus dem Nachlass*, eds W. Huder and T. Koebner. Bonn: Bouvier (2nd edition).

Kesten, H. (1947), *Die Zwillinge von Nürnberg*. Amsterdam: Querido.

Keun, I. (1947), *Bilder und Gedichte aus der Emigration*. Cologne: Epoche-Verlag.

Klee, P. (1920), 'Schöpferische Konfession', *Tribüne der Kunst und Zeit*, No. 13, 28–40.

Koebner, T., Sautermeister, G. and Schneider, S. (eds) (1987), *Deutschland nach Hitler. Zukunftspläne im Exil und aus der Besatzungszeit 1939–1949*. Opladen: Westdeutscher Verlag.

Koestler, A. (1948), *Sonnenfinsternis*. Stuttgart: Büchergilde. English: (1940), *Darkness at Noon*. London: Jonathan Cape.

— (1954), *The Invisible Writing*. London: Collins with Hamish Hamilton.

Krohn, C.-D. (1993), *Intellectuals in Exile. Refugee Scholars and the New School for Social Research* (trans. R. and R. Kimber). Amherst: University of Massachusetts Press. Originally in German: (1987), *Wissenschaft im Exil. Deutsche Sozial- und Wirtschaftswissenschaftler in den USA und die New School for Social Research*. Frankfurt am Main, New York: Campus.

Krohn, C.-D. and Mühlen, P. von zur (eds) (1997), *Rückkehr und Aufbau nach 1945. Deutsche Remigranten im öffentlichen Leben Nachkriegsdeutschlands*. Marburg: Metropolis.

Krohn, C.-D., Rotermund, E., Winckler, L. and Koepke, W. (eds), *Exil und Widerstand*. Munich: edition text + kritik (Gesellschaft für Exilforschung/ Society for Exile Studies, Exilforschung Vol. 15).

Krug, H. (1986), 'Exil und Rückkehr. Hilde Spiel im Gespräch', in Neue Gesellschaft für Bildende Kunst, Berlin (ed.) (1986), *Kunst im Exil in Grossbritannien 1933–1945*. Berlin: Frölich & Kaufmann, pp. 289–95.

Kurth, P. (1990), *American Cassandra. The Life of Dorothy Thompson*. Boston, Toronto, London: Little, Brown & Co.

Langkau-Alex, U. and Rupprecht, T. M. (1995), *Was soll aus Deutschland werden? Der Council for a Democratic Germany in New York 1944–45*. Frankfurt am Main, New York: Campus Verlag (Internationales Institut für Sozialgeschichte, Amsterdam: Quellen und Studien zur Sozialgeschichte, Vol. 15).

Leber, A., Brandt, W. and Bracher, K. D. (1966), *Das Gewissen steht auf. 64 Lebensbilder aus dem deutschen Widerstand 1933–1945*. Berlin, Frankfurt am Main: Verlag Annedore Leber. English: (1957), *Conscience in Revolt; Sixty-four stories of resistance in Germany, 1933–45*. London: Vallentine, Mitchell.

Leuchtenberg, C. J. : see Mendelssohn, P. de.

Link, W. (ed) (1968), *Mit dem Gesicht nach Deutschland. Eine Dokumentation über die sozialdemokratische Emigration* (Aus dem Nachlass von Friedrich Stampfer ergänzt durch andere Überlieferungen. Herausgegeben im Auftrage der Kommission für Geschichte des Parlamentarismus und der politischen Parteien von Erich Matthias). Düsseldorf: Droste Verlag.

Löwenstein, Prince H. zu (1931), *Umrisse der Idee des faschistischen Staates und ihre Verwirklichung. Unter Vergleichung mit den wichtigsten Gebieten des deutschen Staatsrechts* (diss., Hamburg 1931). Kirchhain: Zahn & Baendel.

— (1934a), *After Hitler's Fall. Germany's Coming Reich*. London: Faber & Faber and (1935), New York: Macmillan.

— (1934b), *The Tragedy of a Nation. Germany 1918–1934*. London: Faber & Faber and New York: Macmillan. German: (1934), *Die Tragödie eines Volkes. Deutschland 1918–1934*. Amsterdam: Steenuil Verlag. Dutch: (1934), *De Tragedie van een Volk*. Amsterdam: Steenuil Verlag.

— (1937), *A Catholic in Republican Spain*. London: Victor Gollancz. German: (1938), *Als Katholik im Republikanischen Spanien*. Zürich: Stauffacher.

— (1938), *Conquest of the Past. An Autobiography*. Boston: Houghton Mifflin.

— (1942), *On Borrowed Peace*. New York: Doubleday, Doran and (1943), London: Faber & Faber.

— (1945), *The Germans in History*. New York: Columbia University Press and (1969), New York: AMS. German: (1950/56), *Deutsche Geschichte: Der Weg des Reiches in zwei Jahrtausenden*. Frankfurt am Main: Heinrich Scheffler (1st–3rd edns); (1962), Berlin: Haude & Spener (4th edn); (1976/ 84), Berlin, Munich: Herbig (5th–8th eds); (1990), Bindlach: Gondrom (9th edn).

— (1968), *Towards the Further Shore. An Autobiography*. London: Victor Gollancz.

— (1972), *Botschafter ohne Auftrag*. Düsseldorf: Droste.

— (1983), *Abenteurer der Freiheit. Ein Lebensbericht*. Frankfurt am Main, Berlin, Vienna: Ullstein.

— (with Zühlsdorff, V. von) (1957), *Deutschlands Schicksal 1945–57*. Bonn: Athenäum.

Mallmann, K.-M. (1997), 'Frankreichs fremde Patrioten. Deutsche in der Résistance', in C.-D. Krohn, E. Rotermund, L. Winckler and W. Koepke (eds), *Exil und Widerstand*. Munich: edition text + kritik (Gesellschaft für Exilforschung/Society for Exile Studies, Exilforschung Vol. 15), pp. 33 ff.

Mann, E. and K. (1939), *Escape to Life*. Boston: Houghton Mifflin. German: (1991), *Escape to Life, Deutsche Kultur im Exil*. Munich: Edition Spangenberg. Paperback edn: (1996), Reinbek: Rowohlt.

Mann, G. (1978), 'Festvortrag', in J. H. Freund (ed) (1978), *Unterwegs. Peter de Mendelssohn zum 70. Geburtstag*. Frankfurt am Main: S. Fischer.

Mann, K. (1952), *Der Wendepunkt. Ein Lebensbericht*. Frankfurt am Main: S. Fischer.

— (1989–91), *Tagebücher*, ed. J. Heimannsberg, P. Laemmle and W. F. Schoeller. Munich: Edition Spangenberg.

Mann T. (1935), *Leiden und Grösse der Meister*. Berlin: S. Fischer.

— (1942), *Order of the Day. Political Essays and Speeches of Two Decades*. New York: Knopf.

— (1961–5), *Briefe*, ed. E. Mann (3 vols). Frankfurt am Main: S. Fischer. For a selection of Mann's letters in English, see (1970), *Letters of Thomas Mann, 1889–1955* (selected and trans. R. and C. Winston, 2 vols). London: Secker & Warburg.

— (1977), *Tagebücher 1933–1934*, ed. P. de Mendelssohn. Frankfurt am Main: S. Fischer. English: for an abridged translation of Mann's diaries to 1939, see (1982), *Thomas Mann Diaries 1918–1939* (selection and foreword by H. Kesten, trans. R. and C. Winston). New York: Harry N. Abrams.

— (1978), *Tagebücher 1935–1936*, ed. P. de Mendelssohn. Frankfurt am Main: S. Fischer. English: (1982) *op.cit.*

— (1980), *Tagebücher 1937–1939*, ed. P. de Mendelssohn. Frankfurt am Main: S. Fischer. English: (1982) *op.cit.*

— (1982), *Leiden und Grösse der Meister*. Frankfurt am Main: S. Fischer (Vol. 8 of (1980–86) *Gesammelte Werke in Einzelbänden: Frankfurter Ausgabe*, ed. P. de Mendelssohn). First published (1935) *op.cit.*

— (1986), *An die gesittete Welt*. Frankfurt am Main: S. Fischer (Vol. 20 of (1980–6) *Gesammelte Werke in Einzelbänden: Frankfurter Ausgabe*, ed. P. de Mendelssohn).

— (1988), *Briefwechsel mit Autoren*, ed. H. Wysling. Frankfurt am Main: S. Fischer.

Marcuse, L. (1960), *Mein Zwanzigstes Jahrhundert. Auf dem Weg zu einer Autobiographie*. Munich: Paul List.

— (1979), *Essays, Porträts, Polemiken*, ed. and with an introduction by H. von Hofe. Zürich: Diogenes.

Mendelssohn, P. de (1932), *Schmerzliches Arkadien*. Berlin: Universitas Verlag. Subsequent edns, (1949) Hamburg and (1977) Frankfurt: both Krüger.

— (1934), *Das Haus Cosinsky*. Zürich: Oprecht & Helbling. English: (1936), *The House of Cosinsky*. London: Hutchinson.

— (1935), *Wolkenstein. Ein Roman*. Vienna, Leipzig: R. A. Höger.

Michels, K. (1997), 'Transfer and Transformation: The German Period in American Art History', in S. Barron and S. Eckmann (eds), *Exiles + Emigrés. The Flight of European Artists from Hitler*. Los Angeles County Museum of Art, pp. 304–16.

Möller, H. (1992), 'Die Remigration von Wissenschaftlern nach 1945', in E. Böhne and W. Motzkau-Valeton (eds), *Die Künste und Wissenschaften im Exil 1933–1945*. Gerlingen: Lambert Schneider, pp. 601–16.

Morgenthau, H. Jr. (1945), *Germany Is Our Problem*. New York: Harper & Brothers.

Müller, H.-H. and Eckert, B. (eds) (1995), *Richard A. Bermann alias Arnold Höllriegel. Österreicher – Demokrat – Weltbürger. Eine Ausstellung des Deutschen Exilarchivs 1933–1945. Die Deutsche Bibliothek, Frankfurt am Main*. Munich, New Providence, London, Paris: K. G. Saur (Sonderveröffentlichungen/Die Deutsche Bibliothek, No. 22, ed. K.-D. Lehmann).

Myers, B. S. (1957), *The German Expressionists. A Generation in Revolt*. New York: Praeger.

Neue Gesellschaft für Bildende Kunst, Berlin (ed) (1986), *Kunst im Exil in Grossbritannien 1933–1945*. Berlin: Frölich & Kaufmann.

Neumann, R. (1963), *Ein leichtes Leben. Autobiographie*. Vienna, Munich, Basle: Desch.

Niemöller, M. (1939), *From U-Boat to Concentration Camp. The Autobiography of Martin Niemöller*, with his further story by the Dean of Chichester. London: William Hodge.

Olden, B. (1977), *Paradies des Teufels. Biographisches und Autobiographisches. Schriften und Briefe aus dem Exil*, ed. R. Greuner. Berlin: Rütten & Loening.

Olden, R. (1933), *Hitler, der Eroberer. Die Entlarvung einer Legende. Von einem deutschen Politiker*. Berlin, Prague: Malik.

— (1934), *Das Schwarzbuch. Tatsachen und Dokumente: Die Lage der Juden in Deutschland*. Paris: Comité des Délégations Juives.

— (1946), *The History of Liberty in Germany*, with a foreword by Gilbert Murray. London: Victor Gollancz.

Ondaatje, M. (1992), *The English Patient*. London: Bloomsbury and New York: Alfred A. Knopf.

Papcke, S. (1992), 'Entlastet von Gemeinschaftsmythen. Anmerkungen zur deutschen Soziologie im Exil', in E. Böhne and W. Motzkau-Valeton (eds), *Die Künste und Wissenschaften im Exil 1933–1945*. Gerlingen: Lambert Schneider, pp. 401–12.

Platen, August von (1982), *Werke in zwei Bänden*, ed. K. Wölfel and J. Link. Munich: Winkler.

Roth, J. (1975–6), *Werke*, (4 vols) ed. H. Kesten. Cologne, Berlin: Kiepenheuer & Witsch.

Rothfels, H. (ed) (1961), *Berlin in Vergangenheit und Gegenwart. Tübinger Vorträge*. Tübingen: J. C. B. Mohr.

Sahl, H. (1959), *Die Wenigen und die Vielen. Roman einer Zeit.* Frankfurt am Main: S. Fischer. English: (1962), *The Few and the Many* (trans. R. and C. Winston). New York: Harcourt, Brace & World.

Scheurig, B. (1960), *Freies Deutschland. Das Nationalkomitee und der Bund deutscher Offiziere in der Sowjetunion 1933–1945.* Munich: Nymphenburger Verlagsbuchhandlung. English: (1969), *Free Germany; the National Committee and the League of German Officers.* Middletown, Connecticut: Wesleyan University Press.

Schlabrendorff, F. von (1984), *Offiziere gegen Hitler. Deutscher Widerstand 1933–1945.* Berlin: Ullstein. English: (1966), *The Secret War Against Hitler.* London: Hodder & Stoughton.

Schrader, B. and Schebera, J. (1987), *Kunst-Metropole Berlin 1918–1933. Dokumente und Selbstzeugnisse.* Berlin, Weimar: Aufbau-Verlag.

Schwerin, D. Graf von (1991), *Dann sind's die besten Köpfe, die man henkt. Die junge Generation im deutschen Widerstand.* Munich: Piper.

Severing, C. (1950), *Mein Lebensweg.* Cologne: Greven.

Söllner, A. (1996), *Deutsche Politikwissenschaftler in der Emigration. Studien zu ihrer Akkulturation und Wirkungsgeschichte.* Opladen: Westdeutscher Verlag.

Spiel, H. (1991), *Die hellen und die finsteren Zeiten. Erinnerungen 1911–1946.* Reinbek: Rowohlt.

Stahlberg, A. (1987), *Die verdammte Pflicht. Erinnerungen 1932–1945.* Frankfurt am Main: Ullstein. English: (1990), *Bounden Duty: the Memoirs of a German Officer, 1932–45.* London: Brassey's.

Steinbach, P. and Tuchel, J. (eds) (1994), *Lexikon des Widerstandes 1933–1945.* Munich: C. H. Beck. English: (1997), *Encyclopedia of German Resistance to the Nazi Movement.* New York: Continuum.

Stimson, H. L. and Bundy, M. (1947), *On Active Service in Peace and War.* New York: Harper & Brothers.

Tanenhaus, S. (1997), *Whittaker Chambers. A Biography.* New York: Random House.

Thom, G. (1986), *Rufer ohne Fahne. Der Dichter Jesse Thoor.* Vienna: Österreichischer Bundesverlag.

Thoor, J. (1956), *Die Sonette und Lieder,* ed. A. Marnau. Heidelberg-Darmstadt: Lambert Schneider (Veröffentlichungen der Deutschen Akademie für Sprache und Dichtung Darmstadt, No. 7).

— (1958), *Dreizehn Sonette,* ed. and with an afterword by W. Sternfeld. Stierstadt im Taunus: Eremitenpresse.

US Department of State (Released March 1950), *Germany 1947–1949. The Story in Documents.* Department of State Publication 3556 European and British Commonwealth Series 9 (Division of Publications, Office of Public Affairs).

Villard, H. (1904), *Memoirs of Henry Villard. Journalist and Financier,* 2 vols. Boston, New York: Houghton Mifflin.

Villard, O. G. (1933), *The German Phoenix. The Story of the Republic.* New York: Harrison Smith & Robert Haas.

Walter, B. (1947), *Thema und Variationen, Erinnerungen und Gedanken*. Stockholm: Bermann-Fischer.

Wedekind Regnier, P. (1978), 'Beheimatet in dieser Welt', in J. H. Freund (ed), *Unterwegs. Peter de Mendelssohn zum 70. Geburtstag*. Frankfurt am Main: S. Fischer, pp. 11–12.

Whittick, A. (1940), *Erich Mendelsohn*. London, New York: Faber & Faber.

Willett, J. (1984), 'The Emigration and the Arts', in G. Hirschfeld (ed), *Exile in Great Britain – Refugees from Hitler's Germany*. Leamington Spa: Berg and New Jersey: Humanities Press (for the German Historical Institute, London), pp. 195–217.

Wingler, H. M. (1962), *Das Bauhaus 1919–1933: Weimar, Dessau, Berlin*. Bramsche: Rasch. English: (1969), *The Bauhaus: Weimar, Dessau, Berlin, Chicago*. Cambridge, Massachusetts: MIT Press.

Wolf, F. (1969), *Briefe. Eine Auswahl*. Berlin, Weimar: Aufbau-Verlag.

Zühlsdorff, V. (1986), *Briefe über Deutschland 1945–1949. Hermann Broch. Die Korrespondenz mit Volkmar von Zühlsdorff*, ed. P. M. Lützeler. Frankfurt am Main: Suhrkamp.

— (1998), *In Begleitung meiner Zeit. Essays, Erinnerungen, Dokumente*, with a foreword by Bernhard Vogel. Munich: Kastell Verlag.

— (with Löwenstein, H. zu) (1957), *Deutschlands Schicksal 1945–1957*. Bonn: Athenäum.

Index